FOLKLORE

THE BASICS

Folklore: The Basics is an engaging guide to the practice and interpretation of folklore. Taking examples from around the world, it explores the role of folklore in expressing fundamental human needs, desires, and anxieties that are often not revealed through other means. Providing a clear framework for approaching the study of folklore, it introduces the reader to methodologies for identifying, documenting, interpreting and applying key information about folklore and its relevance to modern life. From the Brothers Grimm to Internet memes, it addresses such topics as:

- What is folklore?
- How do we study it?
- Why does folklore matter?
- How does folklore relate to elite culture?
- Is folklore changing in a digital age?

Folklore: The Basics supports readers in becoming familiar with folkloric traditions and how to interpret cultural expression. It is an essential read for anyone approaching the study of folklore for the first time.

Simon J. Bronner is Distinguished Professor of American Studies and Folklore at the Pennsylvania State University, Harrisburg, USA. He has previously taught at Harvard University, Leiden University, Osaka University, and the University of California at Davis. He is the editor of the *Encyclopedia of American Folklife* for Routledge, the *Material Worlds Book Series* for the University Press of Kentucky; and the *Jewish Cultural Studies* series for Littman. He served as president of the Fellows of the American Folklore Society.

THE BASICS

FOLKLORE

THE BASICS

Simon J. Bronner

LONDON AND NEW YORK

First published 2017
by Routledge
2 Park Square, Milton Park, Abingdon, Oxon OX14 4RN

Simultaneously published in the USA and Canada
by Routledge
711 Third Avenue, New York, NY 10017

Routledge is an imprint of the Taylor & Francis Group, an informa business

British Library Cataloguing in Publication Data
A catalogue record for this book is available from the British Library

Library of Congress Cataloging in Publication Data
A catalog record for this book has been requested

HBK ISBN13: 978-1-138-77494-0
PBK ISBN13: 978-1-138-77495-7
EBK ISBN13: 978-1-315-68838-1

Typeset in Bembo
by Book Now Ltd, London

CONTENTS

FIGURES

INTRODUCTION

This book is about traditional knowledge and practice that people label and study as "folklore." With reference to "folk" as group or everyday life and "lore" as cultural or oral learning and expression, the term gained wide circulation in the nineteenth century to cover a range of material that had been treated separately in historical and literary annals: speech, tales, songs, dances, and customs, for example. The connecting thread was the idea of tradition, and a process of acquiring and transmitting it. Indeed, "folk" could also be construed as an adjective meaning "traditional" to describe lore. As part of the "vernacular," following linguistic usage, folklore evoked an image of intergenerational transmission and localized culture. Unlike the pantheon of literary and art works attributed to a single author, often anonymous folk productions represented variable, multiple existence across time and space. Folklore raised cultural and psychological puzzles to solve because for many social critics it was not supposed to be around after the Industrial Revolution. Yet there it was, even among the elites of society, and for many literati, it held a fascinating aesthetic, and even political, appeal.

The labeling of traditional expressions as folklore has a long history with an evolving meaning in relation to industrialism, nationalism, colonialism, and cultural literacy in addition to modernization.

Medieval Anglo-Saxon manuscripts cited the compound *foldār* (literally "knowledge or learning held in common") to signify oral tradition or popular wisdom in contrast to *bōclār*, meaning academic "book-learning" or "doctrine" (Mazo 1996). In the sixteenth century, European writers produced accounts of exotic customs and cultural alterity, at least by their estimation, after encountering Natives in the New World and Asian communities on trade routes to the East (Cocchiara 1981, 1–43). In the seventeenth and eighteenth centuries, "traditionary lore" identified with folk song, poetry, and narrative (such as the famous fairy tales of Cinderella, Sleeping Beauty and Little Red Riding Hood, published by Giambattista Basile in 1636 and Charles Perrault in France in 1697) became important to European "Romantic nationalist" philosophers such as German writer Johann Gottfried Herder (1744–1803) who in his theory of *Volksgeist* (literally "spirit of the people" in German) made claims for national identity, harmony with nature, and spiritual existence growing out of the rootedness and artistry of peasant folk culture (see Bronner 1986a, 4–7; Sandford *et al.* 1841, 703; Stocking 1996; Wilson 1973).

Herder's philosophy inspired the brothers Jacob and Wilhelm Grimm in the early nineteenth century to produce volumes on German folktales based upon the "collecting" of an array of artistic material (beliefs, verses, and legends as well as fairy tales) as told by *Das Volk* or "the common people" (peasants and artisans who constitute the core of German peoplehood) in the Hesse-Kassel region (Kamenetsky 1992, 55–80). Previous European anthologies of vernacular literature, including Bishop Thomas Percy's *Reliques of Ancient English Poetry* of 1765 and Achim von Arnim and Clemens Brentano's *Des Knaben Wunderhorn: Alte Deutsche Lieder* ("The Boy's Magic Horn: Old German Songs, of 1805–1808) had folk verses that were modified by the editors. The Grimms claimed to render stories and songs faithfully as people told and sang them. They were not the first to refer to German *Märchen*, popularly known as fairy tales, but they innovatively included notes that described the connection of the stories to folk beliefs, myths, proverbs, games, and legends and listed international analogues, toward the goal of showing possible origins, development, and diffusion of the material (Cocchiara 1981, 187–200; Kamenetsky 1992).

Although the presentation of Grimms' tales from *Das Volk* held literary and political interest, it was their comparative folkloristic commentary in a separate volume published in 1822 that spurred a scholarly enterprise to compare folklore globally and to assess national/regional borders along cultural lines. They opened up the debate about the origin of the wondrous tales by theorizing an Indo-European origin in the mythopoeic age for the tales that corresponded to the movement of language into central Europe. More so than other writers, the Grimms bragged that their sources were genuine tradition bearers, and the brothers encouraged field work to capture the genuine "voices of the folk." In the first edition of *Kinder -und Hausmärchen* [Nursery and Household Tales, 1812], they proclaimed that

> [we have] tried to collect these tales in as pure a form as possible ... No details have been added or embellished or changed, for we would have been reluctant to expand stories already so rich by adding analogies and allusions; they cannot be invented.
>
> (Tatar 1987, 210)

In the second edition (1819), the Grimms put a face to the folk artistry. They included an illustration called *Märchenfrau* (fairy tale woman) by their brother Ludwig Emil Grimm as the source for many of their tales (Figure 0.1). She has been identified as Dorothea Viehmann (1755–1815), born Katharina Dorothea Pierson to a family of French Huguenot background in Rengershausen near Kassel in northern Hesse, Germany. At the time the Grimms met her, she was a poor village tailor's wife from Niederzwehren. Thirty stories, transcribed from her oral telling a year before her death, appeared in the edition. The illustration fixed the image of the storytelling German peasant as the authentic folk (Ward 1988, 91–92). Later critics have challenged the association of fairy tales with poor villagers, but it has been a hard one to shake in the public imagination (Dégh 1988; Hearne 1988; Kamenetsky 1992, 113–50; Rölleke 1988; Ward 1988).

Impressed by what the Grimms had accomplished for Germany, British editor, William John Thoms (Figure 0.2) in 1846 in a letter to the prominent literary magazine *Athenaeum* insisted that the inclusive term "folk-lore" would be preferable to "popular antiquities and literature" (or a German term such as *Volkskunde*) used in England

Figure 0.1 Frontispiece of *Kinder- und Hausmärchen*, vol. 2, by Jacob and Wilhelm Grimm, 1837

Source: Courtesy Staatsbibliothek zu Berlin.

to describe the types of traditions gathered by the brothers (Emrich 1946; see also Thoms 1965; Tokofsky 1996). Thoms thought that as an analytical category "folk-lore" could integrate various items that had been treated separately, and consequently drew attention to the connecting thread of expressive tradition as a focus of inquiry. The significance of this kind of knowledge learned by word of mouth, participation, and demonstration, in contradistinction to bookish academic study was that it drove identifications of culture, often along local, regional, national, and ethnic lines. It drew attention because of the continuity of traditions through long stretches of time, passed, as was often rhetorically emphasized in contrast to the novelty of modernity, "from one generation to another." Thoms

Figure 0.2 William John Thoms (1803–1885) with bound volumes of the journal *Notes and Queries*

Source: Wellcome Library no. 14950i. Courtesy Wellcome Library, London.

and others concerned about the rupture with the pastoral past caused by the upsurge of industrialism, the status of spirituality and artistry with the rage for scientism (particularly with the influence of evolutionary doctrine), and the expansion of empires over diverse cultures in the nineteenth century, proposed folklore as a concept as well as a rubric to address tradition-centered communities and imaginative expressions that appeared to defy the wave of modernism washing over industrializing countries of Europe.

In response to Thoms's call in 1846, *Athenaeum* established a "department of folklore," and during the 1850s books using "folklore" in their titles began to appear. By 1876, Thoms and others were using the term "Folk-Lorists" to refer to students of the subject. In 1878, Thoms was among notable public intellectuals such as Andrew Lang, Max Müller, and George Laurence Gomme who organized the Folklore Society in London. In 1886, leading French writer Paul Sébillot adopted "Le folk-lore" as the preferable French term for "Les traditions populaires" (popular traditions or customs of the people) (Sébillot 1886). In 1888, the American Folklore Society was established on the model of the British organization, and three years later an international cast of folklorists descended upon London for the second International Folk-Lore Congress, thus institutionalizing the term that encapsulated the broad subject area of traditional knowledge and practices as "folklore" (Jacobs and Nutt 1892). German writers and professors following the Grimms held on to *Volkskunde* (knowledge or learning of the people) and *Volkspoesie* (vernacular poetics) as operative terms for traditional expressions. Despite the emergence of a global scholarly network, linguistic-nationalistic contingents pressed for folklore work along regional-ethnic lines: in Thoms's English realm, Scotland, Ireland, and Wales, for example, developed significant academic-museum legacies of folklore collection and study emphasizing cultural nationalism (Briody 2007; Fenton 2000–2013; Owen 1991).

In the discourse of this formative era, "folklore" vied at times with "folklife" and "folk culture" which tended to emphasize the everyday life of peasant and homogeneous communities that included customs, crafts, architecture, and art. Folklore in rhetorical usage referred more to the language, narratives, and songs of ordinary people in heterogeneous societies. To suggest a regionally focused study of social and material life, Swedish writers claimed *Folkliv* as early as 1817, and the Dutch and Germans used *Volksleben* after 1776, all of which translated in English to the use of "folklife" (Vermeulen 2006, 131–33). Swedish professor Sigurd Erixon (1888–1968) distinguished folklife study as "regional ethnology" to provide holistic descriptions in contemporary fieldwork of regional-ethnic cultures within complex societies. He held an academic chair at the University of Stockholm with folklife in the title (1934–1954), first established in 1918 to study "conditions of life and ways of representation, their traditions and customs, their spiritual and material cultivations" (Erixon 1943, 228; Jacobsen 2001, 7). In Britain, separate journals arose with the titles *Folklore* (published by the Folklore Society) and *Folk Life* (published by the Society for Folklife Studies; following Erixon's conceptualization, the subtitle of the journal is *Journal of Ethnological Studies*).

Especially influential on the usage of folklife was the folk museum movement led by Artur Hazelius (1833–1901), founder of the *Nordiska museet* (Nordic Museum) in 1880 (originally established in 1873 as the *Skandinavisk-etnografiska samlingen* or Scandinavian ethnographic collection) and in 1891 the outdoor folk museum *Skansen* (literally the Sconce) in Stockholm (Figure 0.3). Skansen later became a generic term in Europe and the United States for a site containing traditional buildings arranged in communities rather than galleries. Within the buildings and outside in working fields, docents demonstrated everyday life, crafts, arts, and customs of regional-ethnic folk cultures. In addition to concerns for exhibiting buildings, many

Figure 0.3 Vårfest, or Spring Festival, at the folk museum Skansen, Stockholm, Sweden, 1893

Source: Nordiska Museets Arkiv och Bibliotek.

of the museums conducted field research to interpret folk culture within a traditional landscape. Closely associated with the Nordic Museum, for example, was the *Institute för folklivsforskning* or Institute for Folklife Studies for research and instruction in ethnological matters of community and region.

European concerns for grasping the ramifications of sociocultural change spread to other parts of the globe facing modernization. In Japan, Yanagita Kunio, who was influenced by English folklorists, led the development in the early twentieth century of *minzokugaku*, which is usually translated as "folklore studies" (literally the study [*gaku*] of people [*min*], or conceptually as "culture that does not depend on writing" (Christy, A. 2012, 7; see also Morse 1990). With the rise of the Republic of China in the early twentieth century, a folklore studies movement spread that was led by Zhong Jingwen (1903–2002). It concentrated on folk song studies, and then expanded to customs and narratives, to rebuild a sense of Chinese peoplehood after the decline of the Manchu Qing Dynasty (1644–1911) and the effects of colonialism. Chinese scholars who had studied folklore in Europe and Japan translated it into Chinese with the holistic term *minsu* (literally people [*min*] and tradition [*su*]). Together with historian Gu Jiegang, Zhong Jingwen organized The Folklore Society at Zhongshan (Sun Yat-Sen) University in 1927 and its publication activity began in 1928 brandishing the folklore label (*Minsu zhoukan*), including translations of articles by English folklorists. In both areas, fieldwork among villagers as the authentic tradition bearers and poetic roots of the nation tended to predominate, as is evident in the launch of the journal *Folklore Studies* at the Catholic University of Peking in 1942 (retitled *Asian Folklore Studies* in 1963 when it moved to Nanzan University in Japan).

The situation in South Asia, especially in India, celebrated for its treasure trove of ancient narrative and religious lore, was influenced by English colonialism, in which European writers, administrators, and missionaries were involved in collecting and publishing folklore about subject peoples (Kirkland 1973; Upadhyaya 1954). Among the ancient texts mined by folklorists for folktale sources of European classics such as Aesop's fables and Mediterranean mythology from the original Sanskrit was the *Jatakamala*, probably dating to the fourth century BCE. Beginning a post-colonial movement of India-born folklorists, D. N. Majumdar established an "Ethnographic and Folk-Culture Society" in 1945 at Lucknow University, that featured ethnographies of village life by natives of that region to open pre-colonial traditions for research, analysis, and public discussion (Upadhyaya 1954). In addition to re-examining the ancient Sanskrit texts, folklorists promoted fieldwork to collect folk songs, sayings, and narratives of the incredibly diverse number of ethnic-linguistic groups for archival research (Kirkland 1973). Responding to cultural tourism, world heritage preservation movements, and campaigns for ethnic-linguistic sustainability, a later development was the public Karnataka Folklore University, which, when it opened in 2011, claimed to be the world's first college exclusively devoted to the study and research of folklore. Another location affected by colonialism that has developed folklore studies to recover as well as analyze native pre- and post-colonial traditions is Africa. A distinguishing feature of many folkloristic academic programs in Africa is attention to oral literature and history in addition to coverage of a wide array of indigenous-linguistic groups.

In the Nordic countries, Finland became the stronghold of folklore studies owing in large part to the nationalistic importance of the *Kalevala* produced by Elias Lönnrot in 1835. As in Germany, collectors were motivated to collect linguistic and narrative traditions directly from ordinary people. Oriented toward the understanding of oral traditions as literature, Finnish scholars developed an analytical method called the historic-geographic method that was intended to uncover the global diffusion of folktales from likely origin points (Krohn 1971; Richmond 1973). Giving academic credibility to the study of folklore was the establishment in 1898 at Helsinki University of the first chair of folklore. Reaching across borders, the holder of that chair, Kaarle Krohn in 1907 organized with Danish folklorist Axel Olrik and German folklorist Johannes Bolte the Federation of Folklore Fellows, which after 1910 published an influential series called Folklore Fellows Communications, further underscoring the global use of the term "folklore" as an encompassing concept for traditional materials.

Distinctive methods under the banner of folklore were also being developed in the Russian Empire but the connections to the West were not as close as they were with the Scandinavians. The Grimm brothers inspired Russian writers in the nineteenth century and their historiographies laud Alexander Afanasyev's massive compilation of folktales between 1855 and 1867 as a rival collection to the Grimms. Not as concerned for questions of origin and diffusion, Russian folklorists became globally important in the discourse of folkloristics for structural analysis, particularly to display the morphologies of folktales, connections of personalities to the style and composition of storytellers, and social-ideological uses of folklore (Oinas 1973; 1975). The word "folklore" was notably adapted into Russian for Yuriy Sokolov's *Ruskii fol'klor* (1938) as a popular college textbook. The thick volume exemplifies the approach to folklore as an umbrella concept for various literary genres such as charms, proverbs, riddles, songs, tales, religious verses, chants, and laments.

Russian researchers tended to make a distinction between ethnographies of village life and minority groups and the literary tasks of folklore studies. Although the study of folklore flourished in Russia and Eastern Europe, scholars typically worked outside of the discourse apparent in Western Europe, America, and Asia until the folkloristic work of Sokolov, along with now classic works of structuralism by Vladimir Propp, personality studies by Mark Azadovskii, and social functionalism of Petr Bogatyrev drew wide discussion after their translations in English appeared in the 1960s and 1970s (Azadovskii 1974; Bogatyrev 1971; Oinas and Soudakoff 1975; Propp 1968; Sokolov 1971).

After the fall of the Soviet Union in 1991, suppressed work in ethnic-national languages such as Yiddish, Belarusian, Lithuanian, Latvian, and Estonian came to light and showed a heightened sensitivity to ethnopoetics, cultural nationalism, diasporization, and subaltern identity (see Bar-Itzhak 2010; Basanavičius 1993–2004; Gottesman 2003; Klotilatviešu Folkloras Krātuve 2015; Klotiņš 2002; Veidlinger 2016; Virtanen 2002). Indeed, folklore played an integral role during the Estonian "singing revolution" in the 1980s when folk-singing demonstrations defied Soviet authorities and led to independence in 1991. Of special note was renewed reflection about large ethnographic collections of the past such as the An-Ski expedition into the Russian Pale of Settlement from 1912 to 1914. It raised timely questions in the twenty-first century about the integration of ethnographic methods and philosophies of migratory community/ethnic identity under the big tent of "folkloristics" or social-science-oriented folklore studies (Veidlinger 2016).

By the mid-twentieth century the kind of material presented under the heading of folklore and the approaches to study it had changed with documentation of significant traditions that marked the dynamics of modern industrial, urban, and organizational groups. Scholars raised on the traditions of cities and factories viewed folklore as part of modernity and examined its place in the formation of identity within plural, complex societies. In the place of archaeological keywords of relic, survival, evolution, and primitive were contemporary, individualistically oriented references to modern, art, context, and performance. Anthologies such as *The Urban Experience and Folk Tradition* (Paredes and Stekert 1971), *Toward New Perspectives in Folklore* (Paredes and Bauman 1972), *Folklore: Performance and Communication* (Ben-Amos and Goldstein 1975), and *Folklore in the Modern World* (Dorson 1978a), set the tone for the new process and present-oriented, discourse. With the identification of emerging traditions, folklorists treated cultural practices less as remnants of the past and more as resources of living creativity and adaptation. Another assumption to fall by the wayside was the rootedness of folk groups, and frequently the presumption of their isolation and primitiveness fostering the maintenance of traditions. In this view, folklore was evident among all strata of society and was not correlated with a lack of education or writing. Additionally, with the increased global mobility of peoples, folklorists theorized about traditions that appeared to travel and adapt in different modern contexts including crowded, cosmopolitan cities and suburban dwellings in their orbit (see Boström and Öhlander 2015).

The acknowledgment of mobility also led to countering the "essentialist" assumption that one's ethnicity of birth dictated the person's cultural profile, often leading to the assignment of attributed or stereotyped traits. Folklorists noted the ways that people understood the cultural coding of different situations and could attain and express different identities in their varied encounters of life. Thus, identity, and folklore, were malleable according to varied contexts, and individuals could even construct their own identities based upon the creative manipulation of traditions. For folklorists recording people in action, such expressiveness included not only familiar items of folklore but frequently focused on the behaviors that produced them. Some behaviors, in fact, were not comparable as textual forms but were noticeable as repeated practices, and in actions referred to colloquially such as playfighting, kidding around, hanging out, and schmoozing, to name a few, appeared to be symbolically significant as situated processes (sometimes characterized by the term *praxis*) that were understood to have cultural associations.

Besides the revelation that folklore thrives within non-communal institutions, another perspective from modern folklore research is the role of the media to channel rather than obliterate traditional practices. The rise of the mass media did not displace the transmission of folklore and subsequently new perspectives arose to explain the idea of mediated traditions. In addition, the spreading discourse of scientific relativity in physics led to applications in culture advancing the idea that groups are not better than one another as cultural Darwinism based upon evolutionary doctrine had suggested. Observers noted differences in practice and explained them within particular historical and geographic conditions. The evolutionary association of folk to peasants or "primitives" was altered to a relativistic conceptualization of everyone possessing folklore. Folklore became understood as a form of learning and expression intrinsic to humanity. Theoretically, this process of knowledge and practice, summarized as tradition, was significant because it materialized and defined culture as a constructed as well as an inherited force in the conduct of everyday life. Folklore as process, the action-oriented argument suggested, was critical for people to denote their individual as well as social identity, difference, and boundaries. Consequently, folklore was not secluded in the past or remote areas, but constantly emerged in everyday social interaction among urban elites as well as rural peasants. The factors behind, and the people responsible for, generating and absorbing traditional practices consequently invited documentation and explanation.

To be sure, folklorists still sought out tradition-centered communitarian groups (e.g., the Amish, Figure 0.4), Bedouins, and Hasidim), often to ask questions of their social and cultural maintenance with the perceived threat of modernization to their distinctive lifestyles. This concern became the foundation of folklife, folk cultural, or ethnological approaches, which could be expanded to groups owing to modernization, such as lifestyle and interest groups (e.g., Goths, neo-Pagans, skateboarders, fan cultures), organizations (e.g., Boy Scouts, Twelve-Step groups, summer camps, military groups), and corporate/professional culture (e.g., nurses, lawyers, firefighters, college campuses). The motivation for, and strategies of, engaging in tradition are often at the center of analysis. If the focus of ethnological lenses turned toward small groups, folklore studies also broadened inquiry to social factors beyond a group's entrenched geographical and class location—ethnicity, gender, urbanity, occupation, age, disability, body type, or sexual orientation.

A way to show the relevance of folklore to everyday lives was to point out the connection of traditional knowledge and practice through the life span. Even before a baby is born, a mother might receive conventional wisdom about signs of the fetus's gender, beliefs about the effects of food on the baby's body, and ways to induce labor. Bestowing a name and ritualizing birth (including the initial "cutting of the cord" before religious rites of passage) are

Figure 0.4 Old Order Amish man driving a horse-drawn buggy amid motor-vehicle traffic in Lancaster County, Pennsylvania, 2014

Source: Photograph by Simon J. Bronner.

often among the first folkloric responses to a new life. In childhood, games, toys, gestures, slang (including nicknames), crafts, and rhymes from tradition often come into play and serve to inculcate values and develop identity as well as amuse and engage youth. Many cultures associate adolescence with coming-of-age rituals, courtship customs humor, pranks, and legend transmission as youth develop social relations and anticipate moving into independent adult status. There can be a public perception that folklore is attached to youth and old age because these are supposedly changeful, vulnerable phases of life devoted to pastimes. Folklorists further point out in young adulthood the critical functions of traditions in the workplace (narrative, customs, visual lore) and formations of family identity through storytelling, holidays, weddings, and crafts are common. Old age has been examined as a time of life review involving narrative and material expressions in preparation for the final passage of death. Folklore is therefore not relegated to a stigmatized caste, remote slice, or racialized segment of society; it is ubiquitous for everyone from the cradle to the grave.

Bridging humanities and social science perspectives, a hybridized discipline, designated as folkloristics or folklore studies and centered on folklore as a common, fundamentally human experience, came into its own in the twentieth century with academic and community centers spread around the globe (Bronner 1986b; Dorson 1973a; Zumwalt 1988). Museums, colleges and universities, archives and libraries, festivals and concerts, public service organizations, businesses, and governmental agencies arose during the twentieth century to address folklore and folklife issues and engage in high-profile projects with ethical and public policy implications. As these institutions entered into discourses on the meaning of traditional knowledge, categorizations of "folk" and "lore" received close, hard looks to see if they remained viable in a post-modern, or what some scholars would call, a popular-culture world (Foster and Tolbert 2015). With the declaration of the digital age in the twenty-first century, new challenges arose to the assumptions of folklore as face-to-face communication and its social basis. Theories of communication and new philosophies with keywords of convergence, hybridity, and networking followed to account for post-industrial phenomena of mass-mediated culture and the role of mobile individual agency in self-actualization and new forms of social belonging (Blank 2013a; Jenkins 2006; Howard 2015; Kapchan 1993; Porter 1996; Stross 1999; Trend 2001). Nonetheless, as readers of this book should appreciate, the original invitation of the Grimm brothers to locate and analyze key cultural expressions globally and the traditions and tellers they represent still holds.

With this intellectual legacy in mind, I address in this book the basic keywords, concepts, and theories of folklore studies underlying the folkloristic research process: (1) establishment of a problem statement or thesis; (2) identification and annotation; (3) analysis and explanation; and (4) formation of implications and applications. Consequently, this book is not a manual of fieldwork, a bibliographic guide, or a history of the discipline, although it contains material on all three. It is not an index to the genres and groups of folklore, but, to be sure, I included an array of practices and communities to show the thread of tradition connecting phenomena labeled "folk." What this book does is survey how, and why, researchers derive the meaning and applications of folklore as a shaping resource in the lives of individuals, groups, and nations. Using illustrative examples from my own research as well as signal studies from the intellectual legacy of folkloristics, my approach is methodologically driven to illuminate the basic scholarly ideas of folklore studies. It invites readers to appreciate, and I hope, enter, "the field."

WHAT IS FOLKLORE, AND WHY DOES IT MATTER?

PROBLEM AND PRACTICE

On the cusp of a new century that promised to bring profound changes to the world, English folklorist Edwin Sidney Hartland in 1899 riveted the attention of his august Victorian audience with a provocative question: "What is Folklore and What is the Good of It?" (Hartland 1899). Folklore had become a popular subject in the land and consumers snapped up books on tales, speech, and songs with the term in the title. By the time that Hartland issued his tract, the term folklore, introduced into intellectual discourse by William John Thoms in 1846, had taken hold on several continents. Thoms later reminisced that his motivation was a fear that the past was quickly giving way to industrialism. He remembered that "the railroad mania was at its height, and the iron horse was trampling under foot all our ancient landmarks, and putting to flight all the relics of our early popular mythology" (Thoms 1876, 42).

Thoms hoped that folklore could integrate many genres that previously had been studied separately: "manners, customs, observances, superstitions, ballads, proverbs." The connecting theme through all of the material was tradition. Under Hartland's watch, scholars calling themselves "folklorists" flourished, a learned society with celebrity writers had been organized devoted to folklore, and the first academic chair of the subject had been created in Helsinki, Finland.

Folklorists, Hartland proclaimed, were engaged in the "science of tradition" (Thoms 1965; Hartland 1894–1896; 1968). Even as methods and theories changed drastically from the Victorians to digital natives who framed tradition arising out of technological interaction, the flag of tradition continued to be waved over the territory of folklore. Surveying folklore's study at the mid-point of the twentieth century, eminent American folklorist Stith Thompson proclaimed "the idea of tradition is the touchstone for everything that is to be included in the term folklore" (1951, 11). That idea still held strong by the end of the century when Richard Bauman declared for a new generation of communications-centered folklorists that "there is no single idea more central to conceptions of folklore than tradition" (1992, 30).

Whereas most Victorians limited lore to semiliterate or isolated "folk," most folklorists by the time the *Standard Dictionary of Folklore, Mythology, and Legend* came out in 1949 agreed with Mamie Harmon that folklore "may crop up in any subject, any group or individual, any time, any place" (1949, 400; see also Dundes 1966a). Folklorists identified multiple existence and variation in the lore as a characteristic of a folk process, rather than its relegation to the remote past or place, as the Victorians were wont to do (De Caro 1976; Dundes and Pagter 1975). To underscore folklore as a type of communication that draws attention to itself, Dan Ben-Amos suggested during the iconoclastic 1960s removing temporal tradition altogether from definitions of folklore. In its place, he advocated for emphasizing imaginative expression emerging from social interaction in a definition of folklore as "artistic communication in small groups" (1972, 13). Yet in 1984 he reflected that "tradition has survived criticism and remained a symbol of and for folklore" (124).

The idea of tradition had evolved even among the Victorians. With reference to tradition, Hartland altered Thoms's emphasis in folklore on literary antiquity to a social application of natural history that followed a hierarchy of progress in civilization. Tradition, as he later publicized it for his fellow folklorists in various guides, was a process of transmission characteristic of the level of "savagery" among unlettered, isolated groups which survives into civilization. In his words, "It is now well established that the most civilized races have all fought their way slowly upwards from a condition of savagery."

Hartland implied in his tract that the "considerable amount of knowledge of a certain kind [traditional]" even if "savage" or unscientific, was nonetheless profound, although he stopped short of calling it artistic as Ben-Amos had. The knowledge was "traditional" in its association with oral and customary communication. In Hartland's view, the folk who passed it on were presumably on the lower rungs of the social ladder. "Civilized" people at the top, he argued, might be quick to dismiss this knowledge, but Hartland urged his audience to study it so as to learn about their cultural progress.

THE MODERN DISCOVERY OF FOLKLORE IN ANALOG AND DIGITAL CULTURE

The modern present or process-oriented conception of tradition in folklore as it developed in the twentieth century owes more to another British folklorist's social-psychological emphasis on the "folk" (Jacobs, J. 1893; see also Fine, G. 1987b). In an often-cited essay simply entitled "The Folk," sociologically oriented folklorist Joseph Jacobs blasted Hartland's laddered natural-history ladder model and assumption of illiteracy as the hallmark of folklore. He asserted several principles that added the individual to group, and space to time, as crucial factors in analyzing the significance of folklore in culture. He viewed the diffusion of folklore, and its suggestion of a multiplicity of cultures, as negating the assumptions of a singular hierarchy of civilization. His points were: (1) folklore is continuously being updated and invented, and therefore folklore involves innovation, and consequently individual initiative; (2) folk is not a level of society, but a group sharing tradition that could be of any stratum; and (3) tradition is not a body of knowledge among the illiterate, but a process understood by following spatial and psychological patterns.

Folklore in Jacobs' perspective became contemporaneous, spread by technology such as telephones and books as well as by word of mouth. Linked to individual needs and social conditions, folklore lost the racial taint applied by the survivalists. Tradition, he implied, was chosen as well as followed. It was created anew as well as inherited from yore. Calling for the study of the lore of the present, Jacobs announced, "We ought to learn valuable hints as to the spread of folk-lore by studying *the Folk of today*" (Jacobs, J. 1893, 237; emphasis added). Hartland was willing to concede the point in establishing folklore study as a science rather than antiquarian pursuit. He broke with his fellow Victorians, who, he said, view "its subjects only in the remains of a distant epoch, preserved less perfectly in Europe, more perfectly in Africa" (Hartland 1885, 120). Capitalizing tradition to separate it as a body of knowledge in contrast to the customary manifestations of plural "traditions," Hartland presaged future scholarly thought by pronouncing, "I contend that Tradition is always being created anew, and that traditions of modern origin wherever found are as much within our province as ancient ones" (1885, 120). Hartland and Jacobs could agree that the significance of folklore, the "good" of it, was its manifestation of the processes of tradition that shed light on how culture worked and how humans conducted their lives.

In late nineteenth-century America, similar definitional debates ensued, and as in Britain, they often referenced the dramatic changes brought by mass industrialization and immigration. The underlying issue driving the concern for folklore as a vernacular product was the effect of rapid social and material changes perceived by the white Protestant elite on national traditions and values. Folklore was not the only location for this question. As abstract art taking inspiration from primitivism took hold in the early twentieth century in response to modernization, art critics raised the issue of a tradition of art. As new forms of writing—realistic and popular— spread, literary circles took up the matter of vernacular or "local color" tradition in literary production. But arguably tradition was most discernible in the persistent quality of folklore and the groups it represented. In the first issue of the publication of the Folk-Song Society of the Northeast, Phillips Barry and Fannie Hardy Eckstorm were among the few folklorists to directly face the matter in their title "What Is Tradition?" They were acutely aware of changes in popular musical tastes and the rise of the urban recording industry. They well understood the preservation instinct in saving the songs of tradition they called folksongs, even as they recognized "that ballad making is still going on" (1930, 2).

Following Jacobs, Barry and Eckstorm significantly distinguished two kinds of tradition: in time and in space. They wrote:

A song may have come down through the ages, like "Hind Horn" [Roud Folksong No. 28] or "Johnny Scot" [Roud Folksong No. 63], traditional in the sense that many generations of singers have sung it. Or, it may be, like "Willie the Weeper" [Roud Folksong No. 977], or "Fair Florella" [Roud Folksong No. 500], merely widely distributed, so that one who sings it may expect to find an indefinite number of persons, over a large territory who know it. Such is tradition in space. Both types of songs are equally traditional; both are species of folk-song. For, despite all that has been argued to demonstrate the contrary, it is tradition that makes the folk-song a distinct genre, both as to text and music.

(1930, 2)

Still, the problem of how tradition fit into technological or mass culture remained along with the additional question of whether "authentic" traditions in modernity needed the qualifier of "folk." American folklorist MacEdward Leach addressed these issues when he observed:

America is rapidly developing a new cultural stratum—alas for folk story and song. This is mass culture, a product of a society ordered and regimented by a technology working through mass media, such as radio, television and graphic advertising; and master-minded by hucksters selling goods, ideas, social behavior, religions—hard and soft commodities.

(1966, 395)

The situation was hardly America's alone, as references spread to the influence of mass media on the rise of mass culture throughout the globe by century's end.

The concept of tradition in the twentieth century was revised to include creativity, individuality, and emergence into the "folk process." In the modern sense of folkloristics, especially, individuals choose and adapt traditions rather than merely following them, as the Victorians imagined (see Bronner 1998; Dorson 1978b; Dundes 1966a). Traditions in this modern view are indeed invented and contested, but still presumed as a kind of shared knowledge and action to be a basic need of life. Traditions are strategically selected and performed for the purpose of changing modes of persuasion and identity.

Equating tradition with submission, however, cultural critic Raymond Williams claimed "tradition" to be a loaded keyword of society that was frequently manipulated to keep the establishment in power. In the midst of modernization, he reflected, tradition became associated with respect for the establishment and duty to follow precedent. In his view, tradition stood in the way of "virtually any innovation" (Williams, R. 1983, 318–20). In the reformulation of tradition advanced by folklorists, the term became intertwined with creativity or "expressive culture." It often was presented as the profound intellectual property of disempowered groups hanging on to tradition as a form of resistance to official authority or to bolster claims to political recognition and advocacy for social change (Bronner 1992b; Limón 1983; Norkunas 2004; Silverman 1983).

In the reformulation of tradition characterized by acceptance of a present accelerating into the future, the standard of persistence through generations no longer held fast. The spread of jokes in short-lasting "cycles," carried through loosely connected "networks," "conduits," and "communities" was one oft-cited example of a "new" or "emergent" tradition (Dégh 1997; Dégh and Vázsonyi 1975; Dundes 1987a; Fine, G. 1979b; 1980; 1983). Indeed, the late twentieth-century folkloristic attention to jokes as a pervasive modern narrative genre was itself a sign of expansion of the concept of tradition, because formerly, according to folklorist Elliott Oring, jokes, a prominent example of a performative "living tradition" used by people in all walks of modern life, "were considered neither to reflect the spirit of the ancient folk-nation nor to indicate the survival of primitive belief and thought" (1986, 9–10). Other newly scrutinized genres in this "living tradition" mode were legends, personal experience stories, youth slang, gestures, and song parodies.

With the explosion of the Internet representing "digital" communication, the question of tradition's role in culture again surfaced. After all, texting a joke to an unseen recipient is a far cry from gesturing and making eye contact with huddled buddies in the usual familiar place (Bronner 2012c). One commonality of both cyberspace and natural space is being "free" and "open" in the sense of being unrestricted. Both invite involvement on common ground and participants form social guidelines to organize themselves. From the perspective of the user, the Internet opens access and is an open medium. Users recognize a fundamental difference between sites identified as "official" or corporate, usually controlling its content and broadcasting information to a passive viewing audience, and those that allow posting, "live" chat, and free exchange among users. For many users, the latter constitutes the folk universe of cyberspace in contrast to a corporate realm. The folk realm is not located in a socioeconomic sector or a particular nation as much as it represents a participatory process that some posters refer repeatedly to as the democratic or open Web.

Folklore as an expression of tradition is wrapped up in the Internet because in "messaging," "connecting" and "linking," if not talking to one another, people incorporate the symbolic and projective functions that folklore distinctively provides. And when people email or post, they often invoke, and evoke, folklore as a cultural frame of reference for creatively relating experience, particularly in narration and image that respond to ambiguity and anxiety. The basis of the claim for the Internet taking on folkloric qualities is the medium's interactive, instrumental quality that differentiates it from television and radio for which people are divided between broadcasters and listeners or viewers. Internet users are captivated by its capability to simultaneously send and receive, produce and consume, write and read; they are "prosumers" (Tabbi 1997; Zukin 2004: 227–52). Precedent can be found in vernacular uses of photography, photocopying, and faxing, which invited manipulation of images and text to create a play frame in which humor, pathos, and memory were shared among members of a social network, often from an anonymous source that signified commentaries that folklorists call "metafolklore" on values and attitudes about the very technology and institutional contexts that made the images and text possible (Dundes 2007; Dundes and Pagter 1975; Fineman 2004; Mechling 2004; 2005; Preston 1994; Roemer 1994). Many of these broadside-type sheets, surreptitiously produced in circulated from photocopy rooms, found their way to bulletin boards and office walls.

The visual practice of Web posting differs from the vernacular use of photography, photocopying, and faxing because it is more widely available, of course, but further, it also could be personalized at the same time. Youth has also influenced the growing compactness of the Internet, which can be utilized on the run, and in private away from home and the watchful eye of authority. Youth are thought to particularly engage the Internet because they have more to say, and fantasize or worry about, and they derive gratification from widening their circles of contacts into definable networked cliques. It enables the transition out of the home, giving them physical mobility and social connection often associated with cultural passage into adulthood. The openness of youthful endeavor is indicated by the number of electronic responses to tell others what one is doing. This linkage of action to age is yet another way that the Internet mediates, and alters, tradition, for conspicuous on the web are efforts to virtualize rituals of change, joy, and grief, such as virtual wedding chapels, church services, and cemeteries (Goethals 2003; Hutchings 2007). The folk Web has not replaced in reality rites of passage, but it often elaborates upon them in virtual photo sites, and arguably has transformed the album-keeping (related, too, to autograph-album writing) and photocopying of humor into digital culture. As the folk Web is embraced by all ages, beginning even before children can read, it becomes part of ritual routine, including creation of electronic family albums, virtual cafes, and support groups composed by parents, niche sites for ethnic-religious networking, matchmaking and chat rooms assuaging loneliness for singles, and memory-making by older adults in scrapbook and memorial sites. The old pastoral model of folklore with wisdom of yore "handed down" by a golden ager may lead people to think that digital culture displaces tradition in this mode, but digital culture can be conceived as fostering a "handing up" by young wired wizards with mythic imagination and social ebullience.

A distinction that arose in the twenty-first century is between analog and digital culture. Digital comes from the Latin *digitus* for finger, suggesting discrete counting, and converting real-world information into binary numeric form. Analog contains a reference to the Greek *logos* philosophizing meaning that comes from the related senses of the word as "word" (or "say") and "reason." Analog culture, often attributed to the touch-oriented world of tradition, especially in pre-modern society, is one whose meaning comes from sensory aspects of perception (Stewart and Bennett 1991: 28–32; Bronner 1986b). In this view, storytelling in analog culture is an event defined not just by a text but by a physical setting and the perceptions between tellers and audience (Georges 1969; Oring 2008). Digital narrative, as indicated by its symbolic equivalence with seeing something "going viral," is often described in terms of spread, immediacy, placelessness, and ubiquity (Wasik 2009). Digital culture, rather than being relational, is *analytical* because users link, arrange, and reconstitute informational elements; folkloric action that is analytical depends on repetition and alteration of images as users simultaneously send and receive (Blank 2012; Buccitelli 2012; Howard 2008; Page and Thomas 2011; Peck 2015).

In his compilation organized around American regions, *The Greenwood Library of American Folktales*, editor Thomas A. Green listed over 80 discrete texts he contextualized as folklore in cyberspace. Many are oral legends and chain letters adapted to the distributive medium of the Internet with the invitation to "forward ASAP," but many use the form of electronic communication to comment about its distinctive qualities. An example is the "email charge" rumor that the federal government will charge a 5-cent surcharge on every email delivered to offset losses by the U.S. Postal Service (Green 2006, 4: 262–64). A variant accuses newspapers and the popular press of repressing the story. It invites users to harness the power of the Internet to "E-mail to EVERYONE on your list." It speaks to the democratizing "freedom" ideal of the Internet and at the same time the belief that superstructures representing the power elite flex control. As one variant states directly, "The whole point of the Internet is democracy and noninterference" (Green 2006, 4: 264). This idealization of the Internet as an untethered, unbureaucratized "commons" suggests that although it is certainly viewed as postmodern in its transcendence of space and time, it is popularly constructed in the model of the premodern village, raising comparisons to a "global village" governed by tradition rather than nationalistic rule of law.

This constructivist outlook of digital conduits of communication which does not have a baseline for the extent, location, economic status, literacy, or antiquity of the group lends itself to the centrality of *network* as the social basis of folkloric communication generally. With the use of network as a term, in the words of folklorists Beth Blumenreich and Bari Lynn Polonsky, is an understanding that

Folklore is individually determined and based, not "group" determined and based. Moreover, the individual's folklore is determined by the nature of his interactions and experiences. This suggests that folklore can be most profitably studied in terms of interactional communicative and experiential networks—ICEN's, as we shall call them.

(1974: 15; see also Augusto 1970;
Fine, G. 1983)

Blumenreich and Polonsky conceptualized networks to be face-to-face connections of choice in which obligations are decentered from family and community to a number of heterogeneous organizations that the individual chooses. Unlike communities in which one resides or interacts with others, networks are infinitely expandable and transcend time and space. Virtual networks, according to a dictionary of "New Keywords" for the information age, are central to the development of choices, and "imagined to be a means of establishing electronic communities (networks of people sharing beliefs and/or interests at a distance) at a time when long-term communities are said to be disappearing" (Webster, F. 2005). Networks are integrally tied to technological change which facilitates increasing, simultaneous flows of information through accumulable, expandable social conduits. Although the buzzword of information makes the communication sound like sterile minutiae, folklore is one of the strategies commonly employed to give a sense of tradition, and hence identity to participants in the network.

AN EXPLANATORY METHOD FOR THE STUDY OF FOLKLORE

Folklore as an expression of traditional knowledge is primary evidence used by an analyst to produce findings and generalizations about tradition as process (Honko 2013b). Victorian authors were well aware that since the materials of folklore were not easily perceived as particles of physics or specimens of biology, there could be skepticism of their application as scientific data. Hartland's important question of "What is folklore and what is the good of it?" addressed the issue of whether folklore studies constituted science by stating

> But here you will tell me: It is impossible to have a science of anything
> which does not fall into method, and is not capable of being classified and
> reduced to rule. Tradition is admittedly shifting, uncertain, chaotic; and
> how can you have a science in tradition?

His answer was that folklore obeys laws and follows patterns. He wrote:

> The aim of the science of Tradition is to discover those laws, by the
> examination of their products, the customs and beliefs, the stories and
> superstitions handed down from generation to generation, to ascertain
> how those products arose and what was the order of their development ...
> (1899, 11)

The modern reformulation of folklore took into account more
flexibility in the authority of tradition, and shifted interest from
development to the generation of folklore. Alan Dundes, a driving
force in the reformulation of folklore concepts arising in the present, called for the identification and analysis of folklore's "patterns"
(1980, x). Other prominent folklorists referred to patterns in different terms. Jan Harold Brunvand referred to folklore's "common
qualities" and proposed that the "findings of such folklore research
are applicable to many fields" (Brunvand 1998, 24). Michael Owen
Jones and Robert Georges suggested that the hallmark of tradition
is "continuities and consistencies"; Richard Bauman offered the
goal of research as "regularities," which he described as "discover-
able uniformities in folklore behavior" (Georges and Jones 1995, 1;
Bauman, R. 1969, 169). The choice of words such as "patterns,"
"qualities," "continuities," and "regularities" to describe folklore
conveyed the notion that folklore can be objectified as material or
content. It then can be ordered and compared, and work with it can
be replicated. In this model, analysts record phenomena and render
them manageable as data. Then they identify connections among
aggregate data. Reflecting on this occupational praxis, Richard
Bauman boasted, in fact, that folkloristics is the most "documentary"
and "aggregative" of the social sciences (1969, 168–69).

For some workers in the field, the organization of a "collection"
of a locality, group, or theme, identification of cultural scenes related
to tradition, or creation of an index to classic texts or artworks is an

end in itself. Any one of these endeavors can demonstrate the vitality of folklore or promote attention to group members who might not otherwise be visible or appreciated. Along these lines, some field-work manuals refer to a method of "shotgun" collecting in which one produces long lists of folk items they encounter in an area. Often engaged in what they viewed as salvage cultural work because folklore inevitably disappeared, these collectors left the task of explanation to others, although it might be argued that they were engaging in analysis by showing that whatever area or group they were working with had a trove of folklore that represented cultural viability.

Hartland's commentary used the strategy of explanation, to show, in his words, "that the science of Folklore is one of real importance, full of interest, full of surprises to those who are unacquainted with it." The expectation of paradigm shift arising from the identification of causation is evident from his comment that folklore "has vast possibilities that will revolutionise our conceptions of human history" (Hartland 1899, 44). History is especially pertinent, not just because of the attraction of evolutionary models in Hartland's era, but also the logical presumption of antecedent causation—what went before explains what occurred later. The idea persists that folklore needs to be rationalized. Interpreted, folklore's patterns are uncovered. Explained, its sources are analyzed.

From where does the commanding rhetoric of interpretation derive? Many historiographers cite as pivotal Clifford Geertz's *Interpretation of Cultures* (1973) and his concept of "thick description" in an "interpretive theory of culture." Geertz distinguishes his "description" from "explanation" by stating that, rather than generalizing across cases characteristic of explanation, description generalizes "within them." Giving the analogy of a patient being diagnosed to interpretation, he was particularly concerned that interpretation would not be predictive but it would anticipate a specific situation. His subjective interpretation gave special attention to

> the meaning particular social actions have for the actors whose actions they are, and stating, as explicitly as we can manage, what the knowledge thus attained demonstrates about the society in which it is found and, beyond that, about social life as such.

(Geertz 1973, 27)

Geertz suggested a structuralist task for the ethnographic interpreter:

> uncover the conceptual structures that inform our subjects' acts, the 'said' of social discourse, and to construct a system of analysis in whose terms what is generic to those structures, what belongs to them because they are what they are, will stand out against the other determinants of behavior.
>
> (Geertz 1973, 27; see also Lévi-Strauss 1963)

Geertz's cultural "interpretation" referred also to his background in literary study, because he conceived of actions as "texts" that could be read differently by various observers as well as participants.

Concerned that Geertz's interpretation could appear arbitrarily derived and narrowly preoccupied with reflections of social structure as explanation, Alan Dundes outlined a folkloristic interpretation after a task of objective identification. Rather than engage in "shotgun" collecting as the means to "thick description," Dundes insisted on the postulation of hypotheses and performing some operation upon data—whether using structuralism, historical reconstruction, or cross-cultural comparison—as a prerequisite step to explanation (Dundes 1965a). Analysts, in his view, strive to gather contextual and behavioral information as well as textual data, and check their results by examining whether the information is consistent through the material they have gathered (internal consistency) and correlates with other comparable situations (external validity) (Fine, G. 1984).

Arguably, labeling folkloristic method "scientific" is a rhetorical strategy to point out that the study of tradition should be empirically based and contribute to explanations of human behavior rather than simulating experimental laboratory science (Brown, M. 2008; Carvalho-Neto 1971, 85–98; Glassie 1983: 124–26; Samuelson 1983). The four-tier ethnographic methodology I will outline that moves from problem statement, identification, and annotation to analysis, explanation, implication, and application is a far cry from the Victorians' natural history in which traditions were collected and classified as biological specimens to construct an evolutionary periodization from savagery to civilization. In the outline presented here, folklore is key evidence of the process of tradition acting as a causal force in culture while still inquiring humanistically into the faith and insight that tradition provides as a type of knowledge or mode of thought (D'Andrade 2008; Edmonson 1971; Pelikan 1984, 65–82). In answering basic questions of why people need and use traditions, why some traditions "catch on" or "die out," and why some people defend or attack traditions, the outline is intended to guide investigation of tradition's connotativeness—its encapsulation of contextualized meanings that may vary as traditions are enacted by participants and perceived by insiders and outsiders.

What happens when the controlled conditions of a laboratory are transferred outside to the wildness of a cultural "field" with human subjects? Kenneth Goldstein's *A Guide for Field Workers in Folklore* (1964), in keeping with the behavioral or ethnographic turn, posed an early answer to the question by adapting "scientific inquiry" to the study of human subjects enacting folklore in its "natural contexts." Goldstein's comparison of his procedure with laboratory science reveals that the use of hypothesis is similarly emphasized, but it appears late rather than early in the process (1964, 16):

1 *Problem statement*: the setting up of a problem to be solved.
2 *Analysis of the problem*: the determination of the relevant data and the methods most appropriate for obtaining them.
3 *The collection of data.*
4 *Presentation of the research findings.*
5 *Postulation of hypotheses, based on the analysis and interpretation of the data.*

One should notice, too, that he suggested "interpretation" as a subjective statement of meaning from the viewpoint of the analyst that differs from "findings." Goldstein made a connection between inference and interpretation in his warning that "since inference involves a considerable amount of interpretation, it is less to be preferred as a field method than interviewing" (1964, 105). Goldstein pointed out that "findings" are evident from direct observation while "interpretation" is deduced from general principles and may not be apparent from the literal content of the collected material. As a narrative structure, Goldstein's method followed a sequence of solving a puzzle, from the opening "problem" to a concluding "solution." This procedure implied that in resolving an enigma, the analyst rationalized folklore together with tradition, since its persistence and use seem irregular, unusual, or draws attention to itself in some other way.

An especially trenchant inquiry into folkloristic method by Kenneth Laine Ketner revised Goldstein's schema for systematic inquiry with the following:

1   Realization of a Puzzling Question or Doubt.

   A   Unsaturated questions. These are the kinds of questions which begin with words like "what," "when," "where," "why," or "how" …

   B   Saturated questions. These are questions of the form "Is S a P?" …

2   Develop One or More Hypotheses.

   A   If the inquiry begins with an unsaturated question, the first step will be to propose a hypothetical answer …

   B   Sometimes the inquiry begins with a saturated question. In that case, we already virtually have a hypothesis at hand, and we can then proceed to 3 and 4.

3   Deduce Consequences.
4   Test the Hypothesis.

(1973, 118–20)

The basis of this revision is a move to the observation of cultural scenes in contrast to Goldstein's emphasis on collecting as an analytical "materialism." According to Ketner, materialism "insists that folkloric phenomena are to be understood as if they were objects, which means that folklore is seen as a static entity, a thing that can be transmitted from one person to another" (1973, 122). The negation of this philosophy is seen in approaches he labels "folklore interactionism," "a view which urges that folkloric phenomena are basically dynamic processes of interpersonal interaction" and are therefore documented through ethnographic "thick description" of events rather than collecting or inventorying texts (Ketner 1973, 122).

Ketner's revision also suggested the use of explanation rather than interpretation to account for the generation as well as the nature of cultural phenomena (Ketner 1973, 126; see also Ketner 1975). The model for explanation would look like the following (with *explanans* representing the material used in explaining and the *explanandum* being the matter to be explained):

Premises, such as ... Statement of one or more general lawlike regularities, and
    Statement of one or more specific conditions
    Constituting *Explanans* (all statements true), leading to ...
    Conclusion ... Which logically implies that which requires explanation
    Constituting *Explanandum*.

(Ketner 1973, 127)

By emphasizing the phenomena, rather than their location, this model, according to Ketner, implies that "folkloric behavior is not a curiosity, not a symptom of inferiority and ineptitude, not a mass of error, not the exclusive property of the stereotyped 'folk,' but a sign of one's humanity" (Ketner 1973, 130). Returning to Dundes's binary structure of *identification and interpretation* as a folkloristic research procedure, one may discern a division between description and analysis. Dundes's critique suggested that interactional approaches are locked into description since each situation needs to be uniquely defined.

There is a way to double Dundes's binary, however, to create a more systematic linear methodology than identification and interpretation by themselves denote. Before identification, the folklorist presents a *problem statement* often expressed as a puzzling question about the pattern or meaning of folklore observed. Working from the assumption that cumulative scholarship begins where others end, the problem statement involves an extended survey of bibliographic sources on the subject and the variations of the material under consideration. This opening establishes the significance of the query by either reconsidering a previous explanation stated as hypothesis; questioning a monocultural limitation which can be addressed with cross-cultural or historical comparison; pointing out an action that had not been considered as a subject for inquiry (e.g., collecting as a praxis by folklorists); indicating an unexpected or enigmatic persistence or decline of tradition and its function (e.g., education, entertainment, cultural validation, social maintenance); showing that an unlikely, usually learned or elite, group was "folk" in the form of a saturated question (e.g., scientists, mathematicians, lawyers); working through the effects of changing units of measure (e.g., motifs on a literary model or functions in a morphological scheme); or testing assessments of folkloric material (e.g., attributions of monogenesis, exceptionalism, and diffusion).

What follows is an *identification* predicated on the description of the item and the genre or genres to which it belongs. For Dundes, identification often involved showing material that had been left out or minimized in previous collections, especially tied to the extent of an item's variations, its various cultural contexts, behavioral (or performance) information, or the available metafolklore. Distinctive to the study of folk traditions is the *annotation* often included in the identification project. The annotation positions the practice in time and place and relates it to, even categorizes it with, similar forms or actions. Folklorist Elliott Oring presented the annotation as essential to the analytic process because it uncovers "some sense of this web of relations" (1989, 361). Oring emphasizes that it illustrates that "folklore collected or contexts observed in the face-to-face encounters at home, in the dormitory, or at work are often related to traditions that have been reported by other collectors in other times and in other places" (1989, 361). The issues that the annotation addresses, going back to the scholarly practices of the Grimms, involve the spread of tradition beyond a single group, class, or level of culture to avoid "cultural parochialism"; identifying sociocultural change and variation, particularly in response to the tendency to view tradition as static; and psychological or social importance of tradition, or in other words, its force and function for individuals and groups as members of society.

Analysis consists of an operation upon the data to signify cultural patterns. In this step, folklorists expose underlying structures, or extract symbols from a text for closer examination, present contextual descriptions of an item's use, use cross-cultural examples to draw comparisons and contrasts, find significance in etymologies and names as signs, or construct a developmental chronology of an item or culture. In an orientation toward tradition, the role of precedent to the present is usually ascertained in addition to determining historic sources for, and reactions to, cultural practices (see Abrahams 2005; Bronner 1982; Knight 2006). The "text"

WHAT IS FOLKLORE, AND WHY DOES IT MATTER? 33

analyzed has expanded from the utterances and objects to the event as a whole and the behaviors that shape the event. Such texts have categorizable forms, patterns, and structures that can be described, annotated, and compared.

The *explanation* is the critical leap from identifying textual or behavioral patterns to recognizing cognition. It typically involves discerning meaning with reference to generalizable statements that can serve to solve intellectual enigmas, resolve apparent paradoxes, and uncover hidden motivations. For instance, folklore might be explained as a way to broach difficult subjects within a frame of symbolic narrative, ritual, and fantasy. Folklore displays cognitive function by involving projections onto familiar expressive forms and practices of emotional or mental conflicts, anxieties, elations, and aspirations. The wedding, for example, is the most elaborate ritual in many individualistic societies because it involves the anxiety, and joy, of moving from the status of an individual to becoming part of a union. Many of its traditions deal with issues of fertility, gender roles, family relations, and future prosperity that can be symbolically read within various practices (throwing of bouquet, showering with rice, exchange of rings, the elaborately dressed bride being "given away") as projections into a ritualized social frame. Wedding traditions might also be enacted to display symbols of ethnic and regional identity in socially recognized food, dress, bodily decoration, music, and dance. They might also be adapted to social changes, such as same-sex and intercultural marriages, and their public enactment can also make a political statement about social, as well as, marriage equality. Not all married couples engage in "traditional" weddings, but for many who participate, an important aspect is the engagement with folkloric processes to make a critical life transition (Caton 1993; Foster and Johnson 2003; Greenhill and Magnusson 2010; Hamon and Ingoldsby 2003; Ochs 2011; Theophano 1991).

Frequently the conclusion constitutes a final phase of what I call *implication*. Implication is different from many folklorists' *application* (the basis of applied or public folklore) because in application one usually proposes programming to edify the public or implementation of pragmatic actions in areas such as medicine, government, social work, and education that address personal or societal needs (see Jones, M. 1994). Analysis can be used, for example, to consider the social and political significance of the outlooks one uncovers or symbolic relationships among apparently diverse forms or traditions. In my study of the common folk art form of carving chains and caged balls with a pocketknife out of one piece of wood, for example, I found that curators and art historians dismissed the work as "whimsy" and mere "whittling." I hypothesized from my experience with living carvers that the forms held a greater social and psychological significance (Bronner 1996; 2005b). As a problem statement, I questioned that if it was ephemeral, then why did the art persist so widely and why did carvers spend extended time on the apparently tedious task of making chains and caged balls? In fieldwork, I *identified* a pattern of simulating the look of iron chains, pliers, and cages but leaving the wood unpainted so as to show their fragility. Surveys of carvers in the present day indicated that older men who often had rural backgrounds primarily created these forms. Using historical sources for *annotation*, I determined that the form was widespread on several continents and in the European-American version had uses in spinning devices, sailors' gifts for sweethearts, and as playthings for children. Its association with non-utilitarian purposes in the modern period did not reduce its creation into the present day.

Although the annotation showed the utilitarian precedents for, and traditionality of, the crafts based upon a comparison of forms, it did not reveal the meanings as carvers expressed them. Using interviews with carvers, I *analyzed* the connection between their life stories and their decision to use their traditional knowledge that they learned typically in childhood of making chains in old age and found that they remarked on it relieving anxiety associated with physical, cognitive, and social decline. Watching how the chains, cages, and pliers were made and trying my own hand at it, I realized that the key "trick" connecting the different forms' creation is the process of "cutting in" the wood with the knife rather than the visual expectation of cutting wood out or using connecting screws (Figure 1.1). Carvers mentioned the paradoxical metaphors of the chains and cages representing entrapment and exclusion and at the same time their agency in creating forms that depend on the praxis of inclusion by "cutting in." In surrounding themselves with chains and cages they produced metaphors for their anxiety about being old in a youth-oriented society and the symbolically empowering actions of carving.

Figure 1.1 Folk artist Earnest Bennett demonstrates carving wooden chains and caged balls from one piece of wood with a technique of "cutting-in" at his Indianapolis, Indiana, home, 1982

Source: Photograph by Simon J. Bronner.

I ethnographically observed in ritualized scenes of carvers encountering recipients of the chains that they presented the forms as visual riddles (made of parts but without connections, wood but not wood, utilitarian but not utilitarian, strong but not strong) to be figured out. The unstated answer was that the maker representing old, traditional skills held power. They gave the forms away to represent their values and provide a memory of them as they contemplated their end of life. I *explained* their urge to create these forms in old age and share them in ritualized frames of action by pointing out the psychological need for "riddling art" in the projection of conflicts. The particular outlet of carved chains and cages out of wood was a behavioral mode that was appropriate; it was contextualized in their rural backgrounds and masculine uses of tools and wood. Other explanations are possible, certainly, with considerations of different human subjects and contexts, and I generated hypotheses about the creative uses of tradition by older men that could be tested. I concluded by pointing to the *implication* of the gendered needs of men who were socialized to be productive and managerial to have expressive, productive outlets in retirement associated with social withdrawal (Bronner 1992c; 2005b). I checked the validity and consistency of the findings by checking if the explanation held in other settings and if metaphoric claims are not contradicted within the scene examined (see Elster 2007; Fine, G. 1984; Honko 2013a; Wojcik 2008). I have pursued the *application* of these findings in programming in centers for older adults, public exhibitions of creative work by older men and women, and work with counselors to apply folk art as therapies (Bronner and Gamwell 2014; see also Hufford *et al.* 1987; Mullen 1992; Shuldiner 1994; Siporin 1992, 194–95).

Modern folklorists investigate tradition as meaningful, purposeful activity that is an instrument of knowing and navigating through social life. In contrast to presentations of tradition that emphasize its ethereal, mystical, or ancient characteristic, the modifier of "folk" clarifies this tradition as measurable, comparable, analyzable—and explicable. Folklorists reveal folk tradition as continuous and chang-ing, and therefore in need of explanation. Using "folklore" as a label does not presume that tradition is anachronistic or restricted to faith and falsehood. In sum, folklore problematizes tradition.

A HANDY DEFINITION OF FOLKLORE IN PRACTICE

Underlying the four-step folkloristic method is the "handiness" of tradition. The way people *perceive* the hand—active, immedi-ate, instrumental, gestural, and visible—particularly in relation to the mind—passive, remote, non-productive, individualized, and unseen—dictates the way analysts conceive folklore as perva-sive, relevant, contemporary, functional, expressive, and ultimately meaningful. Being a cultural resource *at hand*, tradition represents everyday processes of social control and expression, and these pro-cesses are often set in contrast to modernization associated with standardization, commercialization, discontinuity, and artificiality. The idea of tradition is "handy" or effective in the sense that people regularly invoke it to refer to a purposeful, creative process of sus-taining social connections through cultural expression, whether literally in greeting traditions of shaking hands and celebratory customs of clapping hands for applause or figuratively in handing down stories and songs—and values—between generations. That is not to say that the influence of tradition on life is easily averred, particularly by an intellectual elite. Because of a modernist concern that tradition restricts individualism, progressivism, and free will, the force of tradition has been denied or even protested (Adorno 1993; Giddens 1994, 66–74; Williams R. 1983, 318–20).

Stith Thompson's classic academic statement of folklore being socially "handed down" and therefore equated with tradition in *Funk & Wagnalls' Standard Dictionary of Folklore, Mythology and Legend* (1949, 403) echoes through most introductions to folklore during the mid-twentieth century: "The common idea present in all folklore is that of tradition, something handed down from one person to another and preserved either by memory or practice rather than written record." His contemporary Archer Taylor revised the handing process to be more historical when he defined folklore as "materials that are handed on from generation to generation" (1949, 402–3). The synchronic concept of "handing over" to expand the definition of folkloric transmission across space as well as time gives as a key to folklore the notion that it has multiple existence and variation over space as a sign of traditional processes at work (Barry and Eckstorm 1930).

Scholars of later generations continued to invoke the hand to describe the communicative process of tradition in folklore. Jan Harold Brunvand referred to folklore as "unrecorded traditions" characterized as "communication from person to person" (1998, 3). In a kind of motific substitution, Brunvand abstracts Thompson's emphasis on the hand in "handed down from one person to another" in the use of "communication," presumably to draw attention to transmission of traditions by records, telephone, photocopiers, facsimile machine, television, and computer (1998, 3). Remaining in the concept of "passing" is the generation of repeatable, varied expressions arising out of social interaction. According to Brunvand, folklore is "passed on" figuratively, if not literally hand to hand, or person to person and from elders to their juniors: "Folklore is oral or custom-related in that it *passes* by word of mouth and informal demonstration or imitation from one person to another and from one generation to the next"

(1998, 12; emphasis added). In the twenty-first century, Martha Sims and Martine Stephens in *Living Folklore* (2005) characterize folklore as "knowledge ... *handed on* orally from person to person" (2005, 131; emphasis added) and "expressive communication within a particular group" (2005, 6), thus suggesting the semantic equation of "handing" with "communication," "circulation," "transmission," "expression," and "sharing" as essential generative processes resulting in traditional material usually summarized as folklore.

No wonder, then, that folklorists emphasize "fieldwork." This scholarly labor outside the formal environments of institutions and archives implies that observation of the action of handing, the thing being handed, and the hands (that is, participants) who are involved, need documentation. Fieldwork presumes that folklore embodies tradition by revealing people in cultural production or metaphorically in "handwork," whether analog or digital. Folklore as a kind of expressive gesture therefore carries meaning that is discerned from recordable, repeatable practices. Folklore's traditionality presumably distinguishes it from other kinds of practices that are restricted to fixed forms of a solitary creator or are deemed culturally inert (as in "routines" of brushing teeth or putting on socks). Folklore, as with stylized hand motions of which the person is not aware, might become significant to record if it signifies a form of cultural inheritance and body of traditional knowledge. As a competitive athlete, ritually putting on socks before a game, in fact, took on significance for me because of an awareness that others had engaged in this kind of practice framed as traditional and given personal meaning in my actions.

Although approaches to fieldwork certainly vary (such as questionnaires, individual interviews, focus groups, collections of short items), a field approach essentially differs as an analysis from a literary reading or mathematical proof. Trained to discern manifestations of tradition, the analyst of folklore tends to frame events into repeatable, variable actions (such as singing, telling, and making), extrapolate knowledge gained and symbols communicated through the action, detect the exchange or direction of the transmission, and infer the character of people and settings in the exchange. The analysis frequently rationalizes activity that may appear out of the ordinary and aestheticizes material that might be construed as usual or routine.

Folklorists apply fieldwork strategies to the study of the past, typically through archivable documents, by tracing social transactions resulting in an expressible product or practice and finding relationships of a present practice to other times and places.

What about the distinction I claimed for folklorists annotating lore to discern relationships of material to tradition-bearers, groups, expressive precedents, and contexts? The annotation locates cognates of a practice and determines if their contexts are comparable in time and space to establish its "traditionality." In other words, the annotation provides evidence of social transactions resulting in the practice or memory becoming culturally embedded. The annotation raises questions in its paucity or abundance about the agency, persistence, change, structure, and function of lore that by definition involves "passed," or traditionally gained, knowledge. Tradition therefore implies an element of time, in the sense of folklore representing precedence of knowledge and presence of an expressible product or reproducible practice. Tradition also involves space because the transaction is located or situated and the folklorist infers social connections that make it possible for the expressions to diffuse as a result of cultural transactions and exchanges. A relational factor sought in the annotation is the cultural association of tradition to folklore by determining where the knowledge passed from and where (and by whom) it became planted (another reference to the hand).

Most linguistic as well as philosophical considerations of tradition begin with a singular source citing the Latin root *tradere*, "to hand over or deliver" and adapting it to the popular idea that tradition is "handed down" from generation to generation, especially by oral means. This gap between the linguistic root and popular discourse raises the question of how speakers moved from the Roman conception of a social act involving contemporaneous transfer of material goods to the dominant narrative of receiving knowledge from a predecessor. The source of the term "tradition" is typically traced to Roman jurisprudence, suggesting a literal meaning of tradition as a material transaction (Gross 1992, 9). Roman laws of inheritance dealt with goods considered valuable and meanings arose from the root *tradere*, including *traditio* for the process by which transmission occurs and *traditum* for the thing transmitted. Historian David Gross points out that *traditio* implies that "(a) something precious or valuable is

(b) given to someone in trust after which (c) the person who receives the 'gift' is expected to keep it intact and unharmed out of a *sense of obligation* to the giver" (1992, 9; emphasis in original). As an inheritance, the gift or *traditum* often comes from a predecessor or ancestor, and with it is the expectation that the thing would be cherished and preserved and considered valuable enough to be passed on to someone else (Gross 1992, 9). The obligation to keep and honor the item is driven presumably out of respect for the memory (and wishes) of the predecessor, whose name may be obscured over time as the *traditum* is passed on generations later. This sense of obligation shows up in an alternative meaning of *traditio*, "surrender," and suggests an association with authority because the recipient submits to the sway of the elder.

Getting to the abstraction of tradition from Roman law, a metaphorical shift occurred from thing to knowledge, which was probably based on the symbolic connotations of transmitting the *traditum*. A major clue is provided by rituals accompanying the transmittal. To mark the transfer of a piece of land, an agent physically handed over a clod of dirt from the property to the recipient; to legally recognize the acquisition of a house or a shop, keys would ritually pass from one person to another (Congar 2004, 9). The earth and the keys not only act as a synecdoche for something larger; they also inspire memory and narrative of the possession and the figures associated with it. Enacting *traditio* drew attention to itself by the use of a repeatable symbolic practice that relied on a shared knowledge between agent and recipient about the consequences of the act. The tradition became noticeable in the flow of life because it was ritualized and framed as time out of time. In that special occasion differences between present and past collapsed. One was aware in the tradition that the action had precedent, but especially important was a transcendent concern about what it stood for. Other actions including telling a story or singing a song that evoked the transference of something expressive or valuable received could be attached to the process of *traditio*. In this way, both tangible and intangible "gifts" recognized by their expressive and connotative characteristics became equated. Recalling what these things represented constituted a narrated knowledge that was not so much institutionally taught or read as it was socially engaged in practice. It connoted socialized or localized knowledge popularly designated as lore.

Setting the process of *traditio* apart is its consecutiveness. In a business deal, an agreement is concluded; it does not have to be reenacted to be valid. The business deal is a matter of record. In tradition, transmittal needs to occur repeatedly often by word of mouth and practice, which further sets it apart from modernization characterized by the rule of official law and record. The socially communicative characteristic of a transaction in tradition is crucial to the perpetuation of lore. Every action in *traditio* involves a giver as well as a recipient, and the participants are aware that something like it has occurred before and will happen after they are gone. They understand that the action of *traditio* is consecutive from one person and one moment to the next. A commonly used metaphor is that they are links in a chain, each separate but connected to one another in a consecutive pattern. Tradition requires agency to continue, and part of the obligation to keep the *traditum* intact is to re-enact the process. Traditions can disappear and be revived after lapsing, but psychologically, a fear exists that the chain, or the order, of tradition will be broken if it is not enacted consecutively (see Dundes 1966b).

Referring to tradition suggests not only that cultural reproduction occurs, but also that a meaning may be changed by an individual agent who varies a precedent to create a version for a particular situation or locality. This broadening of the social implication of tradition is a semantic development beyond the one-to-one relationship implied in Roman law. As lore, traditions can be transmitted to a crowd and move in different directions with the travels of the recipients. When individuals engage in the process of *traditio*, traditions vary as they are adapted to different settings or are recalled with changes in content and meaning, even if they are structured similarly to the lore that went before them. As populations move and social needs change, traditions inevitably permute, increasing or altering by fusion with other traditions, or declining in practice and memory. Cognitively, there may be an inclination to believe that traditions by their nature as valued social artifacts grow from simpler to more complex forms in an evolutionary pattern, but this may be countered by a devolutionary belief that modernization and the passage of time render traditions fractions of what they once were (Dundes 1969a). The mechanical-sounding action of handing down may not be deemed intellectual, or more accurately "scholastic," but it suggests active participation and hence authenticity in culture by the passing of something socially significant involving memory and narrative (Bourdieu 1990, 127–40). It is often "practical" in the sense of being applied to lived experience and variable in social situations (Bourdieu 1990, 80–97).

Habit, in contrast with tradition, appears impractical. A habit is an action, often a mannerism that is regularly repeated until it becomes involuntary (see Aboujaoude 2008). Rather than constituting a connotative message, habit is typically considered "routine" by being unvarying, or a rote, even an addictive procedure for an individual. Its manifestation in individual behavior is often differentiated from custom, which is a repeated social occasion (Duhigg 2012). Although *traditional* and *customary* are often used interchangeably to refer to the prescriptive repetition of activities based on precedent, customary activities do not have the degree of consecutiveness and connotation expected of tradition. One does not hear of the *chain* or *authority* of custom in the way these terms are applied to tradition. Indeed, an event might be intentionally referred to as a custom to imply that it does not have as strong a consecutive hold on its participants as tradition or that it is irregularly enacted. Social psychologist Edward A. Ross includes the criterion of involvement in the distinction that he insightfully draws between custom and tradition: "By custom is meant the transmission of a way of *doing*; by tradition is meant the transmission of a way of *thinking* or *believing*" (Ross, E. 1909, 196; see also Clark, M. 2005, 4). The commonality of tradition and custom is their involvement of action in the form of practice, but tradition often brings into play a mode of thought or social learning associated with lore. Tradition—more than custom—brings out the handing down and over of values.

Separating brushing one's teeth in the morning as a daily routine or custom from the tradition of the tooth fairy is a quality that has been labeled *phemic* by philosophers, particularly those incorporating theories of language developed by J. L. Austin (1961; 1968; see also Warnock 1989). For some observers the imaginative content of the tooth fairy along with other beliefs, rituals, games, and narratives sets it apart as a tradition. However, many utilitarian practices that are socially or geographically situated such as craft, medicine, and agriculture would not be perceived as fantasy or play and yet are viewed as noticeable traditions. *Phemic* material denotes an implicative message that is impelled to be transmitted and the material becomes associated with the process of its transmission. Austin approaches the analysis of these messages similarly to pragmatic gestures to account for the way they are *ordinarily used*, that is, transacted with others, to produce symbols and elucidate meaning.

Austin's contribution to a theory of tradition based upon practice is to rubricate forms of transmission that result in actions (he called them "illocutionary acts") that people recognize as traditional. Austin calls the production of sound a *phone*, whereas a *pheme* is a repeated utterance with a definite sense of meaning (a subset of a *pheme* in his system is a *rheme* to refer to a sign that represents its object). Colloquially, the *pheme* may be said to "say something" that might be used on different occasions of utterance with a different sense (Warnock 1989, 120). The nuance to tradition as "regularities" that Austin introduces is that the illocutionary act is one performed *in saying something*; the locutionary act is one in the act *of saying something* while the perlocutionary act occurs *by saying something*. Indeed, the example in everyday life that Austinian philosopher John Searle uses to exemplify this distinction among the acts invokes the role of the hand as the response that signals a transaction and the occurrence of a tradition. The locution might be a query of whether salt is on the table and the illocution is of requesting it. The perlocution is causing someone to hand the container of salt over or "pass it" (Searle 1969, 53). The rules or traditions governing the transaction are often unstated and learned by participation in cultural scenes or regular responses to what Searle calls "the presence of certain stimuli" or "intentional behavior" (1969, 53; see also Cothran 1973).

The term *pheme* comes from the goddess Pheme of Greek mythology who personified renown and was characterized by spreading rumor. Symbolically important to the idea of folklore as phemic is her status as a daughter of the earth and one of the mightiest, if not the most elegant or beautiful, of the goddesses (Burr 1994, 231). She had a proclivity to repeat what she learned for better or worse (in art, she is often depicted with multiple tongues, eyes, and ears or with a trumpet broadcasting messages), to the point that it became common knowledge. Along the way, though, the information had varied greatly and was often made larger or stylized in proportion to the original bit of news. Pheme did not fabricate knowledge; her skill was in framing material in such a way that it would be passed around in ways that drew attention to themselves. She was a relay station of sorts, serving as both recipient and transmitter of earthy material that, in being shared from person to person, became aestheticized and elaborated. The knowledge transmitted was known as much for the process it went through as for its content; in its expressive forms, it carried a message, often judgmental, or connotative. Because it was subjected to this verbal and non-verbal transmittal process associated with earthy rumor, the content invited evaluation of its truth and value. In its "larger" form, the material raised questions about its sources and its combinations and reconfigurations, forming a whole with multiple connotative layers created along the path of transmission.

Phemic transmission can be distinguished from *phatic* communication in what anthropologist Bronislaw Malinowski characterized as a "type of speech in which ties of union are created by a mere exchange of words" (Laver 1975, 215; see also Warnock 1989, 120–22). As action, *phatic* speech corresponds to the routine intended, according to linguist John Lyons, "to establish and maintain a feeling of social solidarity and well being" (1968, 417). Tradition often serves this social function as well, but it is distinguished as purposeful activity with a repeatable, multilayered message that can be called *phemic* because it compels "handing down/over" and variation in the long term by means of social, especially face-to-face, interaction. Saying the greeting "how are you?" might appear routine/phatic (characterized with the folk term of "small talk"), but the responses of "hunky dory," "just ducky (peachy, dandy)," "fair to middling, mostly middling," "couldn't be better," "can't complain," "still among the living," "still breathing (standing, living)," "fine as a frog's hair," "fine as a frog's hair and twice as fuzzy," "not dead yet," and "old enough to know better, and you?" often ritually signal a special social connection between the speakers/texters. Further, the practice contextualizes *phemic* or connotative meaning characteristic of a folkloric frame of action (such as reference to aging, anxiety/"troubles," lifestyle choices, medical inquiries, friendship or family relations, and insider, localized knowledge) (see Coupland *et al.* 1992; Coupland *et al.* 1994; Rings 1994; Wright 1989).

The fact is that every day, people are involved in events they recognize as traditional and at the same time look to establish precedents for traditions of the future (Georges and Jones 1995, 1; Jones, M. 1997). It signifies in countless gestures of speech, play, and rituals scripts embedded with values, symbols, and anxieties in their live—and the heritage from which they come. In short, tradition's "handiness" informs people where to begin and guides them on how to proceed. But they may be troubled by engaging in practices about which they do not have background. That is why so often one hears questions about common rituals and customs such as "how did this start?," "why did it last?," "why do we do it now?," and "what does it mean?" These questions are evidence that tradition is so pervasive that it is hard for people to separate from it so as to recognize it, no less analyze it. And apparently getting answers to these questions are more than to satisfy curiosity; they relate to one's sense of belonging and judgment of behavior.

In the twenty-first century, several world service organizations define folklore as traditional, indigenous, or local knowledge in need of protection because of threats to native habitats. The World Intellectual Property Organization, for example, established an Intergovernmental Committee on Intellectual Property and Genetic Resources, Traditional Knowledge and Folklore to develop international legal instruments for the protection of traditional knowledge, which it defined as "a living body of knowledge that is developed, sustained and passed on from generation to generation within a community, often forming part of its cultural or spiritual identity." Traditional expressions of knowledge, according to the WIPO, are "forms in which traditional culture is expressed" (WIPO 2015). The reference to culture underscores the proximity of tradition-bearers near one another, usually within a distinctive environment. In these definitions, the "handing down" process and continuity over time within a stable, rooted community are emphasized. Folklore, however, manifests in various forms traditional knowledge that is "handed over," mobile, and can be individualized. To be sure, traditional knowledge draws attention to a body of cumulative, transmitted ideas that are expressed in the practices of ritual, narrative, speech, craft, building, singing, and play known within a group. But traditional knowledge properly refers to the process of creating tradition.

That is, folklore is produced from one's cognition of precedent, a repeatable, variable practice recognized as connotative. This might mean that the content might be new but the structure of the rhyme or proverb is familiar. This concept of practice is not dependent on face-to-face interaction and is especially apt for investigations of digital culture as repetitive expressions generated by and shared with users. At the same time, it guides work in literary and historic sources because of the identification of expressive material that draws attention to itself by its repetitive framing with cultural or connotative meaning.

Arguably, the term "practice" by itself does not indicate the kind of learning that produced the activity or its transmission that resulted in perception of it as a tradition. Practice also suggests human agency and practical action. A commercial movie might depict a folk practice or express a traditional tale but the practice would probably not be viewed as integrated into folk culture unless it is repeated in everyday or ceremonial life. The folkloristic conceptualization of practice comes closest to philosopher Theodore Schatzki's notion of practice as "arrays of activity" that call upon "skills, or tacit knowledges and presuppositions, that underpin everyday and ceremonial activities" (2001, 2; see also, Bronner 2012b). With this concept, analysts seek constructed "cognitive frames" that direct, embody, and contextualize these activities as something deemed to be expressive, symbolic, and cultural—and therefore meaningful. Based upon this idea, I propose a practice-centered definition of folklore that retains a consideration of context but focuses attention to the knowledge domain, or cognition, at the basis of tradition. Simply put, folklore is *"traditional knowledge put into, and drawing from, practice."*

The definition begins with the identification of knowledge gained or learned typically from phemic processes of repeated, perlocutional communication in visual as well as oral and written means, and imitation and demonstration (often for social and material traditions). Knowledge or lore is perceived or constructed as traditional, characteristically through its repetition and variation, and connotative evocation of precedent. It can be viewed as distinct from, although, sometimes integrated into, the notion of popular culture as fixed in form and commercialized (folklore can also be "popular" and broad-based beyond the small group or subculture). Reference to the actions of "put into and drawing from" suggests the framing of connotative, purposeful enactments as an adaptation from precedent or an outcome of repeatable behavior. This outcome can be material and social as well as verbal. It can be constructed by and enacted for the individual.

Think for a moment of the practice of hitting one's head with the palm of the hand and saying, "What was I thinking?" The words alone might be rendered literally but framed in action and intent as folklore, the symbolic gesture in words and action that are recognized from precedent, carry meaning, usually of having made a preventable mistake. The tradition-bearer hits the head to indicate that the brain was not working right, much as one might in fact, hit a machine to get the gears moving. The interrogative phrase might not even be heard by another person, but constitutes a framed, stylized, repeatable, variable action along with an uttered text that is based on precedent, even if it is individualized. It can be visualized on the Internet and sent to a friend who probably recognizes the reference to tradition. It might be used in popular culture by writers and filmmakers but they use "folklore" rhetorically whereas individuals hitting their foreheads with their hands are enacting, or practicing, the lore.

Even without the utterance, the gesture of hitting one's head could be construed as a signal of consternation. Combining the gesture toward the thinking "head" with the line "What was I thinking?" (and typically facial gestures of dismay), persons symbolize the precarious connection of their reasoning to action. The practice based upon traditional knowledge connotes motivations occurring in various circumstances or contexts that need explanation and persons might not be fully cognizant of their reasons for saying or doing what they did. The folklorist helps to discern what people are thinking, how they think with tradition, and why they act with, and on, tradition. Folklorists investigate a variety of questions in relation to the meaning of folklore, but fundamentally, they address why people repeat and express themselves.

WHAT DOES FOLKLORE DENOTE?

IDENTIFICATION AND ANNOTATION

The rhetoric of "fieldwork" in historic tomes of folklore might give the impression that the few remaining precious nuggets of folklore are mined in the deepest, darkest recesses of the earth. Or that folklore blasts into global consciousness only on special, often exoticized occasions such as Mardi Gras, Day of the Dead, and the Pamplona Bull Run. The likelihood, however, is that if you listen closely, folklore is evident in most conversations you hold. You pepper daily speech with slang, sayings, and humor. In greeting and parting, you probably utter familiar words accompanied by gestures such as a handshake, slap, bow, nod, wave, hug, or kiss. The actions are contextualized as traditional in different settings, including the corporate office, family reunion, and theater stage. You can also watch for social and material evidence of tradition that can be called folklore. A gold band on someone's left hand might signal the status of being married. You could also see passersby wearing headcovering indicating ethnic-religious, occupational, or age identity: *hijab* (headscarf worn by Muslim women), *kippah* or *yarmulke* (Hebrew and Yiddish terms, respectively, for skullcap or headcovering worn usually by Jews), "plain cap" (fabric headcovering worn by Old Order Mennonite and Amish women), "dixie cup" hat (white canvas with an upright brim worn by sailors in the United States),

African headwrap (colorful fabric shaped into a vertical bundle), and baseball cap (soft cap with a rounded crown, often with an embroidered insignia, and stiff front peak worn by many Americans).

Such observations might lead to a project to analyze one or more of the folk practices in cultural contexts. Doing so suggests that the meaning of practices is relative to the particular setting in which it is enacted. Or it is possible to examine the group and setting in which these practices occur to ascertain ways in which they foster tradition, invite participation in traditional events, apply traditional knowledge, and provide purposes for the tradition. The problem statement for such a project can vary, but as noted earlier, the use of folklore often raises questions of traditional process including motivations and structures for invoking tradition and the creative agency for changing it, relationships of cognition to expressive, symbolic action, functions of lore for individuals and for groups and societies, the connections of identity to the kinds of material people choose to express as folklore, and the cultural, philosophical, and political implications of the material. In short, folklore carries meanings that need explanation.

A first step is to identify the material and assess its traditionality through annotation. As the above examples indicate, the material comprises not only words, images, and gestures, but also actions to communicate them and the scenes of which they are a part. Each item might be analyzed as a separate action with a distinctive set of circumstances, and then aggregated with others to allow comparison and analysis. Folklorist Alan Dundes proposed in a seminal essay that any given item of folklore should be analyzed for its texture, text, and context (1964b). By texture, he meant its linguistic features such as stress, pitch, juncture, and tone, but a broadening is needed of the stylistic, aesthetic, or performative qualities of verbal communication to bodily and material genres including dance, music, and craft, for example. I would suggest that "mode" defines such qualities better than "texture." It is possible to describe a mode of practice that is characteristic of an individual as well as a group or setting. Mode can be conceptualized to describe an expressive quality such as sarcasm of an utterance, sturdiness of a structure, or playfulness in a design. A modal description helps someone who was not present appreciate the distinctiveness of the material beyond its form and construction.

The text is often thought of as verbal material, but the term actually derives from the image of a woven pattern. Metaphorically, it can describe the way a thing as well as a word appears, and indicate the formation, or weave, of components into a thing or narrative for onlookers or listeners to understand. A text invites inquiry into the structure and components of the item that might include for a craft the procedure for making it. Folklorists refer to a single item as a textualized "version" of an expression, which can be classified into genres usually defined by structure and purpose. An "etic" classification (from "phonetic") is one devised by the analyst with attention to comparable units of measure; an "emic" classification (from "phonemic") is conceptualized as a "native" category (Ben-Amos 1976; Dundes 1962a; Feleppa 1986; Headland *et al.* 1990). For example, folklorists use "beliefs" as a neutral, enumerative term for a statement of a condition and a result, but many people will refer to "superstitions" as a credulous prediction, often with a supernatural component. The significance of making a division between etic and emic terms is that the native terminology can be a sign of tradition and reveal cognitive categories. There can also be movement between etic and emic terms such as the case of "urban legend" introduced by folklorists to differentiate a contemporary narrative from a historic legend. As folklorists worked with the urban legend they realized the characteristic texts was not restricted to urban locations. Folklorists referred to such material as "contemporary legends" or "belief legends," while "urban legend" entered popular parlance as a bizarre story told as true but which was actually false.

In the classification of texts, items might be labeled a "variant" of a textual type. Whether a statement of belief, a recipe for a traditional dish, or an iconic decoration on a work of folk art, the variant implies that collected texts bear similarity to one another and could be traced back to an original source. Folk buildings and narratives are often arranged into structural typologies to suggest the historical and geographical development of one form into another and the visualization of those forms as variants of one another (see Glassie 1968; Noble 1984). Items can also be thematized with key words, actions, and designs such as love, violence, work, and play, and conceptualized to reflect "folk ideas" or core outlooks of a group or society, sometimes termed "worldviews" (Dégh 1994b; Dundes

1971a; 1995). Folklorists frequently arrange proverb collections, for example, by theme to locate the concerns of folk wisdom, and games by actions such as chasing, guessing, and daring to facilitate cross-cultural comparison (Knapp and Knapp 1976; Mieder 1986; 2012; Opie 1969; Roud 2010; Schipper 2003; Sutton-Smith and Roberts 1972).

Many practices that are called folk such as believing and playing, modern folklorists have argued, are not easily translatable, or comparable, as formalized texts. They might be referred to as behaviors, processes, and performances that are identified ethnographically, that is, described as part of socially framed cultural scenes. Whereas texts are presumed to be read or viewed as final outcomes, many practices can be documented as structured activities that proceed from a beginning to their conclusion. Patterns can be discerned, often with the help of photographic tools, in behaviors such as "play fighting" or "rough play" that is distinguishable from aggressive fighting (Mechling 2008; Reed 2005; Sutton-Smith *et al.* 1988; Smith 1997; Smith *et al.* 2004). Often there are contextual factors such as the location (e.g., the beach, playground, gymnasium), people involved (e.g., long-time friends, parents), and time (e.g., summertime or childhood) that signal the perception of the activity or tradition as appropriate and therefore culturally "framed" (Bronner 2010; Goffman 1974; Mechling 1983).

Dundes defined "context" as the "specific social situation in which that particular item is actually employed" (1964b, 23). The significance of the context to the identification of the item is that it might be associated with a specific group of people and performative venue (family dinner, concert stage, art gallery, or campfire) or will vary according to the audience. Dundes emphasized the social situation because of his definition of "folk" as a flexible social unit, "*any group of people whatsoever* who share at least one common factor" (1980, 6). Folklore, he argued, is consequential for providing "traditions which help the group have a sense of group identity" (1980, 7). Context, or that which literally "surrounds the text" can also be physical or psychological (see Hufford, M. 2003). The physical setting such as a hunting cabin guides the kind of practices that occur within it and the psychological refers to the perception of a location, frame, or scene as appropriate to playful, aggressive, work, ritual, or sacred activity.

It might also refer to the personalities or cultural backgrounds of the participants. Folklorist W.F.H. Nicolaisen (1980) has suggested that a linguistic term of "register" is useful to distinguish practices in a context that exists as a background for an activity and a setting that dictates it. Folklore, he theorized, is a variety of expression that can be invoked for a particular purpose or in a specific setting and is therefore associated with a cultural register people choose to put into practice in response to events and groups. People learn various registers in their lives and part of the cognitive strategies and "traditional knowledge" for living they acquire is the employment of a register to enact from their available repertoire at certain times and places (Nicolaisen 1984, 260–9; 2006).

It is possible to think of a group sharing a factor that it does not traditionalize (people on a bus, shopping at a store, driving the same car or persons in a room wearing glasses and belts). The key test for the "folk group" is whether folklore signals, or emanates from, social experience. Often overlooked, therefore, as Dundes's definition became standardized within folkloristics is his qualification, "what is important is that a group formed for whatever reason will have some traditions which it calls its own" (1965b, 2). Thus the unstated part of the definition is that two or more persons who share a linking factor use *traditions* to bond, so to gain, in Dundes's words, "a sense of group identity" (1965b, 2; see also Bronner 2007, 20–22; Fine, G. 2012; Noyes 2003). A concept of folklore arising out of the group extends and democratizes the concept of folklore by affirming what Dundes called a "flexible" notion of tradition and thereby negates folk as "monolithic" and "homogeneous" (1980, 8). With this emphasis on social interaction, one has to question, however, whether a group of two or more persons is necessary for folklore to be put into practice. Based on identifications of traditional human play with animal companions Jay Mechling pointed out that lore can be produced between a person and a pet, an imaginary object, or even oneself (Mechling 1989b; 2006). A social relationship is implied, if not actualized. The key is the perception that connotative activities construed as expressive, variable, and traditional become repeated.

An example of distinguishing folklore from what it is not is the structural comparison of games to narratives. Although games and narratives are typically separated into social and oral genres, respectively, Dundes found a similar sequence moving from a "lack" (something missing) to "a lack liquidated" (something found) prevalent in both (1964a). The implication for Dundes, therefore, was that they could and should be studied together as related traditions connected to cognitive patterning. He related organized football with backyard games, Disney movies with orally transmitted tales, and television commercials with old sayings. This treatment of all things cultural as relying on folklore raises the question of authenticity, that is, how to differentiate folk from popular materials. Dundes's structural answer is that a production *based upon* a folk model can be compared to, but distinguished from, "the folk model itself" (1965b, 1–2). The folk model, unlike the popular production, which tends to have a commercialized, fixed form, is more variable. The folk model also has precedent and displays continuity over space whereas the popular production is defined by its contemporaneity and typically, its novelty.

Jan Harold Brunvand suggested thinking of popular as "normative" cultural circulation by "formal means" (print and electronic media) whereas folk represented a group-oriented and tradition-based transmitted by custom and oral means; another level of elite signified for him selective academic and institutional training (1998, 8–10). The normative label can be relative, however, to the cultural scene and group, since communities create frames in which folk or traditional social structures predominate. And that is the point of creating analytical categories of folk and popular: to discern cognitive and behavioral processes at work in the formation of cultures and their implications for the conduct, and meaning, of life. The connection of folk materials to traditional knowledge, learning, and practice within social frames can be used as criteria for folk culture, even though many phenomena in modern society will display both folk and popular cultural influences. This view suggests a folk-popular continuum or weave rather than a dividing wall and invites identification and annotation that make comprehensible the cultural interplay, and shades of difference, among folk-popular-elite cultural processes, productions, and values in everyday and ceremonial life (Abrahams 2005; Bausinger 1990; Bluestein 1994; Craith *et al.* 2008; de Caro and Jordan 2004; Foster and Tolbert 2015; Mechling 1989a; 1993; 2002; Mieder 1993; Narváez and Laba 1986; Schoemaker 1990; Sherman and Koven 2007).

IDENTIFYING AND ANNOTATING ITEMS

Fieldwork represents a process of gathering data by observation and documentation of people engaged in folk practices. Continuing the naturalistic metaphor of fieldwork, folklorists refer to "collecting" folklore, by which is meant recording texts and noting their contexts and modes of expression. Collection raises images of viewing biological specimens that can be aggregated, classified, and compared by type. Kenneth Goldstein preferred the model of a farmer reaping the fruits of labor with the suggestion that folklore is a renewable resource that people need. He wrote that folklorists "harvest the crop of folklore materials and data without which the others would be unable to carry on their work." Goldstein warned that

> Collecting must be more than merely an enjoyable experience that can be pursued during holidays or vacations ... The researcher-analyst may apply the most rigorous methods during the later stages of investigation, but unless the primary data have been properly obtained with a full understanding of context and process, the most scientific of methods may not retrieve the situation later on.
>
> (1964, 24–5; see also Sims and Stephens 2011, 206–31)

Fieldwork methods are not restricted to inventorying items. Folklorists have used life-history approaches involving intensive interviewing with significant tradition-bearers, polls and surveys of individuals, often resulting in statistical analysis, visual recording of daily life in a particular setting, and participant-observation in rituals, occupations, and customs. Folklorists have less frequently but nonetheless significantly used experimentation with transmission of folk items within a group, reconstructions of historic conditions to engage in folk practices such as thatching and food preparation, and clinical tests to gauge responses to folk material. These non-field methods of identifying folk material simulate "natural" conditions and often supplement inventories of folklore in diaries, novels, local histories, legal proceedings, newspaper accounts, medical records, and governmental reports, to name some common sources.

Many folklore documentation projects have been designed to be housed in archives and primarily classified material by genre, location, tradition-bearer, and contributor. With digital environments, identifications as part of "databases" frequently cover more areas such as age, ethnicity, occupation, and family as well as including more contextual material. The following template from the folklore archives at the Pennsylvania State University, Harrisburg, based largely upon student collections in the Central Pennsylvania region, demonstrates considerations for collecting folk items.

ITEM:

This is the verbatim text as you heard or saw it. An example that you might hear from college folklore that might come up in a conversation you hear is: "If your college roommate commits suicide, you will get an A in all your classes for the semester."

CATEGORY:

This identifies what you heard and saw in a category or genre. The above example, for instance, could be classified analytically as a belief. The speaker might comment on the statement in emic terms of a "story" (indicating that it is unconfirmed), rumor or news. If you hear "the early bird catches the worm," you might write "proverb" as the genre, or if in response to the above belief, you hear, "that's an 'old-wives tale,'" you could write "folk speech" or "slang."

SUBJECTS: *keywords*

This identifies the keywords or subjects to which the item refers. This will often be the group, location, or theme to which the item relates. Examples for the college roommate belief might be "college student, death, suicide, Penn State University."

TRADITION BEARER AND BACKGROUND INFORMATION:

Give the name of the person or persons from whom you heard or saw the item. Give a description of the tradition bearer(s). An example is "white male, born in 1979, from Philadelphia, Pennsylvania, and now in his second year at Penn State."

MODE AND COLLECTION INFORMATION:

This provides the date and circumstances under which you heard or saw the item. This includes the way the tradition-bearer related the item to you. An example from the roommate belief is "Recorded in Stacks Cafeteria at Penn State Harrisburg, April 7, 2015, while discussing student competitiveness. It was not an interview situation. It was a friendly meeting and in the conversation I noticed that he prefaced this example with the comment, 'It's like the old story of ....' He smiled when he told me the belief, and used a sarcastic tone of voice, as if to indicate that he did not really think it was true, but had heard it often from other students."

CONTEXTUAL INFORMATION:

This gives any information that could be useful to understand the meaning of the item in a broader context. An example from the roommate belief is "There was an assumption that Penn State was a competitive institution, and there was too much concern for grades. There also was the background in his relating the item that the administration was impersonal and dealt with students according to formulas. When I asked him where he had heard the story, he could not recall a specific person, but said that he heard it from many people, often around final examination time."

COMMENTARY:

This gives any observation you have to make as the "collector." An example from the roommate belief is: "I had heard the item previously as a student at Penn State, but I had thought that it was true, and was in some policy manual. Upon reflection, it does seem to indicate that someone believes that getting good grades is ample compensation for the distress of having a roommate die. It seems to express the shallowness of human relations in college."

ANNOTATION:

This gives references to the item in print and on-line sources. By giving this bibliographic information, you are showing that the item has been recorded in tradition and has attracted analysis. Be sure to use full documentation of the source. Here are examples: An example of an annotation for the roommate belief is:

"Reference to the belief as a commentary on students in overly large classes and the formulaic thinking of large campus administrations can be found in Simon J. Bronner, *Piled Higher and Deeper: The Folklore of College Students* (Little Rock: August House, 1995), p. 12; William S. Fox, "The Roommate's Suicide and the 4.0," in *A Nest of Vipers*, ed. Gillian Bennett and Paul Smith, pp. 69–76 (Sheffield Academic Press, 1990). It is also the subject of a movie, *Dead Man on Campus* (1998).

COLLECTOR INFORMATION:

Give your name, address, email and any pertinent information (age, ethnicity, location) on your relation to the tradition-bearers or scene. Future researchers can consult this information to consider possible "filters" through which you heard or saw the tradition and its context.

An example of the discourse over such item collections is the analysis of the famous hookman legend. JoAnn Stephens Parochetti first reported the narrative with the emic term "scary story" in print from collections she made in the fall of 1963 among fellow students on the campus of Purdue University. She reported a typical narrative as:

Late one night a young couple was "parked" in a densely-wooded area of town listening to the radio when a news flash came on. A man with a "hook" hand had just escaped from a mental institution and was thought to be in the same vicinity as the couple. Just at that moment, the couple heard rustling noises in the bushes nearby. They decided to leave immediately. Upon returning to the girl's home, the boy walked around the car to open the door for her—when he discovered a HOOK hanging on the door handle of the car!

(Parochetti 1965, 49)

She informed readers that what she called "The Hook Story" was the most frequently reported narrative in her collection. Finding that recording her fellow students as a group to simulate a "bull session" was unsuccessful, she approached tellers individually for their stories. Most of her contributors, she wrote, opened up to her because they were sorority sisters. Setting "The Hook" apart from other narratives was that it was "nearly always believed" to be true and its geographical distribution of the reported setting stretched from California to New York whereas other stories were more localized. Other collections followed from campuses in Kansas and Indiana, and in the annotation for the latter, folklorist Linda Dégh reported 44 variants from the Indiana University Folklore Archives. Treated as "typical" in the story were the plot elements of the hook on the attacker's hand, the couple parking, the narrow escape, and the discovery of the hook on the door handle.

In her observations of the telling of the legend in the 1960s, Linda Dégh mentioned that the legend was frequently told by men to scare girlfriends while they parked in lonesome spots, while other tellers elaborated on the natural dread of the handicapped (1968, 98). Alan Dundes made a case that from the viewpoint of the women relating the legend, the story is a warning about the aggressive sexual advances of men:

> The "hook" could be a hand as in the expression "getting one's hooks into somebody," but a hook could also be a phallic symbol. The typical fear of the girl might then be that a boy's hand, signifying relatively elementary necking, might suddenly become a hook (an erect, aggressive phallus).
>
> (1971b, 30)

Dundes supported his claim by pointing out that

> If the hook were a phallic substitute, then it would make perfect sense for the hook to be severed as a result of the girl's instigating the sudden move to return home. The attempt to enter the "body" of the car is seemingly a symbolic expression of the boy's attempt to enter the body of the girl.
>
> (1971b, 30–31)

Skeptical of the sexual interpretation of the hookman legend, Dégh noted that if the story demonizes the aggressive male, why would the telling of the "scary" story by the man, as she observed, result in the woman drawing closer to the man, "seeking protection from the 'fearless male'" (Dégh 1971, 65–66)? One answer might be that the story has in it a social map of teenage transition between childhood and adulthood. The car, a sign of teenage mobility and maturity, is parked on the fringes of the community, far from authority or constraining forces. Indeed, the car is often narrated to be located near an "insane asylum" or "mental institution," indicating that rationality is absent in this outlying zone. The radio bulletin, emanating from town, warns the couple to head back to the fold; the female, usually stereotyped as more cautious and homebound, typically insists that the couple return. When the couple returns home, the male acts more sedate. They have traveled the road of transition from the home to the edge of the community, from childhood to the freedom of adulthood. In some versions, the narrator comments that the young woman "was laughing at herself for being so silly" as to have childish fears, but discovers in her driveway that the dangers are real and she need not feel embarrassed about wanting to go home (Bronner 1989, 311–12).

A later annotation of the story was provided by folklorist Bill Ellis who tied the emergence of the legend plot to publicity given to the arrest of Caryl Chessman in 1948 in Los Angeles (Ellis 1994, 63). Chessman, whose nickname was "Hooknose" because of facial deformities, was linked to lovers' lane robberies. Ellis finds significant to the spreading story that Chessman after pulling a handgun on the couple and threatening them with death, occasionally demanded that the girl perform oral sex on him and leave in his car. In what Ellis describes as "an odd act of gallantry" Chessman brings the girl to her house (1994, 63). The detail of the radio announcement might owe, Ellis speculates, to the detail of frequent broadcasts on the case during what Ellis calls "near-hysteria" in the area during the 1950s.

Whether or not the Chessman case is the origin of the story, the questioning of context and meaning perceived by the teller and audience addresses the significance of the practice of telling an apparent cautionary narrative on a college campus away from home. Tellers did not have an awareness of the Chessman case but believed that indeed a danger existed in lovers' lanes from deranged attackers. One way to validate the interpretations is to check for reports of the collected items. Surveying seventy versions of the hookman story deposited in the University of California, Berkeley, folklore archives, Ellis presented historical trends that previous folk-lorists could not assess. He found that the stories peaked during the early 1960s and while persisting in less frequently reported versions through the 1970s, collections of hookman narratives virtually disappeared after 1980 (1994, 65–66).

Many of the interpretations hinge on the gendered telling of hook-man stories. Ellis found in the Berkeley corpus a preponderance of women telling other women the story (46 percent) but a surprisingly high number of male-to-male transmissions (33 percent), considering that the story is often identified as a woman's narrative (1994, 66–67). He could also assess the claims for the typicality of plot motifs. A romantically occupied couple in a lovers' lane is indeed central to most versions, but he finds variability in other features: put on guard by a radio announcement, 54 percent; lunatic escaped from a mental hospital, 39 percent; convict escaped from prison, 15 percent; girl insists on leaving while boy is unwilling to leave, 36 percent; driving off in a hurry, 49 percent; hook found by the boy, 58 percent. Ellis concludes that "The Hook" is a contemporary legend "only in the loose sense that it has actively circulated in fairly recent times, and reflected the cultural reality of adolescents at that time" (1994, 70). In later versions, it could even be heard as a joke or an incredulous narrative rather than a "legend" told as true.

With the mediation, and often parody, of the hookman legend in film and television, the character has arguably become less scary, and more of a nostalgic reference to sexual anxieties of a more innocent generation. A short list of films featuring the hookman, for exam-ple, includes *Meatballs* (1980), *Campfire Tales* (1991), *I Know What You Did Last Summer* (1997), *Lovers Lane* (1999), and *The Hook-Armed Man* (2000). The theme continued into episodes of television show *Supernatural* (2005) and the video game *Campfire Legends—The Hookman* (2009). In the video game, the hookman ruins the romantic getaway of a female protagonist by the name of Christine. Apparently confirming the predation of the hookman on women, the game involves her escaping and finding life-saving objects. Although the hookman character is prominent in popular culture, he has been less evident in folklore that is the kind of socially framed expressive events in dorm settings described by Parochetti among her fellow students during the 1960s. Twenty-first-century collections at Penn

State Harrisburg report that college students become aware of the hookman early in their adolescence and report a hidden hook pulled out as a prank played on unsuspecting or sleepy roommates. They may be arrogantly making fun of the need of previous generations to park to get the privacy to engage in sex, but still retain anguish over the risks of evening trysts away from campus.

Even as a "playlike legend," as folklorist Bill Ellis has called the hookman narrative circulating after 1980, in the twenty-first century, it nonetheless still attracted comment, perhaps with a tinge of humor, if not frightfulness. Ellis suggests that playfulness about the hook constitutes "a rich vocabulary of convenient language that allows teenagers to discuss a range of feelings and emotions about the fears, ambiguities and thrills of adolescent courtship" (1994, 71). Another function of the hookman moving into the category of camp and children's folklore from his previous campus haunt is that he becomes a point of reference for supposedly more realistic characters encountered in contemporary campus frights. Most of these characters are not disfigured or beastly, although they may be guilty of monstrous deeds. In early twenty-first-century collections, they are often the unassuming kid next door who keeps to himself or the trusted brother inflicting a fatal initiation. Whether related deadly seriously or in fun, they typically get a reaction that is likely to reflect on one's adolescent vulnerability in love and life.

One question in textual approaches that is difficult to answer is the necessary number of versions to venture valid analyses. In the digital age, more archival databases have been formed with accessible texts and supplemental contextual information to help comparative content, thematic, and structural analysis with larger samples and wider geographic and historical reach. More compilations of contemporary narratives in print and online have answered a need to identify legend types in ways that had been previously reserved for folktales. The issue of identifying traditional legends as quickly forming, and often disappearing, contemporary material also extends to jocular material. Stith Thompson (1955) felt obliged to leave out many erotic motifs in jokes under his "X" category of the motif-index, although he recognized their wide use in folklore. Frank Hoffmann (1973) offered a supplement specifically for Anglo–American erotica culled from joke collections in print, and the bookshelf of other motif and type indexes is long enough to fill a book-length bibliography (Azzolina 1987). Other major enumerative indexes have been standard references in folklore studies for beliefs, songs, proverbs, riddles, jump-rope rhymes, counting-out rhymes, singing games, and non-singing games (Abrahams 1969; Abrahams and Rankin 1980; Brewster 1953; Hand 1952; Mieder 1986; Opie and Opie 1985; Taylor 1962; 1951; Whiting 1989). Their roots were often tied to a period of massive "shotgun" collection in the late nineteenth and early twentieth centuries. With the contextual turn in second half of the twentieth century, their utility came into question, although they are still important as distinctive reference works of folklore studies that indicate the global ambitions of comparative study.

Folklorists Stith Thompson and Antti Aarne, who worked on grand indexing projects for folktales, broadcast a primary goal of objectifying traditional knowledge by organizing all the reported expressions into subjects and themes (Aarne and Thompson 1961; Thompson 1955). Their classification has been likened to the Dewey decimal system of library classification, because the numbering scheme uses decimal points for expansion, and these numbers are arranged under broad subject headings which are assigned letters such as "A Mythological Motifs; B Mythical Animals; C Tabu; D Magic." Structurally, there was often an attempt to show the clustering of items/motifs into types or abstract categories that could raise sociological questions about ethnic and religious associations (such as the hero patterns in saint legends) and psychological issues about the appeal of certain repetitive themes (such as Oedipal attractions). Thompson and Aarne were particularly interested in historical and geographical information for items to assess developments of classic stories such as Cinderella, which is found on several continents.

The reference works also showed the extent and persistence of traditions, although some critics also took this project as a sign that encompassing all the types is an impossible task. Theoretically, the indexing enterprise implied an evolutionary assumption that all the world's folk literature derives from a limited corpus of possibilities. The last volume of Thompson's motif-index contained over 10,000 main terms; Hans-Jörg Uther's revision (2004) of the Aarne-Thompson tale-type index (1961) contains 2411 separate narrative types. Filling in holes in their project that depended on their access to European-language materials, Hasan M. El-Shamy (2004) composed a type index for the Arab world drawn from Arabic sources and offered 8700 newly developed motifs (see also El-Shamy 1995). Reviving the indexing project, he and other folklorists in *Archetypes and Motifs in Folklore and Literature* (Garry and El-Shamy 2005) proposed revisions to the concept of motifs and types by avoiding the designation of ideal or correct plots, identifying tale-types by their core of action as the unit of measure, imposing standards of quantification (incidences of a tradition within a culture) for identifying an item as a repeated "tradition" (and therefore creating a more accurate hierarchy of themes), and locating "motif spectrums" representing various themes that seem to cohere (and facilitating therefore psychological analyses of archetypes and contextual investigations). Yet they also opened the references to criticism because the agents of this material were often left out and it was even uncertain whether an item was truly representative of a teller's or believer's typical rendition of a tradition.

It appeared from the indexes that the texts had lives of their own and the indexes could not reveal much about the process of their composition or performance. As "etic" units of measure, motifs also drew suspicion as part of a systematic method, because of doubt that the world's traditional knowledge had been uniformly represented (Thompson's motif index was accused of being Euro-centric), that it could be compared as equivalent units in different contexts, and that it could be precisely defined (motif could variously refer to theme, actor, action, and object) (Dundes 1962a; 1997c; Georges 1997). According to Alan Dundes: "it is not a standard of one type of quantity (e.g., units of heat, length, and so forth)" and therefore would be invalid for statistical analysis (1962a, 96). Critical questions also arose about the "textualization" of the items because collectors could render items differently or subjectively make them conform to ideological or linguistic standards, particular for oral items in various languages (Fine, E. 1984; Honko 2000).

Thompson's subjective identification of themes, critics claimed, did not reflect the use of folktales in everyday life, no less cognitive categories. Thompson's *Motif-Index of Folk-Literature* devotes sections to sex, religion, and drunkenness as deserving their own range of motifs because presumably they inspire narrative commentary. One might also surmise that such categories involve conflicts and guilt, leading to symbolization in narrative. He chose not to create separate rubrics for hunting and fishing, although many people refer to these activities generating abundant stories, beliefs, and rituals (emic references to a "fish story" or "hunting tale" suggest exaggerated narratives). Perhaps Thompson considered hunting and fishing stories to be too personalized and therefore not as indexable in the way that formulaic folktales and myths were. Folklorist J. Russell Reaver, however, surveying manuscript archives of 2378 American tall tales from thirty-two states collected from 1949 to 1951, concluded that the most popular motif in the corpus was X1110, *The wonderful hunt* (Reaver 1972, 370; tale type 1890 in Uther 2004, 2: 478–79; see also Baker 1986, 3–12; Burrison 1989, 169–75; Creighton 1950, 136–38; Lindahl 2004, 102–5, 479–80; Roberts, L. 1955, 145–47; Sackett and Koch 1961, 15–17). The most prevalent story using this motif is described as a person shooting many animals with one shot.

The motif of the wonderful hunt figures prominently in folklore collector Vance Randolph's summary of hunting yarns from the Ozarks in *We Always Lie to Strangers* (1951, 95–130). Although the motif gives the impression of a single set of variant stories, the documentation suggests a structural difference between the single-shot wonder or accidental kill and the remarkable pursuit. As an example of the former, Randolph documented stories told as a third-person narrative about legendary hunter Abner Yancey, who, armed with a single-shot rifle, was trying to get two squirrels lined up so as to kill them both with one bullet. The squirrels fell when Ab fired, and just then he heard turkeys in a nearby tree. Seven hens and a gobbler were sitting on a branch, and Ab's bullet had sped on to split the limb and catch their feet in the crack. Ab climbed the tree and wrung the turkeys' necks, but on his way down he fell into a brush pile, killing two big rabbits and a covey of quail. On the story goes, following the structure of a catch tale, until a button popped off his shirt and killed a big buck that Ab never even saw (Randolph 1951, 120–21).

Regarding the second form, Randolph stated that "every backwoods child has heard of the hunter who chased a giant buck, which always dodged around a knoll before he could fire" (1951, 117). Many of these stories prompt listeners to think about the significance of firearms to the hunt; as the machine that empowers the hunter, the gun is the physical extension of the person that invites exaggeration. Randolph related, for instance, the story of the man who asked the blacksmith to bend his rifle barrel so that he could shoot around the mountain. He pulled the trigger just as the big deer disappeared, and the animal ran completely around the hill four times, with the rifle ball in hot pursuit. Finally, the exhausted deer slowed down and was killed by the bullet. Closure to the narrative is provided by noting that the buck fell dead "at the hunter's feet" (1951, 117; see motif X1122.3.1 and type 1890E in Baughman 1966). Variations of this "lie" are hunters who bend a gun to conform to angles on a fence (and hit all the birds sitting on it) or to curves on a stream (shooting all the ducks on a winding waterway), and the ones who change barrels of a double-barreled gun to shoot sideways (the bullets round up all the game on both sides of the hunter) or twist them to shoot up and around a tree trunk. The incongruity in these different lies is that the gun is unnatural by virtue of being straight and mechanical but is naturalized by bending and curving to match the contours of streams, mountains, and trees. One indication of the symbolic opposition of the straightness of the machine and the circularity of nature is the motif for "hunter bends gun barrel in curve, shoots game standing in circle" (X1122.3.3 in Baughman 1966; Baker 1986, 9; Lindahl *et al.* 1997, 219). The exaggeration works because the machine that is out of place in the wilderness becomes integrated into the landscape between human and animal. It playfully inserts the mechanistic gun in the primitivistic picture of the hunting scene. One commonly reported variant even has the bullet substituting for the man chasing down the deer: "hunter bends gun in curve, *bullet chases deer* around mountain several times before catching up with, killing deer" (X1122.3.2 in Baughman 1966; emphasis added).

In his annotation, Randolph points to the meaning given to the stories by Ozarks residents by noting that they begin with an exaggeration of the abundance of game in the old days. Another significant pattern in the stories is the hierarchy of animals from the pigeon and squirrel, usually considered deserving of slaughter, to the monarch of the woods, the buck, highly regarded as a dangerous opponent. Another factor in evaluating the yarns is that Randolph, like many collectors and indexers, was primarily looking for set fantastical pieces that also go by the term "fabulates," hardly taking into account the more prevalent deer camp tradition of narrating the personal experiences of hunting. In the set pieces often intended as humorous, what is laughable—that is, cognitively incongruous—is the success of the hunter. Human dominion over the land and its creatures is extraordinary, drawing attention to the ordinary routine of human struggle in the woods. The buck is arguably the monarch in these narratives told by men for other men because of its rack of horns, imagined as a weapon as well as a crown, and its manly attributes.

An "emic" alternative to annotating the text with "etic" motifs and types is to represent the range of symbolic and thematic choices and the cognitive structures within a culture that compose and express them. For example, building on Russian folklorist Vladimir Propp's syntagmatic analysis of a limited number of functions (actions and dramatis personae) within a sequence of folktale narratives, Alan Dundes called such functions motifemes as features of a text that mark the advancement of the narrative and provide functional slots, thus constituting the "syntax" of the story. An allomotif, he offered, is a specific textual component that fills those motifemic slots. Wanting to show that emic units had a contextual aspect, Dundes maintained that the allomotif is usually limited to a few versions within a "motifemic context." Within those slots, the options are presumably symbolically equivalent and allow for an explanation of their relationship to one another. Allomotifs would bear the same relationship to motifeme as phonemes (distinct units of sound in a specific language that distinguish one word from another) and allomorphs (a variance in sound that does not change the meaning of an utterance) in linguistics to morphemes (the smallest grammatical unit in a language). Dundes maintained that storytellers operate with a sequence of motifemes in mind that need to be identified rather than the kind of atomized listing of options suggested by the motif-index. In his words:

Comparative studies of folktales have been primarily concerned trying to establish which allomotif is older or logically prior rather than attempting to show how culturally relative allomotifs might signal oicotypes [localized variants that respond to surrounding social and environmental conditions] which might in turn provide significant clues to national character, regional penchants, or individual idiosyncracies.

(Dundes 1987b, 169; see also Azuonye 1990; Carroll 1992a; 1992b; Dundes 1964a; 1980; 2007; Georges 1997; Jones, S. 1990; Lovell-Smith 1996)

Whether a folktale, myth, game, rhyme, or proverb, symbolic equivalence can be posited with the identification of allomotifs in a narrative sequence. The proverb "The bird flies high, but always returns to earth [water]" has been reported in Africa (Freeman 2014, 259), in Denmark as "However high a bird must soar, it seeks its food on earth" ("What They Say" 1895, 1), the Netherlands as "Bird never flew so high but it had to come to the ground" (Christy, R. 1893, 79) and also in Indonesia as "No matter how high a stork flies, it always comes back to water [wallow, water buffalo]" (Fanany and Fanany 2000, 105). One can discern the minimal structural units of a topic and comment, and the syntactical pairing of words for up/high/lately and down/low/previously that presumably is an opposition holding metaphorical meaning (Dundes 1975; Gibbs and Beitel 1995; Mieder 2004, 1–32; Milner 1969; Norrick 1985, 51–57; Silverman-Weinreich 1994; Taylor 1962, 143–50; Winick 2003; Zholkovski 1978). The motifeme is an action suggesting that the bird comes "home" or symbolically down/back to its roots/heritage where it comes from or was nurtured/raised. The key to the meaning is that the earth and water are symbolically equivalent as allomotifs representing something ordinary and fundamental to identity and culture. Context can be used to verify the equivalence and clarify the meaning in a geographic area or social situation, but the structure can be viewed as driving the communication and perception of the utterance.

The equivalence of earth and water is "emic" because in Dundes's words, "the symbolic equation is being made by the folk themselves … the equation comes from within the culture, not from without" (1987b, 171). The symbolic equivalence can be traced across genres and within narratives, according to Dundes:

> The symbolic equivalents of one tale type might well turn out to be found in another tale type ... Such rich comparative data would also serve to indicate whether a given symbolic equation was oicotypical, that is, found exclusively in one particular geographic or cultural area, or whether it was more widespread, e.g., found throughout Indo-European or American Indian cultures.

(1987b, 177)

In the European context, for example, the symbolic equivalence might refer representatively to social mobility, whereas in Indonesia the collector noted the significance of physically moving away from home and the influence of modernization. It indeed could be used as a metaphorical statement within a location undergoing cultural change to associate folklore with one's "grounding."

The study of an allomotific gamut within a structural (motifemic) matrix can be extended to visual and behavioral material, analyzed as part of a sequence of icons, such as the functional placement of motifemes in a gravestone, certificate, quilt, ritual, and rug (see Bronner 1992a; Forrest and Blincoe 1995; Pocius 1979; Weiser 1980). Or the gamut can consist of formulaic phrases, structural patterns, and expressive modes that guide performers in their oral composition of culturally situated forms such as street "raps," sermons, blues songs, ballads, and epics. This emic approach often goes by the label of "oral-formulaic" theory to point to folk traditions as creative processes that arise in performance. In the case of Pennsylvania-German illuminated manuscripts, the structural formula carried a meaning of progressing through seven stages from earth on the bottom to heaven at the top. Gravestones also featured this sequence and represented a reminder of passage at the end of life to match the baptismal certificate (*Taufschein*) at the beginning of life (Weiser 1980). In the midst of Anglicization during the mid-nineteenth century, Pennsylvania-German minister Isaac Stiehly (1860–1869) in the town of Rough and Ready, Pennsylvania, exaggerated the design to emphasize commitment to ethnic German identity in his region. In addition to carving gravestones (Figure 2.1), he also created illuminated birth, baptismal, and wedding certificates representing the transitions of life tied to the church (Bronner 1992a). Pennsylvania-German viewers "read" his stones not only for a memorial to the deceased, but also a wider cultural statement of ethnic distinctiveness.

Figure 2.1 Gravestone of Peter Knorr carved by Pennsylvania-German minister Isaac Stiehly (1860–1869) in Rough and Ready, Pennsylvania

Source: Photograph by Simon J. Bronner.

Followers of "emic" approaches to the text who were critical of the "inventory" of the etic motif-index that purportedly had limited use as a basis to analyze the creation of tradition, sought analyses ultimately of the mental generative grammar that produces expressions. In architecture, etic typologies based upon historical and geographic benchmarks such as the Georgian house (a double-pile house popular during the period of King George II from 1760 to 1801) or the English barn (a bilaterally symmetrical ground barn with an entrance on the non-gable end) have been challenged by emic structural approaches that identify "base concepts" such as a square "pen" and circle in a culture from which variants develop into forms (often bilaterally symmetrical following the metaphor of the human body) that follow cognitive rules (such as no more than two rooms across the front so as to emphasize the idea of a house as a result of a social union of two persons) (see Glassie 1973; 1974; Kniffen 1965; Noble 1984). The base concept also identifies folk ideas or values that can be thematized as "worldview" or cultural outlooks. The square base concept and bilaterally symmetrical aesthetic which dominated British-American housing, for instance, has been symbolized as one that is individualized and expansive, whereas the circular base concept often associated with many Native American structures fosters communal and localized values (see Demos 2004).

Etic approaches such as the motif-index, its proponents countered, are of literary and historical value on a global scale and help circumscribe traditional knowledge and organize as well as annotate an expressive repertoire. Even harsh critics such as Alan Dundes admitted that motific and typological indexes provide useful broad-based tools for generalizable research (Dundes 1997c; see also Georges 1997; Jones, S. 1990). The emic approach is often localized, and admittedly less comparative, partly because it does not accept the universality of motifs and themes, and leans toward the particularistic, or contextualized definition of cultural areas. Etic approaches are probably most evident in visual analyses of historical developments and geographic distributions from aggregates of objectified crafts, buildings, dialects, and customs. These studies often result in maps and charts organized into "folk atlases" compiled based upon theories of origin and diffusion. They visualize paths of tradition correlated with cultural movements. The relevant information has usually been collected either with the aid of questionnaires sent to correspondents in selected locations or by trained fieldworkers; sometimes the methods have been combined. A concern for "sense of place," "homeland," and "cultural landscape" in the twenty-first century, perhaps fueled by increasing mobility and wireless electronic communication, has inspired renewed efforts to map traditions and interpret the patterns in light of modernization (see Vellinga *et al.* 2008).

On a more localized level, folklorist Timothy R. Tangherlini wedded algorithmic approaches to digitally interpretative problems of historic collections such as the Danish corpus of Evald Tang Kristensen (1843–1929, often called the most prolific collector of folklore ever (Abello *et al.* 2012; Broadwell and Tangherlini 2015; Tangherlini 2013). Working from 24,000 manuscript pages, including a quarter of a million stories, songs, proverbs, riddles, rhymes, and descriptions of everyday life, a team extracted from Tang Kristensen's memoirs, letters, and personal papers the names of 4000 informants and the places these people lived. These places, along with places mentioned in their stories, were geo-coded (i.e., finding geographic coordinates from spatial reference data) using historical gazetteers. The team extracted Tang Kristensen's collecting routes through Denmark indexed to places, people, and time. Moreover, team members searched census data and church records to situate his informants in both space and time. By connecting the three main actors of the folklore equation—people (storytellers and scholars), places (where stories were collected and mentioned in stories), and stories (or folkloric expression in general)—a researcher can discover not only specific texts but also patterns in the network data not readily apparent if the collection is presented in a disconnected fashion (Abello *et al.* 2012).

Such computational approaches that move away from "single-classifier schemes" of indexing to "multimodal network representation" arise from greatly expanded digital databases containing many thousands, if not millions, of texts. For contemporary materials, the advent of geographic information systems computer software, which digitizes cultural maps and allows unprecedented access to information, has also spawned projects to visually record cultural resources and combine tangible and intangible cultural surveys into comprehensive databases (see City Lore 2008; Historical Society of Pennsylvania 2009). Indeed, a special field for the formation, digitization, and quantitative analysis of huge electronic databases and development of analytical software programs devoted to folk traditions has coalesced around the term "computational folkloristics" (Abello *et al.* 2012). According to Tangherlini, this movement involves algorithmic methods for corpus study, including visually detailed approaches that fuse statistical representations of the data with appropriate historical maps for annotation, as well as techniques for producing combinatorial graphs (Tangherlini 2013, 10–11).

IDENTIFYING AND ANNOTATING ACTION

Many folklorists insist on the observation of folk practices as a singular event rather than a quantifiable or comparable text or form. Driven by an ethnological desire to holistically examine cultural life in context, behaviorally oriented folklorists utilize digital age technology that makes the recording of traditional events easier and less obtrusive than in pre-industrial scholarship. Thus, in theory, such ethnographic recording allows participants to more naturally interact rather than performing, or not, for the camera and microphone. Or the camera produces the event such as the mandatory "selfie" at a concert or a staged photo of revelers in formations such as a pyramid on the beach (which is then often posted on social media to attract commentary). Texts are not extracted from events or "itemized" but the scene could be considered a cultural text, or else a framed set of expressive actions and social interactions that is analyzed for symbolic communication and behavior. The "frame" of the event, whether abstracted by the participants or bounded physically by a setting, contains behaviors that often would be perceived or constructed differently outside that frame. Before Erving Goffman applied the terminology of the "frame" drawn from the work of anthropologist Gregory Bateson, he used the looser terminology of "situation" to refer to a recognizable context, or at least recognizable by participants, that drives distinctive forms of expression, and impression, people convey to one another. He was ultimately drawn to "frame" because it suggested more agency by participants who frame their activities and expressions. Goffman was interested in the attempts of participants to manage situations, often through symbolic communication in talk and action, to advance their own interests. A proposition he advanced that drew consideration in scholarly circles is the idea that in these situations boundaries as well as connections are established through symbolic communication often embedded in artistic performances, including the use of proverbs, slang, and "body language."

Goffman outlined an ethnographic goal of analyzing through observation whether the inflected communication that occurs within among people is dictated by the setting, often outside the awareness of participants, or strategically guided by one or more figures in the frame (Scheff 2006). Setting up a metaphoric frame is an attempt by interacting participants to gain social order by emphasizing connections among one another and moving potential conflicts to the margins or edges of the frame. Goffman declared that this constant negotiation of different social settings is a function of modern everyday life in which identities are open to alteration in response to conditions of high mobility, social diversity, and extreme individualism. He conceptualized modern society as one in which people are strangers to one another and consequently create social frames constantly to establish familiarity and construct an identity appropriate to the situation (see Kim 2002; Packard 1972; Sennett 1977). Identities are not shaped by family line or locality alone therefore, but are flexible and overlapping. Modernity offers individuals choices for who they want to be or how they appear to other strangers, but with those choices comes the often difficult cultural work of formulating and managing their identities in various social relations on a daily basis. Forced into this role of presenting themselves, individuals become actors to one another and learn from culture the dimensions of acts they can ply variously to communicate and impress others. To this sociological premise, other scholars into the twenty-first century have added historical and psychological inquiries into the experiences and drives that shape socially framed behavior, particularly in multicultural and heterogeneous contexts where issues of stereotype, migration, boundary, and difference abound.

Sometimes the seriousness of the matters raised on such socially framed stages is masked as humor or play, and Clifford Geertz referred to such events as "deep play" because they represent core issues in a society that within the event are "metaphorically refocused" or channeled. For Geertz, a prime example is the cockfight in Bali, which by native testimonies takes central importance as a male pastime in the society. Geertz viewed the cockfight as a performed text, "imaginative works built out of social materials" (1972, 83; see also Ancelet 2001; Bronner 2005a; Niehaus and Stadler 2004; Pass 2015). Geertz claimed that the basic values of the society are articulated in the Balinese setting by men through symbols of the text. Geertz compares this reading of cockfights as supporting local social structure and male domination with other events in Bali to underscore the point that symbols will occur in cultural systems and the ethnographer's task is to interpret those systems, not just record the events. In an act of annotation, he finds verification for his interpretation of the cockfight as playing out divisions of social hierarchy—in festivals at village temples and in consecrations of Brahman priests. For Geertz, the cockfight was a text, because it constituted "a Balinese reading of Balinese experience; a story they tell themselves about themselves" (Geertz 1972, 82).

Yet this "reading" of action as text through the lens of social structure can be challenged and the annotation of comparable action texts becomes especially important in validating an explanation. Folklorist Alan Dundes, for instance, annotated the cockfight outside of Bali as "one of the oldest, most documented and most widely distributed traditional sports known to man" (Dundes 1994, 242). Dundes claimed that the central "unread" action by Geertz in the traditional play of the cockfight was of two "cocks" doing battle and the adolescent age of the participants. The text of the "cock" serving as a surrogate for the male owners suggests their extension of the male phallus. He located the cockfight in a continuum running from competitive games to actual warfare because in these activities a male "demonstrates his virility, his masculinity, *at the expense of a male opponent*," whom they feminize (1994, 250). Based upon available ethnographies, Dundes speculated that there were a number of contributing factors to the concept that men had a greater need to prove their masculinity than women did to reaffirm their femininity. One was the infantile conditioning of boys growing up in a "maternal-female environment" (Dundes 1997b, 41). Boys broke away from the world of women and joined the world of men, by engaging in all-male puberty rites. He also hypothesized that in adolescence, the time when male sexuality peaked, the only sexual objects immediately available were other males (Dundes 1997b, 40). As a result, Dundes surmised, all-male competitive sport teams, and the military, were organizations where sexual energies could be expended on other males within the group, or on males construed as opponents. Dundes also proposed a biological factor, the male phallic erection.

Because an erection is a temporary state, he thought that males felt the need for proving, repeatedly, that they were able to achieve this "indisputable demonstration of masculinity" (Dundes 1997b, 41). Dundes claimed that winning one match or one game probably was not enough: "One has to prove one's ability to feminize or emasculate one's opponent again and again" (Dundes 1997b, 41).

Even if ethnographers do not read the symbolic communication of the scene in the same way, the methodological point is to identify the components of an event that affect its perception outside the frame as well as its generation within it. One position is that as a humanistic experience, each event will be unique and needs to be interpreted as a singular occurrence rather than as comparable types or categories. An attempt to facilitate cross-cultural or cross-scene studies is the Human Relations Area Files, composed of ethnographic descriptions of over 400 cultures. Each distinct culture in the list of cultures covered is assigned an Outline of World Cultures (OWC) number. Indexers created subject descriptors to index ethnographic texts in an Outline of Cultural Materials and assigned subjects three-digit numeric codes. Designers of its electronic version promised researchers the ability to find information quickly across a broad range of cultures, such as the cockfight. A search reveals 81 descriptions of cockfights in ethnographies in 26 cultures, with the majority located in Asia (22 documents in 10 cultures) followed by North America (9 documents in 6 cultures). With questions raised about the comparability of such documents, the American Folklore Society developed an "Ethnographic Thesaurus" to suggest a shared online vocabulary for ethnographies (American Folklore Society 2015). Cockfighting, for example, is classified under blood sports in a terminological tree beneath sports and entertainment and recreation. For cultural historian Forrest Pass, the emic categorization of cockfights as "rough sports" was especially important in Victorian Canada, where the cockfight became central to resistance to state regulation in a national controversy over the domestication and massification of Canada into a "modern, civilized society" (Pass 2015).

The "thick description" of sports, customs, and rituals as complex events influenced the similar consideration of stories, speech, music, and songs. This kind of identification raised the possibility that the text was not as consequential as the event for the communication of meaning. An influential sociolinguistic perspective on identifying folkloric events came from Dell Hymes who suggested structuring them into components of a sender (addresser), a receiver (addressee), a message form, a channel, a code, a topic, and a setting (Hymes 1962). Communication, in this view, behaves as a cultural system; the goal of identification is to describe the operation of the system which is probably outside of the awareness of participants. In his analysis of African-American preaching, for example, Bruce Rosenberg claimed that each sermon was a unique event, which was influenced by audience, actor, and stage, that is, the church (Rosenberg 1970). The preacher's references to images could be altered to address particular congregational members or political events of the time. Rosenberg claimed that the texts of the sermons were not literally comparable but he found evidence of a similar underlying structure that allowed preachers to improvise. They began with a biblical text and followed with a social context in which they provided the circumstances in the biblical period for the text such as the moral issues faced. This led to an emotional conclusion bringing those issues to the present day. He hypothesized that the sermons were "traditional" not in their content but in their stylistic conventions. Following his study, folklorist Elaine J. Lawless questioned whether performance structures of sermons varied by gender and noted the heightened use of personal narratives in sermons by female Protestant ministers (1997, 16).

Folklorist Haya Bar-Itzhak identified in her ethnographies non-verbal aspects of storytelling events as critical for immigrants making a transition to Israeli society. In the case of Jewish Moroccan narrators and audiences, she observed, non-verbal aspects of performance of saints' legends such as the swaying motion of the body while reciting the story served as criteria for defining the genre even in the absence of a verbal text. Utterance of the saint's name by tradition requires a gesture of kissing the hand. She noticed that in a mixed audience, the older listeners made the same gesture as the teller spoke, but the young locals did not. They giggled, while looking at other students their age. By the end of the story, however, she observed that the young people mimicked the gestures of the narrator. Her conclusion was that the young people were more comfortable with their ethnic culture within their affinity group than in a mixed audience that includes those whom they view as representative of national culture. She wrote, however, that "the young people's return to the body language of the world of holiness, typical of the genre, attests to this [identification with the ethnic culture] better than a thousand witnesses" (2005, 166).

If telling saints' legends and cockfights appear removed from everyday life, even though they have been used to extrapolate patterns of age, gender, religiosity, and nationality expressed in framed ritual activities, consider an "ordinary" event like making a toast. Often initiated by the cue of "let's make a toast," glasses, suggesting construction of a collective social "frame," and in many cases signaled as appropriate because of the prompt of curvaceous shapes of wine or champagne glasses, drinking vessels will be raised and "clinked" together as an action to honor someone, celebrate a special occasion (formalized especially for a wedding or part of holiday customs such as New Year's Eve), or to signal camaraderie within a small group. The toast associated with adult behavior often creates a sense among the participants of the event proceedings starting. Participants will probably not be aware of the historical ties of the toast to sacred offerings to gods or seventeenth-century customs of flavoring drinks with spiced toast (French 1881). They will probably recognize, however, the toast as a tradition with expected behaviors carrying social meanings, although these actions and associations can vary greatly (see Kotthoff 2013). The text of the toast might follow the precedents of "here's to your health" and "cheers," or non-English expressions that have crossed ethnic lines of "l'chaim" (to life from Hebrew), "salute" (to your health from Italian), and "skol" (cheers in Norwegian). Or it might categorically refer to a narrative poetry tradition among African Americans of black heroes and tricksters such as "The Signifying Monkey," "Stack-o-Lee," and "Shine and the Titanic" (Abrahams 1970; Jackson 1974; Jemie 2003; Wepman *et al.* 1976).

Many organizations, including the British Royal Navy and Elks Lodges in the United States, mark their continuity with the past by dictating distinctive toasts at certain times and days. Both designate toasts for "absent friends"; the Royal Navy tradition is to do this on Sunday while Elks Lodges ritualize it at 11 p.m. (McKenna 2005). Of ethnographic interest is the presentation of a non-memorized toast on special occasions which follows conventions of praise. At many weddings, in fact, individuals identified as having close relationships to the honorees are called up to present toasts with the expectation that they will provide personal testimony to the quality of the union and usually close by symbolically invoking magic to provide best wishes for longevity and marital bliss in the future. The use of the toast to signal a transition and insure a good future is also evident on New Year's Eve when individuals "toast in" the new year that they wish to be better than the last.

Participants in an event might also invert the seriousness of the toast by creating a "roast" for an individual who is usually honored. Within the frame of the event permitted disrespect couched within humor is allowed and indeed encouraged. Or a person leading a toast might signal the joviality of the gathering by uttering a parody and perhaps ignobly downing a drink (often a lowly beer instead of wine and champagne perceived to be more genteel). Jocular toasts might include "down the hatch," "here's mud in your eye," "bottoms up" or the rhyme that ignores an honoree and emphasizes self-indulgence (or destructiveness), "Through the teeth, past the gums, Look out stomach, here it comes!" Many follow the opening cue of "here's to" such as "Here's to those who wish us well; all the rest can go to hell" or "Here's to you and here's to me, the best of friends we'll ever be, and if we ever disagree, screw you and here's to me." Observing activity in the framed context of the male "bachelor party," one might hear sexualized sayings such as "Here's to honor! If you can't come in her, come on her," "Here's to our wives and girlfriends, may they never meet," or "Here's to the top, here's to the middle, here's hoping we all get a little" (see Williams, C. 1994). As an event marking the departure of a mate from the "guys" to a committed relationship, the party often uses irreverent sexual humor to comfort those remaining in a single state by humiliating the groom. The symbolic importance of the drinking toast is indicated by the classification of the toastmaster as leading the events even if he or she does not make an actual toast.

In an ethnography of toasting as a cultural scene, Amy Milligan (2010) described a German expatriate group who met regularly in a public restaurant in the United States and separated the event by a toast with a distinctive action of locking eyes for the duration of the movement of glasses together and apart. The locking of eyes was often exaggerated—with the participants peering over eyeglasses or making their eyes as wide open as possible. Each time glasses touched, the two individuals said, "*Prost!*" (cheers). Although not aware of the history of the "locking eyes" ritual, they perceived that it was distinctively German and therefore demarcated their *Stammtisch* ("regulars' table" in German) (Figure 2.2). They jokingly mentioned a belief to reinforce the oddity, at least in the American context, of the ritual: if you do not look into your partner's eyes when clinking glasses, seven years of bad sex will follow. Milligan noted comparative reciprocal toasting rituals such as having your partner fill your glass in Japan and in many places in China having each partner provide a toast rather than having a toastmaster. Part of her observation was a situation in which someone did not follow the ritual and noting the group's negative response, since it undermined

Figure 2.2 Toasting *Prost* ("may it be good [for you]") and holding steins in a folk manner at a *Stammtisch* (German for "regulars' table"), Mount Joy, Pennsylvania, 2011

Source: Photograph by Amy K. Milligan.

the bond of the boundary between others and themselves in that situation. Even though the person was fluent in German, her failure to lock eyes created a barrier within the group. In Milligan's words, the action related to the toast was a "test of membership."

Identifications of folk process seek repetitive practices to represent traditions whereas earlier scholarship applied the primary criteria for folklore consisted of textual similarities. In Japan, my students clearly recognized various festivals, customs, and arts as traditional in a country where "folk cultural properties" are governmentally recognized as national treasures and draw attention to the distinctiveness of Japanese identity. Around the country tall stone markers officially designate the locations of revered "intangible heritage" that continue to be enacted. In Fukuoka, for example, the Hakata Gion Yamakasa Festival held during the summer feature *Yamakasa*, colorful one-ton floats crafted by master Hakata doll makers (Figure 2.3). Townsmen carry the floats on their shoulders and race the floats along a 5-km course to the sound of large Taiko drums and cheering of as many as one million spectators. The floats remain on display at the Kushida-jinja Shrine all year round with explanations of their value as a folk cultural property to remind viewers of the local tradition.

Yet the students were less aware of other folk behaviors in which they engaged every day until differences with my actions drew their attention. My students thought I laughed "like an American," and when I asked what that meant, they pointed out that I reared my head back when hearing something humorous and associated that with a learned American behavior (cf. Davidson 1993). I had not previously heard this cultural connection but realized after observing gestures at "joke telling" sessions with Americans that there was something to it. I could identify phrases that indicated humorous responses such as "knee-slapper" and "belly laugh" and noticed that affirmation of a "good one" was expressed with a pat on the back, soft punch in the shoulder, or an exchange with the hands such as a "high-five" (slap of raised open palms) or "fist bump" (meeting of two clenched fists). I asked the Japanese students in return why when they hear something funny, especially the women, they cover their mouths. They were aware of this, although not as conscious that when they laughed they leaned their head down toward the ground. Somewhat taken aback they pointed to their nose as if

Figure 2.3 Yamakasa (decorated ritual floats) for the Hakata Gion Yamakasa
Festival on display in the Kushida-jina Shrine, Fukuoka, Japan

Source: Photograph by Simon J. Bronner.

to say "who, me?" and I suggested that I would express that by
placing my finger on my chest. One might note that in discussion
the explanations given for the various apparently culturally specific
practices were couched as "metafolklore." Most generally they ech-
oed a cultural value on politeness and thought that laughing aloud

was rude. Thinking of the root of this attitude, they related hearing that covering mouths related to Confucianism which teaches that public displays of emotion should be repressed, but I asked, then, why did it apply more to women than to men? Some answered that historically it was considered impolite to reveal the lips and teeth when laughing and as a praxis, laughing was considered unfeminine intrusive behavior.

The identification and annotation stage of the research process establishes material as folklore, usually with reference to its variable, repetitive practice in a cultural context. Its folkness is significant analytically because it suggests a learning and transmittal process that denotes a distinctive cultural meaning with reference to tradition, whether followed or chosen. It often involves continuities across time and space, and within groups and situations, that are charted by the analyst, before proposing explanations for what it does in our lives, our minds, and societies.

WHAT DOES FOLKLORE CONNOTE?

ANALYSIS AND EXPLANATION

The multiform presence, and absence, of folklore in cultural practice equally invite analysis. Compilers of ethnographic reports concentrating on framing actions frequently show folklore as a "living" tradition or renewable cultural resource. Whether using item or action as the central feature, the discernment, and arrangement, of material as folklore and its aggregation into social categories such as community, group, network, family, region, and nation, and expressive references such as scenes, frames, genres, structures, styles, and performances underscore the defining characteristic of folklore as repeatable, transmittable, and variable. By separating folklore from other types of cultural communications and registers, the analytical approaches implicit in the contextual collection, or ethnographic framing, of folklore suggest further that traditions compel closer scrutiny, especially for meanings that might explain folklore's existence, spread, use, and disuse.

Text-based approaches often begin with inspections of content to determine underlying structures and themes. Texts might be scanned, and coded, for symbols, keywords, motifs, themes, motifemes, and allomotifs leading to a non-literal interpretation, that can be thought of as a translation of inferences into evincive meanings. Images and objects as well as verbal texts are given "close readings," by which is often meant rhetorical or iconographic probes of material for connotative meaning within the specific version or a broader genre of communication. Texts, objects, and images also might be classified and compared cross-culturally for their mode and form to bring meanings into relief. They might be sorted historically and geographically, and mapped and otherwise visualized, to raise questions of origin, dominion, and diffusion. Events described in legends, rituals, and visual arts might be checked against the historical record for their verisimilitude.

Contextual analysis often establishes a setting or group whose history, values, and environment are correlated with the uses of traditional knowledge. Based upon the analysis that includes consideration of related groups and settings in addition to checking cognate forms, the researcher hypothesizes the distinctiveness of folkloric patterns within their social and material surroundings. Behavioral analysis might entail connections of actions and gestures in relation to verbal communication and the construction of a play or ritual frame (see Bremmer and Roodenburg 1992). Analysts also compare performances of material in different venues to assess the influence of audience and location on the expression of folklore. If life-stories of participants have been recorded, they might be correlated with the tradition-bearers' practices, attitudes, experiences, and emotional states. Modes of social interaction and ritualized events are often highlighted in behavioral analysis, especially in visual media, to account for the processes of generating and enacting folklore. These different approaches have in common the production of findings, usually not explicitly evident from the surface evidence, in an operation on the data that indicates how folklore works.

Explanation answers why folklore in thought and action occurs, or does not. It proposes causes for, or factors in, the selection, generation, and consequence of folklore. But in arriving at this goal, analysts often disagree on the relevant questions that lead ultimately to the source of folklore's existence or absence, creation and re-creation, and conveyance and representation. That is not to say that the questions cannot overlap or the quest for answers cannot take different forms. One division that has been proposed is between diachronic (questions of historical context and change) and synchronic (questions of a situation set in space) inquiry as models of causation.

Analysts usually have the advantage of aggregate data that participants do not have, but participants in the events recorded by folklorists often have their own ideas about the practices in which they engage. Some psychologically oriented observers might claim that these rationalizations mask ulterior motives or are the results of inherited narratives misdirecting underlying causes. Some folklorists have suggested that as a human endeavor, folklore fieldwork is intrinsically a collaborative process between the researcher and participant in tradition (Cothran 1973; Mortensen 2005; Mullen 2000; Russell 2006). They point out that as traditions people choose to enact, folklore is often self-consciously invoked, and evoked. Analysts can therefore inquire about the understandings of participants about their traditions as well as document their texts and actions. Nonetheless, the analyst is frequently in the position of evaluating their reasons, and assessing possible meanings and strategies outside of their awareness.

I surveyed folkloristic scholarship to arrive at half-dozen basic modes of questioning that I will discuss in this chapter: (1) time and space; (2) content and authorship; (3) function and purpose; (4) projection and association; (5) performance and communication; and (6) power and conflict. The order moves from historical and literary questions to those that are social and psychological. Some analysts would characterize the different concerns as proceeding from uncovering manifest to latent meanings inherent in folklore.

QUESTIONS OF TIME AND SPACE

Often a starting point of folkloristic inquiry is to uncover the genesis and spread of folklore. This questioning offers a form of explanation because of the assumption that either the origin of an expression dictated the evolution or devolution of the tradition, or it designated a central point from which traditional knowledge diffused. Folklorist Theodor Gaster's presentation of "the oldest stories in the world," for example, such as the Babylonian epic of Gilgamesh, the Hittite numskull tale of "master good and master bad," and the Canaanite nature myth of the contest between the lord of the air and the dragon who ruled the waters, suggests phylogenetic "Ur-forms" (reference to Ur from the birthplace of Abraham in the Book of Genesis) from which other narrative plots derive (Gaster 1952, 3–18; see also Claus and Korom 1991, 46–73; da Silva and Tehrani 2016; Roberts, W. 1958; Swart 1957; Thompson 1977, 428–48; Ziolkowski 2011). Classical scholars often note, for instance, the probable origination of Aesop's fables in South Asian stories in the oral traditions reported in *The Pańćatantra* two centuries earlier (Adrados 1999; Barret 1948; Rajan 1993; Temple, Robert 1998). There is dispute, however, whether the connection is enough to generalize that India is the chief source of fable literature worldwide and explain the content of animals used for moral lessons (Cosquin 1892; Jacobs, J. 1892; Lach 1977, 99–108; Thompson 1977, 375–84).

Presumably finding the tradition's beginnings will shed light on sometimes puzzling content that can be explained by its original context. Further investigation of the content and its contexts along the path of diffusion in different historical periods might reveal groups (migratory communities such as Jews, Sumerians, and Romani are often cited) and occupations (such as seafarers and traders) who might have had a hand in the tradition's relocation and adaptation (Groome 1892; 1899; Jacobs, J. 1896, 135–61; Newell 1895; Swart 1957, 73–75; Utley 1974). A monogenetic answer to questions of origin often implies that some stories, songs, and other traditional material show cultural influence and integration. Some scholars note from evidence of multiple locations of traditions the possibility of polygenesis, several independent points of origin, suggesting common cultural responses to the human condition and environment that transcend cultural differences (Fine, G. 1979a; Georges 1986; Goldberg 1984; Hartland 1899; Lang 1893, 10–28). They suggest that such examples develop "lives of their own" and spread because they contain important human lessons or are based upon elementary thematic archetypes. This view was especially held during the Victorian period related to a psychic unity of humankind, which has given way for the most part to explanations rooted in factors of the particular historical and social conditions of cultures (Dorson 1968, 199–200; Köpping 1983; Wierzbicka 1994).

When used to relate the past to present cultural practices, the monogenetic explanation of a time and place of origin indicates the popular view that tradition carries authority. Participants in customs, for example, might answer a question of why they engage in a certain practice with the declaration, "That's the way we have always done it around here." The implication is that the precedent, whether individually or communally composed, dictates what follows. An example of this explanation in regard to the formation of cultural regions is the "doctrine of first effective settlement" formulated by cultural geographer Wilbur Zelinsky (1973, 13–14). He proposed that the first ethnic group to sustain a self-perpetuating settlement establishes cultural traditions in a region that other successive groups tend to follow. On this basis folklorist Henry Glassie (1968) proposed that American cultural development could be explained by the establishment of four "cultural hearths" in various ports of entry on the east coast: New England, Pennsylvania and Delaware Valley, Tidewater and Chesapeake, and Lowland South. In these hearths, different ethnic cultural combinations mixed to form New World cultural hybrids that emanated along paths of westward movement. The Lowland South tended to have more of an African-American influence, for instance, while Pennsylvania and the Delaware Valley showed more integration of German, Scots-Irish, English, and Welsh traditions. Although the Pennsylvania cultural region was the last to be settled by Europeans, it arguably had the most cultural spread and influence because traditions such as the bank barn, use of the Christmas tree, and foodways such as the pot pie diffused south (into Appalachia and the Ozarks), west (fanning into the Midwest), and north (into the "New England extended" region). After analyzing the connection of architecture, foodways, and dialect into regional cores (central concentration of cultural features), domains (high frequencies of cultural features), and spheres (intermittent appearance of cultural features), it was possible to show objectively the unofficial boundaries of cultural regions in the United States, with the implication that sometimes conflicting values and worldviews emerge (see also Fischer 1989; Gastil 1975; Woodward 2012).

The significance of folk material for historic-geographic analysis, according to Glassie, is that it tends to be variable over space and stable in time. Therefore, even if surveyed in the present, the rural landscape reveals the historical roots of regional culture more effectively than popular culture, which tends to be shorter in duration but stable over large expanses of space. However, when change occurs in folk cultural forms such as the replacement of the fireplace with the stove or the move in gravestone design from designations of the deceased's body to mourning memorials in the nineteenth century, it is usually a sign of social upheaval that bears explanation (Glassie 1992). The objective evidence can also be compared to the subjective data of how residents identify themselves to assess the effect of earlier cultural development. Doing this survey reveals that the etic category of the Middle Atlantic is far less significant than a broader perceptual identification with "the East." Although Glassie found significant cultural differences between the Lowland and Upland South, perceptual studies indicate a broader identification with a southern label.

Critics point out the conjecture about the processes of acculturation in such diffusionist studies based upon the formation of phylogenetic typologies. Suspicions arise whether a similarity of forms in different places can be interpreted as the result of equivalent cultures. And if the forms indicate a prior cultural influence, can one reasonably conclude that the ideas and values from that culture are evident in the new structures? Folklorists might question reasons within communities for the retention of cultural traits and whether those traits necessarily move together as people migrate. Disputed, for example, have been explanations of the emergence of log construction in the United States (Cooper 1991; Gregory 1936; Jordan 1985; Weslager 1969). The answer has been at the heart of a debate about American exceptionalism, for the hybridized log "cabin" has become an icon of a distinctive American frontier mythology. Glassie proposed in answer to the view that the log cabin was a unique American type the influence of settlers from the German Palatinate, and perhaps Moravian migrants, but a rival theory in defiance of the doctrine of first effective settlement suggested that although the colony of New Sweden did not last, it was instrumental in the adoption of log construction. Respondents questioned whether the Scandinavian models feature the interstices and corner notching found in American models. Much of the speculation centers on the regional spread of log construction among British setters in Appalachia and the South, although few antecedents can be found in the homeland (Kniffen and Glassie 1966). Glassie surmised that Germans migrating down the Great Valley into the South and Midwest introduced the building techniques.

Spatial reasoning is also used to explain the persistence of subregional traditions such as the Delta blues which appeared to retain more

African features than folk musical traditions elsewhere, according to folklorists, because of the segregation of the African population on plantations and their isolation from outside sources (Oliver 1969). Similarly, the sensational news of finding medieval-vintage ballads in Appalachia and the Ozarks after they had declined in popularity in the homelands of the British Isles was linked to the isolation of the descendants of English and Scots-Irish settlers in the mountainous regions (Scarborough 1937; Sharp 1932). Rather than a transplantation of a set form into a remote location, the ballads in the New World reflected a process that folklorists called oikotypification, the formation of an expressive subtype tied to a particular cultural setting. So-called "Appalachian ballads" often emphasize shorter versions stripping stories of their aristocratic labels than their lengthier British antecedents and they tend to lose their supernatural elements. Issues of hybridization within space are raised, however, by emergent American forms such as the "blues-ballad" of John Henry, Stagolee, and John Hardy performed by both African and British-American performers (Wilgus and Long 1985).

Do not presume that isolation in rural and ethnic enclaves is singularly responsible for the persistence of folklore, for folklorists also point to spaces where swarming people encounter one another or interact with media as factors in the generation and maintenance of folklore. Responding to the view that children's folklore was threatened by television watching and urbanization, Peter and Iona Opie (Opie and Opie 1969) and Steve Roud (2010) in different generations underscored the role of the ample social encounters in crowded playgrounds as pivotal in the constant renewal of folk games and rhymes among youth. Folklorist Jay Mechling also theorized the appropriation of popular culture by children to form their own expressive culture. It is evident in parodies of commercial power such as "McDonald's is your kind of place" and Internet legends and humor often resounding in social media (Mechling 2002). Observers noted, for example, the rapid production of material identified as folkloric in the wake of celebrity Michael Jackson's death (Blank 2013b, 83–98). Indeed, the traffic of commentary from users became so great that services such as Twitter fell, leading to further folk commentary on stories that "broke the Internet" (Blank 2013b, 4).

A challenge in explanations of the presence of lore as a result of diffusion is to document the process of encounter and exchange that results in adaptation of lore across cultural divides. William Bradford's *Of Plymouth Plantation*, written between 1630 and 1651, clearly recounts the Wampanoag as the source for maize cultivation among the Pilgrims, in addition to other regional folk practices such as the dugout canoe, maple sugaring, moccasin making, and clambake (Baker 1980; Bradford 2006, 55; see also Glassie 1972–1973; Hallowell 1965; Lockhart 2008; Neustadt 1992). Some paths of diffusion need elaboration in historical events, such as the diffusion of the African banjo to British-derived country and bluegrass music in the early twentieth century, while it fell from favor from African-American performance around the same time (Conway 1995; Gura and Bollman 1989; Linn 1991). A historical perspective suggests the negative association of the banjo with minstrelsy in African-American communities that probably affected its disfavor. A modern example of a historical event used as explanation is the children's play complex of "cooties" representing an invisible ailment that youth accuse individuals of having. Folklorists have identified an origin of the term in references to cooties, possibly Anglicized from the Malay word for lice of *kutu*, by soldiers from the Pacific theater returning to their homelands after World War II. The panic caused by the polio epidemic during the 1950s might have resulted in its entrance into the slang and play of children who devised cooties shots, cooties tag, and cootie catchers all around the idea of the contagion of the affliction and its removal by inoculation. After the epidemic was over, folklorists hypothesized the adaptation of cooties as an othering by social status during the civil rights movement during the 1960s and subsequently as a channeling of fears about fatal viruses related to the AIDS epidemic after the 1980s (Bronner 2011, 213–17; Samuelson 1980).

Historical conditions might be given to explain the uses of folklore, and in other cases folklore is the explanation for the retention of historical memory. Folklore, particularly the genres of legends and ballads, is often presented as historical evidence in the absence of a documentary record, especially for groups whose presence is marginalized. This approach stands in contrast to the dismissal of folklore as untruthful. To be sure, historians looking for documentary evidence often are skeptical of claims based upon local legend for houses as stations on the African-American "underground railroad," but the traditional knowledge passed through generations is cited by residents to explain architectural features such as hidden passages and rooms (Gara 1961; Kammen 1999). In the calendric custom of the Jewish Passover, the Exodus story as a lesson of freedom and struggle against bigotry is recalled in a reading of the *Haggadah* (Hebrew for "telling") during a ritual meal called the *seder* (Gaster 1949). More locally centered is a historically oriented folk event such as the 3 October Festival in Leiden, the Netherlands, commemorating the anniversary of the 1573–1574 siege of the city by Spanish invaders (Figure 3.1). During the modern festival, the key feature of eating of herring and white bread signifies the feeding of Leiden residents of these foods by the army of *Watergeuzen* ("Sea Beggars") and these events are recounted in an annual service in the historic *Pieterskerk* (St. Peter's Church, traced to an original chapel, c. 1100). For many contemporary residents the festival, touted as traditional, also builds local identity and reinforces the importance of the city, often considered in the shadow of the larger metropolises of Amsterdam and Rotterdam (Nas and Roymans 1998).

The problem that critics cite of historical explanations is that the process by which present-day activities evolve is sketchy or presumed to follow naturally from prior events. Questions of the individuals who initiated or promoted the construction of historical memory based upon folk traditions often remain. One famous example is the report of John Smith, leader of the Jamestown Colony in 1609, who heard a legend that the "Lost Colony" of Roanoke Island was slaughtered by Chief Powhatan and reported it to the Royal Council. Historians note that subsequent attitudes toward the Native Americans as hostile were shaped by this belief. In the absence of any recorded history, legends persist to the present that settlers of the colony were captured and integrated into the tribes, and tribes claim partial descent from the Roanoke settlers. Even if it is impossible to tell what really happened, or who initiated, altered, and perpetuated the folklore, scholars use the folk memory as evidence of emotional attitudes and social relations that help contextualize, if not explain, the course of history and the lay of the land (Horn 2010; Johnson and Parramore 1983).

Figure 3.1 Raw herring and bread distributed to residents of Leiden, the Netherlands, to open the 3 October Festival, also known as *Leidens Ontzet* (Relief of Leiden), The Netherlands, 2005

Source: Photograph by Simon J. Bronner.

QUESTIONS OF CONTENT AND AUTHORSHIP

Related to the establishment of folklore's genesis in time and place is credit to authorship. Folklore is often treated as the intellectual property of a collective rather than an individual, but one of the explanations for its existence is a person's creation, which through transmission and diffusion often becomes altered, sometimes losing the original's imprint. For example, a familiar theme in twenty-first-century pottery of the American Southwest is the "storyteller." It depicts a black-haired seated woman with an open mouth surrounded by small figures of youth on her shoulders, arms, and legs. Folklorist Barbara Babcock with Guy and Doris Monthan documented the first storyteller made by Helen Cordero of the

Cochiti Pueblo in 1964, in honor of her grandfather, Santiago Quintana. The clay figure, based upon Pueblo techniques to make pots, shows her grandfather with an open mouth and five children clinging to him. She adapted a "singing mother" motif of a woman with an open mouth holding one or two children, but Cordero's figure drew attention as being categorically different because of its multitude of small children listening to a man or woman. Other Native American craftsworkers picked up the theme in variations including the addition of a drum, enclosure in a clay blanket, and use of mythological animals. The storyteller image in clay has become ubiquitous, and symbolic of Pueblo traditional culture (Figure 3.2), although Helen Cordero's name is not attached to it (Babcock *et al.* 1986; see also Congdon-Martin 1999).

Questions arise about the changing social association of lore. A mainstay of children's hand-clapping rhymes in British and

Figure 3.2 Clay pottery figure of the "storyteller" by Caroline M. Sando, Jemez Pueblo, New Mexico, 2011

Source: Photograph by Simon J. Bronner.

American collections, for example, is "See, See, My Playmate" (Roud Folksong No. 16805):

> See, see, my playmate,
> Come out and play with me,
> Under the apple tree,
> And bring your dollies three.
> Slide down the drainpipe
> Into the cellar door,
> And we'll be merry friends
> For ever more, more, more.

I documented these verses used exclusively by girls, usually between the ages of 8 and 10, who in their handclapping routines strive to keep singing in unison with the synchronized movements until one of them makes a mistake (Figure 3.3). The girls delighted in being able to extend the clapping routines while chanting numerous verses. I could observe that the textual stability of the verses was due to the need of the girls to chant the same words. Improvisation, however, was evident as the girls became more practiced and then would agree on variations in the rhyming couplets.

Figure 3.3 Ten-year-old girls in Harrisburg, Pennsylvania, demonstrate handclapping routine accompanying the singing of "See See My Playmate," 2010

Source: Photograph by Simon J. Bronner..

Folklorists Iona and Peter Opie trace the song meant for adults to a duly registered composition of 1940 with words and music by North Carolina native, Horace "Saxie" Dowell (1985, 474–5):

> Play-mate—come out and play with me,
> And bring your dollies three,
> Climb up my apple tree,
> Look down my rain pipe,
> Slide down my kitchen door,
> And we'll be jolly friends
> For ever more.

Dowell's originality, however, has come into question because of the relation of the chorus of "I Don't Want to Play in Your Yard" by American composer, Henry W. Petrie in 1894:

> I don't want to play in your yard
> I don't like you any more
> You'll be sorry when you see me sliding down our cellar door,
> You can't holler down our rain barrel
> You can't climb our apple tree
> I don't want to play in your yard, if you won't be good to me.

Although the Opies provide the source of the rhyme in this popular parlor song, they do not provide an explanation of how and why the song became integrated into children's lore accompanying a hand-clapping routine. It is also difficult to know the composer credit to innumerable parodies although folklorists have observed that they are often a matter of improvisation within an easily remembered formulaic structure:

> Playmate, come out and play with me
> And bring your tommy gun three
> Climb up my poison tree
> Drown in my rain barrel
> Fall down my cellar door
> And we'll be enemies
> Forever more, more, more.

Or

> See see my playmate
> I can't go out to play
> Because of yesterday
> Three boys came my way
> They gave me fifty cents
> To lay across the bench, bench, bench.
> They said it wouldn't hurt
> They stuck it up my skirt
> My mother was surprised
> To see my belly rise
> My father was disgusted
> My sister jumped for joy
> It was a baby boy
> My brother raised some shit
> He had to babysit.
>
> (Bronner 1989, 61–2)

The last parody raises the question of authorship or of "intertextual relations" that suggests a meaning as well as a reference interjected from another text. In this case the references of "They gave me fifty cents" related to family and pubertal dynamics of the performing girls with an expressed anxiety about teen pregnancy and possible sexual abuse. Another common hand-clapping rhyme usually known by performers of "See See My Playmate" is the formulaic "My Mother Gave Me Peaches"

> My mother gave me peaches
> My father gave me pears
> My boyfriend gave me fifty cents
> And he kissed (kicked) me up the stairs
> My mother took my peaches
> My father took his pears
> My boyfriend took my fifty cents
> So I kicked him down the stairs.
>
> (Bronner 1989, 62)

Yet another connection used to validate the sexual connotations of the texts, is a version of jump-rope rhymes introduced as the coming-of-age "Cinderella":

> Cinderella, dressed in yella
> Went downtown to see her fellow
> On the way her girdle busted
> How many men were disgusted?
> (Bronner 1989, 70–71)

Another example of intertextuality is the use of ribbons tied around trees and other public columns to signify various causes. In the wake of the storming of the U.S. embassy in Tehran by Iranian revolutionaries in 1979, publicity was given to the action of Penelope "Penne" Laingen, wife of United States ambassador Bruce Laingen. She tied a yellow ribbon around an oak tree in her front yard to remind onlookers of the plight of her captive husband. Subsequently, families of the hostages formed the Family Liaison Action Group to encourage tying of ribbons and wearing of yellow ribbon pins around the country. Afterward, other organizations adopted the strategy with pink ribbons for breast cancer awareness, red for AIDS, and multicolored puzzle design for autism. Laingen told interviewers that she was inspired by the memory of the wife of convicted Watergate conspirator Jeb Stuart Magruder covering her front porch with yellow ribbons to welcome her husband home from jail. The yellow ribbons referred to the commercial hit record "Tie a Yellow Ribbon Round the Ole Oak Tree" by Dawn featuring Tony Orlando in 1973.

Folklorist Gerald E. Parsons (1991), working for the Archive of Folk Culture at the Library of Congress, found that the significance of the yellow ribbon goes back much further to a legend of a convict, who, after a considerable absence, is about to return home. Concerned whether he would be wanted back, the prisoner wrote to his relatives to put a white ribbon in the big apple tree and if he did not see it, he would continue on his way. When the train got close, he (or a companion) sees that the whole tree is covered with ribbons. Religious publications that printed the story from oral tradition often noted the similarities to New Testament parables of the "prodigal son." In tracing the chain of events leading to the diffusion and variation of the tradition from legend to song to custom, Parsons was able to explain the presumptive agent of the modern tradition but not the circumstances of the legend's origin. He was careful to note that additional explanation is needed for the persistence of the tradition beyond the circumstances of the yellow ribbon in the twentieth century and the subsequent proliferating use of ribbons in the twenty-first century representing victims of disease and tragedy (Parsons 1991, 11; see also Pershing and Yocom 1996; Santino 1992; Tuleja 1997).

Tying a yellow ribbon around a tree has been ritualized by various military groups as a rite of passage before deployment. In Santa Fe, New Mexico, for example, the commander and senior enlisted leader of Charlie Company, 1st Battalion, with their wives, tied a yellow ribbon around a small potted pine tree with the rest of the battalion and their families looking on before deployment to Kuwait (Figure 3.4). Family members tie small ribbons with names of soldiers and messages such as "love ya" to the branches of the tree. Other units host Yellow Ribbon events for returning soldiers and their families.

An inquiry of authorship frequently entails the investigation of the creative process, because of evidence of material in oral tradition prior to the alleged date of composition. Credit is given to Homer as the author of the *Iliad* and the *Odyssey*, but during the 1930s classicists Milman Parry and Albert Lord recorded contemporary bards in southeast Europe who sang material reminiscent of Homeric texts. They proposed that Homer was aware of pre-existing traditional tales that he refined into creative compositions. They further hypothesized that much of the Homeric corpus was orally composed probably prior to the time that Homer, "the blind poet," from pre-existing stories (Foley 1988; 1995; 1999; Jensen 1980; Lord 1960; Parry 1971). There is also the possibility that the Homer is a mythical character or representative of a group of performers. It is significant that long epics with Homeric elements persisted to modern times. Parry and Lord used the contemporary evidence to hypothesize about the circumstances of the epics' creation. Other folklorists have used their explanation of the ability of bards to recite and sing long epics by utilizing performative formulas rather than relying on rote

Figure 3.4 Commander of Charlie Company, 1st Battalion, National Guard, USA, ties a yellow ribbon on a pine tree in a ceremony in Santa Fe, New Mexico, before leaving in 2015 for deployment in Kuwait

Source: Defense Video and Imagery Distribution System, Source: Photograph by Sgt. 1st Class Anna Doo.

memory in a number of other genres including preaching, blues music, and children's play (Evans 1982; Marsh, K. 2008; Rosenberg 1970; see also Foley 1985; 1990).

On a broader scale, the work of Parry and Lord raises questions about the literary creation and oral traditional creativity. Creation, as it is used in the arts, represents the idea of producing an unprecedented image whereas creativity implies a process of innovation and re-arrangement from pre-existing materials (Bronner 1992d, 2–7; Kristeller 1983). Folklorists posit creativity as part of the concept of tradition and in literary analysis seek the roots of tradition that artists adapt and recompose. The philosophical implications of this kind of study is evident from the debate in the early twenty-first century over the origin of so-called fairy tales. Much of the discourse surrounds the claim for Giovanfrancesco Straparola as the possible "inventor" in 1551 of "rise tales" about heroes and heroines who began their lives in real poverty, but who achieve riches and attain a throne, catapulted upward by a marriage mediated by magic (Bottigheimer 2002). Many of these stories have been identified popularly as "fairy tales" or more academically as *Märchen* and presumed to have borrowed from popular oral origins (Bottigheimer 2002, 2).

The evidence, mainly presented by Ruth B. Bottigheimer, for a single literary origin involves an assessment of Straparola as an original writer who produced story "creations" and a particular reading of his texts as unprecedented in oral tradition and then adapted into other forms such as his "Constantino and His Cat" that bears a resemblance to later iterations of "Puss in Boots" (Bottigheimer 2002, 125–28). The context of Venice in the mid-sixteenth century, according to this theory, fostered the kind of discourse about urban/rural tensions and issues of a rise from poverty that informed the stories. Subsequently, Bottigheimer argues, the genre of rise tales became models for other writers, especially the French, who through print literature disseminated the stories which reached the peasantry (see Bottigheimer 2010).

The counter to the theory is that Straparola owed the success of his book *Le piacevoli notti* (The Pleasant Nights) to borrowings from many Latin tales and a sensationalistic use of eroticism and anti-authoritarian irreverence (Zipes 2012, 159–63; see also Ben-Amos 2010b; Da Silva 2010; Ziolkowski 2011). Little is known of his biography and what is known suggests ample evidence among Greeks and Romans as well as other European, Asian, and African groups telling tales during the pre-Christian era and early antiquity, laying the foundation for circulation in vernacular culture that was only slowly appreciated by literati and Romantic philosophers. Folklorist Jack Zipes gives as a case in point the development of *Thousand and One Nights*, originally Persian, stemming from oral storytelling traditions of the eighth and ninth centuries and possibly India before then (2012, 170–72; see also Naithani 2004). Chronicles suggest that travelers, merchants, and soldiers on trade routes from the Balkans to the China Sea engaged in the swapping of stories in caravanserai along the way. Tellers modified them rather than repeating them verbatim. They adjusted them according to regional customs and added cultural details from their backgrounds. Entertainers and professional storytellers called *rawi* catering to audiences of commoners helped further disseminate tales, particularly among the lower classes.

According to Zipes, travelers thus brought the tales to the world and made them international types well before they appeared in print and appealed to a literary elite. Although difficult to pin down a location, date, and author for the creation of oral wonder tales, plots and fragments in early ancient manuscripts reveal a constant "phemic" creative process of imagining, and commenting on, the world through fantasy, metaphor, and ritual. Tales were not named or categorized according to genre, but folklorists analyzing these documents claim that most of the fairy-tale motifs, characters, plots, and conventions existed in oral traditions long before a class of scholars crafted and categorized narratives (Zipes 2012, 170).

Folklorists often identify the influence of what have been called "strong" or "active" bearers of oral tradition and their performative venues (Duilearga 1999, 160–72; Niles 1999; Von Sydow 1999). Where their work can be located, they are presented to explain regional and community styles and content. A prominent example from folk musical study is a figure such as mandolinist and singer Bill Monroe (1911–1996), who is often called the father of bluegrass music (Ewing 2006; Smith, R. 2001; Rosenberg and Wolfe 2007). Steeped in the old-time traditions of his native Kentucky and attracted to the blues stylings of influential African-American fiddler and guitarist Arnold Shultz, Monroe, in working with a group he called the "Blue Grass Boys," crafted a sound characterized by fast tempos, high tenor harmonies, and improvised instrumental sections. He composed songs that entered into the "standard," and arguably traditional, bluegrass repertoire such as "Blue Moon of Kentucky" and "Little Cabin on the Hill" while others such as "Uncle Pen" because of their personal connection (about his fiddle-playing uncle Pendleton Vandiver) are signature Monroe pieces that are often imitated (Rosenberg and Wolfe 2007, 162–65). Folklorists have noted the wide range of his influence on musicians and the ritual centers of activity for a bluegrass community such as the Brown County Jamboree in Bean Blossom, Indiana, and various bluegrass festivals (Adler 2011). In such analyses, rather than treating folklore necessarily as an outgrowth of anonymous communal composition, folklorists seek out explanation in the creative spirits and social conduits that forge recognizable traditions and genres.

QUESTIONS OF FUNCTION AND PURPOSE

Even if an analyst of folklore determines the source of creativity that gave rise to a cultural movement or social conduit of influence, a question that remains concerns the persistence of the tradition well past the time of the promulgators' lifetime. A related question is the connection of one tradition with others in a cultural system for a location, group, network, or community. Are the traditions mutually exclusive or do they depend on one another to constitute a culture? These questions held particular vibrancy as observers noticed that rather than being a purposeless survival of past epochs, folklore provided social and psychological benefits for those who engaged in them and was associated with a matrix of traditions at the center of the culture. Presumably this positive reinforcement encouraged people to continue the traditions, or conversely if the customs no longer served a group's needs, they would dissipate.

Bronislaw Malinowski, who studied Trobriand Islander customs in the early twentieth century, is often credited with proposing functionalist explanations for the significance of folklore as a critical part of an integrated cultural system (Adam 1946; Kluckhohn 1943; Malinowski 2002, 67–74). He theorized that folklore persists because it actively fulfills essential human needs that he called synthetic. Folklore is "functional" in this view in the way that a biological organ functions in a body in relation to other parts. Theoretically, folklore is an activity that is the heart of the culture, and the uncovering of its vitalizing function explains not only its presence, but also the reliance of a community upon it. Malinowski wrote that functionalism is

> [the] explanation of ... facts ... by the part they play within the integral system of culture, by the manner in which they are related to each other within the system, and by the manner in which this system is therefore related to the physical surroundings. The functional view ... insists therefore upon the principle that in every type of civilization, every custom, material object, idea and belief fulfils some vital function, has some task to accomplish, represents an indispensable part within a working whole.
>
> (Malinowski 1926, 132–33)

He explained the persistence of magical beliefs, for instance, as "a remedy for specific maladjustments and mental conflicts, which culture creates in allowing man to transcend his biological equipment" (1926, 136). He compiled a list of beliefs that demonstrated the prevalence of magic, but observing when they were used, he noticed that islanders going out to fish invoked magic as they sojourned further from shore, thus having the function of warning against danger in their ecological system (Malinowski 1918).

In work among Texas coastal fishermen, folklorist Patrick Mullen (1969) found a similar functional pattern that separated the fishing community from the non-fishing community. The fishing lore included omens, blessings of the fleet, word taboos, and luck devices. This is not to say that they are "superstitious," Mullen declared. "They know that not many positive actions beyond the realm of science and technology can bring them success," he wrote (1969, 221). Yet they expressed taboos and beliefs to relieve anxiety or to provide a convenient scapegoat for bad luck in a venture full of uncertainty. Mullen generalizes from this experience comments about the function of folklore as an explanation for persistence in a complex, post-industrial society that is different from the homogeneous setting of the Trobriand Islands studied by Malinowski. Noting that folk beliefs have persisted in modern American society despite the "encroachment" of urbanization, scientism, and formal education, Mullen observes that folklore within a cultural system shared by modern occupations considered dangerous, particularly in environments associated with anxiety, can be explained by the lore's instrumental functions. He reflected that "the case of the fishermen of the Texas coast illustrates how one occupational group can hold on to a body of folklore because they have a need for it, while the rest of society rejects the validity of the same lore" (Mullen 1969, 224–25; cf. Poggie *et al.* 1976). Other groups that he cited with similar functional patterns are farmers, gamblers, students, construction workers, soldiers, and competitive athletes.

George Gmelch (1971), for instance, questioned the label of baseball players as superstitious, evident visibly in situations in which teammates wore caps inside out to encourage a hitting "rally." Upon closer observation, he found many more beliefs for hitting than fielding, and concluded that folklore served the function of giving players a sense of control over hitting, which had a higher failure rate (an excellent hitting average of .333 means that the player fails two out of three times!) than fielding. Accordingly, players reported few, if any, magical beliefs for fielding. The "rally caps" (baseball hats worn inside out to spur a batting streak for consecutive players) drew attention to the failure rate by sympathetically inverting the usual rate of hitting. Gmelch explained the more frequent expression of beliefs among baseball players than other athletes as a function of risk in the run-producing effort in hitting (see Gmelch 2006, 129–43; Webster, R. 2008, 22–23). Gmelch showed folkloric functions at work in complex societies much as they served the needs of homogeneous peoples in isolated locations (Gmelch 1971; see also Felson and Gmelch 1979).

A form of functionalism emphasizing the social bonding function of folklore as more important than others owed to British anthropologist A.R. Radcliffe-Brown, who in an ethnography of Andaman Islanders carried even further than Malinowski the analysis of the role that customs play in the maintenance of an organization (Homans 1941; Radcliffe-Brown 1952). Function for Radcliffe-Brown revolved around the role that social solidarity plays in shaping a culture. He played down Malinowski's biological and psychological motives and emphasized instead the social functions of status and cohesion to explain the persistence of folk practices (Radcliffe-Brown 1935). Radcliffe-Brown denied the evolutionary view that myths arise out of native explanations of natural phenomena. The Andaman Islander, he asserted, "has no interest in nature save in so far it directly affects the social life" (Radcliffe-Brown 1968, 49). The motives that Radcliffe-Brown inferred also ran toward utilitarian needs but were social rather than material in their characteristics. On this basis, Meyer Fortes in his study of the Tallensi in West Africa proclaimed that the tribe has an "ancestor cult not because they fear the dead—for they do not—or believe in the immortality of the soul—for they have no such notion—but because their social structure *demands it*" (Fortes 1960, 39; emphasis added). Edmund Leach, however, criticized the assumption of unity in the social structure and claimed that any social system contains opposing factions. Using the example of myth, he found that different myths validate rights of different groups of people within the same society. He concluded that myth is a "language of argument, not a chorus of harmony" (Leach, E. 1968, 198).

Also an ethnographer of African tribes, William Bascom (1954) proposed to American colleagues that functionalism is important in folklore studies to relate traditions to the culture of which they are a part. He pushed Malinowski's agenda of analyzing the needs within a culture that folklore fulfilled and appeared to privilege Radcliffe-Brown's overarching function of folklore maintaining social stability. He delineated four basic functions to explain folklore's persistence in modern society: (1) amusement; (2) validating culture; (3) education; and (4) maintaining conformity. Beginning with the first function, to say that folklore is entertaining remarks on its attractive quality but also suggests that in invoking play and humor, people use folklore for expressing "deeper meaning" (Bascom 1954, 343). In his view, amusement allows persons to find escape from the repressions imposed by the society. In language reminiscent of Malinowski's reference to "maladjustments and mental conflicts," Bascom pointed out that folklore provides a safety valve for the expression of difficult subjects in humor and play. Rather than undermining the system, however, this outlet for anxieties and fantasies provides a release so that outside of folkloric situations, persons in a society can ease their frustrations and return to the prevailing order. Second, folklore validates cultural activities such as rituals and institutions for those who perform and observe them. Third, folklore educates persons in the values of the society, particularly from elders to children, so that cultural continuities can be built across generations. Fourth, folklore maintains conformity to dominant patterns of behavior.

More than serving the purpose of education, folklore can apply social pressure and even social control, in forms such as proverbs, slurs, and taunts. The similarity of the second and third function has led some folklorists to combine them into a single function, resulting in three basic functions (Oring 1976). With his overarching function of stabilizing society and making it cohere, Bascom took into account Leach's postulation of disharmony as well as harmony, which are evident in the social effects of folklore. Bascom argued that folklore integrates society by giving expression to the values of factions in a society, but by offering the safety valve of this expression, the larger society reduces sources of open conflict and it therefore coheres. As a result of the cohesion of the society, suggesting Radcliffe-Brown's primary structural function, culture remains stable.

Perhaps as a result of the special American concern for the dissenting individual's role under pressure from a mass culture, Bascom's functionalism held that folklore is often generated out of the negotiation between individuals' volition and a cultural "mainstream." Bascom concluded his famous article "Four Functions of Folklore" by asserting that

> [Folklore] is used to inculcate the customs and ethical standards in the young, and as an adult to reward him with praise when he conforms, to punish him with ridicule or criticism when he deviates, to provide him with rationalizations when the institutions and conventions are challenged or questioned, to suggest that he be content with they as they are, and to provide him with a compensatory escape from "the hardships, the inequalities, the injustices" of everyday life. Here indeed, is the basic paradox of folklore, that while it plays a vital role in transmitting and maintaining the institutions of a culture an in forcing the individual to conform to them, at the same time it provides socially approved outlets for the repressions which these same institutions impose upon him.
>
> (1954, 349)

Debate ensued whether folklore can be more functionally subversive than Bascom posited (Barnes 1995, 37–60; Fine and Wood 2010; Meyer 2015, 21–42; Mintz, L. 1999). Funeral wakes, expected to be melancholy and intended to provide social unity, have attracted considerable folkloristic commentary on the function of convivial activities at them (Abrahams 1982; Harlow 1997; Morris 1938; Súilleabháin 1969; Thursby 2006). In his study of house wakes in Newfoundland, for example, folklorist Peter Narváez (1994) addressed the apparently sacrilegious practices of smoking, drinking alcoholic beverages, singing, dancing, fighting, game playing, and pranking in Catholic wakes for the dead. Narváez considered functionalist arguments that the frivolity at the wake placated the deceased whose departure could threaten the solidarity of the community. He recognized Malinowskian rhetoric in the observations of writers who called wake amusements a "cultural imperative," serving the function of normalizing relations with the corpse to prevent the deceased from harassing the living in the future. (1994, 266). But observing the disruptive amusements, Narváez did not find this functional argument convincing, nor after speaking to participants did he find strong evidence for the alternative Marxist function of frivolities representing a counter-hegemonic display against the dominant official Catholic Church that allowed the participants to return to the fold. Narváez complained that these functional explanations did not take into account the intentionality of the participants, that is, the conscious purposes for engaging in particular activities that tradition-bearers have articulated. Narváez received statements from participants emphasizing the pleasures of expressing antagonism in these events and he interpreted them to mean they displayed the social consciousness of a subordinated group engaged in rebellious acts against dominance and dominators. While not functioning to integrate social relations, the unruly acts were, he observed, vitalizing for participants and provided them a sense of empowerment.

Elliott Oring (1976) summarized growing criticism of Bascom's functionalism in folkloristics by declaring that unintended effects of a cultural tradition cannot account for its origin. Further, functions that allegedly generate effects may be falsely generalized as causing all instances in which certain conditions are present. Function, however, from a contextualist perspective varies according to the circumstances of a specific situation. Oring argued that a function is logically a consequence, not a cause, of folklore. That is not to say that folklore is non-functional; it clearly produces effects that are linked to its appeal and persistence by tradition-bearers (Burns, T. 1969; Walle 1977). Disputes arose, however, when functionalist theory assumed a stable social system as an ideal; cultural expressions in this view validated the establishment and status quo. Yet folklore as a pronounced possession of disenfranchised groups could appear to be less accepting and less collective than functionalism implied.

To be sure, functionalism continued to be used to account for the persistence of a cultural item because of the social and psychological benefits or practical utilities it provided to its bearers. In conjunction with ethnographies of cultural scenes, it also was used to evaluate the strategic purposes, or intentions, of participants within the context of that specific event or setting. The analysis, in fact, might look for different purposes among participants suggesting varied reasons for being there. In my analysis of drinking games among first-year college students, for example, I noted that the manifest function of the games appeared to discourage excessive consumption of alcoholic beverages. In memory games such as "Thumper," "Fuzzy Duck," and "Drink While You Think," students had difficulty remembering previously uttered words and coordinating the movements required to play the game as they imbibed drinks. Yet the lesson of the game seemed to get lost in the enactment of the game because students reported being encouraged to drink by having "fun" in the game. Key to their attitude was the idea that by being willing to be humiliated by others who were less debilitated by alcohol consumption, they bonded themselves to the group in a cultural definition of friendliness as convivial, obliging, and mirthful (Bronner 2012a, 229–34). The function of the tradition in practice from the vantage of the participants facilitated drinking to make congenial connections within a campus context characterized by new peer-group acquaintances. At Mormon college gatherings that prohibit alcohol consumption, students play the games as social ice-breakers purposefully to create a play frame that encourages social bonding.

In my analysis of a protest of pigeon shoots in the small Pennsylvania-German hamlet of Hegins, Pennsylvania, I found that both opponents and advocates of the event wanted attention that its staging brought. Animal rights protestors thought that media would broadcast the barbarism of the practice, particularly with use of young "trapper" boys to round up the dead pigeons, while many residents imagined that the involvement of the boys emphasized the wholesome continuity of tradition in families from generation to generation (Figure 3.5). Organizers of the event meant the shoot to be a fundraiser for a needed park that symbolized pigeon shooting, once a ritual event of the fall season, to stand for small-town American life at the heart of national heritage. Other participants saw the function of the shoot as an expression of libertarian rights and hunting culture. I also viewed a potential function outside of their awareness regarding the disputed symbolism of the pigeon in relation to a rural-urban conflict and the view by residents that as rural Americans they have been subordinated by urban values. As a result of the different views of the event's proper function, a discourse arose over the meaning and purpose of the event that I called

Figure 3.5 A shooter with "trapper boys" behind him takes aim at traps holding pigeons at the annual Labor Day picnic in Hegins, Pennsylvania, 1992

Source: Photograph by Simon J. Bronner.

"semiotic layering." The significance of this multiple perspective is that participants' motivations were not guided by a single motivation or purpose and that the functions of the event changed as protests arose (Bronner 2005a; 2008, 99–170).

Critics complain that the contextualist pursuit of a "microfunctionalism" (positing of functions that are particular to the situation) avoids an analysis of patterning and discourages generalization from the scenes. One often-cited contextualist example of functional explanation is the persistence of "camp legends" about scary figures in the woods in summer camp settings (Ellis 1982; Mechling 1999). A camp might have its own circumstances for the emergence and use of the legends. Indeed, many camps have their own names and descriptions for the figure, although analysts might notice that the legends are patterned after Native American mythology, scary creatures, and criminals in the news. The performative venues for the stories might be their dramatization around a campfire. In this context, they might be viewed as providing a social identity for the camp's particular location, but more generally folklorists might analyze similarities to widespread "boogey-man" stories at home often told to children to keep them in their beds at night, serving the function of enforcing social control over youth (Smith, J. 2004; Warner 1999, 42–47; Widdowson 1977). The persistence of the stories is functionally explained by the need of the authorities to keep the campers away from the woods when they are away from the watchful eyes of the counselors. Then in certain situations, do campers, or later college students in rustically situated dormitories, engage this tradition of telling scary legends to one another for different purposes such as social bonding, amusement, and relief from the anxiety of transition? In these situations, many folklorists assert, participants engage in folklore with different intentions and awareness about the effects of their actions. Analysts might find some functions as particularly consequential on the perception, if not explanation, of the events (Bauman, Z. 1999, 115–16; Mahner and Bunge 2001).

QUESTIONS OF PROJECTION AND ASSOCIATION

A theoretical position that addresses the last question is that folklore exists because it provides a socially sanctioned outlet for the expression of what cannot be articulated in the more usual, direct way. This process serves to deal with anxieties, emotions, and conflicts by sublimating, redirecting, and disguising them through the symbol and fantasy-laden content of folklore. Indeed, it could be argued that folklore emerges and endures because it provides a source for symbols that people need in their communication, and those symbols are adaptive devices in the conduct of their lives as they age and change. Analysts taking a symbolist approach offer psychological explanations of individuals' use of folklore to deal with emotional issues—both of joy as well as dread. A key term in this approach is that of "projection" in the sense of individuals projecting their feelings symbolically onto an external oral or visual form. Projection of pent-up feelings to folklore suggests a transference, and in the process of externalizing often troubling thoughts, the feelings become transformed into expressions that might take the shape of fantasies, images, and rituals characterized by symbolic content.

In the process of externalizing feelings onto expressions, desires can become inverted in the symbolic content of lore. Alan Dundes defined "projective inversion" this way: "a psychological process in which A accuses B of carrying out an action which A really wishes to carry out him or herself" (1991, 353). He found that projective inversion is especially prevalent in folktales and legends, suggesting that their narrative elaboration relates a heightened level of taboo. Examples include the themes of incest and infanticide evident in the classic Oedipal plot in which a father-king attempts to kill his new-born son, a projective inversion of the son's wish to kill his father. Dundes's contribution was to view such a tale according to female projection and take early analysts to task for their male-centeredness because they missed the significance of a father-king's act of locking up his daughter to protect her. Dundes proclaimed that early readings assuming that this merely reflected a father's wish to marry his own daughter were mistaken. He asserted instead that the daughter would like to marry her own father. Examining the folktale plot underlying Shakespeare's *King Lear*, Dundes concluded,

> The daughter's wish to marry her father is transformed through projective inversion into the father's wish to marry his daughter, just as the son's wish to kill his father is similarly transformed into the father's wish to kill his own son. Both transformations leave sons and daughters guilt free. Fairy tales, after all, are always told from the child's point of view, not the parents'. I concluded that King Lear was essentially a girl's fairy tale told from the father's point of view.
>
> (1987b, 37)

Dundes's approach depends greatly on the assumption that wishes and feelings are disguised in the form of textual symbols and expressed through the "safe" outlet of narrative and belief. Because of this masking, interviews with tradition-bearers might not reveal their conflicts. The content of folklore as a form of symbolic autobiography can be analyzed systematically, however, for signifiers of projection and projective inversion (Dundes 1962b, 32). Unexpurgated field documentation with contextual information is desirable to arrive at what he called a "depth" community psychology of folklore rather than the "literal" historical or aesthetic reading of texts. Dundes was particularly concerned for identifying the roots of deep-seated prejudice and thought that folklore was prime evidence not only for bringing issues to the surface but also in that process allowing for them to be addressed and remedied (Dundes 1987a, 28).

Dundes proposed a modern folkloristic approach that focuses on symbolic patterning in cross-cultural variants while questioning for the purposes of explanation the particular symbols and specific projections that are culturally relative. The key psychoanalytic premise he applied is developmental and gendered: "There is a relationship, perhaps causal, perhaps only correlational, between the initial conditions of infancy and early childhood (with respect to parent-child relations, sibling relations, etc.) and adult projective systems, which include myth" (1984, 270–71). Complaining that construing myths and legends as responses to historical events or generalizing social functions did not explain the symbolic content of creation myths, Dundes addressed the cross-cultural use in many myths of animals who brave floodwaters to scoop up mud which expands magically to form the earth. Using the concept of "male-birth" or "womb" envy from psychologists Karen Horney and Bruno Bettelheim, Dundes commented that "it was a classic case of male anal erotic creativity (in which males attempt to compete with females by creating from a substance produced by their bodies)" (2002, xiv).

Projections and projective inversions can occur in material form as well. Folklorist Michael Owen Jones in his study of traditional Kentucky chairmaker Chester Cornett explained the craftsman's construction of an unusual rocking chair at a difficult point of his life, and possibly his maintenance of an "old-time" legacy of chairmaking, in Cornett's projection of "protective seclusion" within the solid sides of the chair. Correlating Chester's life story of moving from his rural environs to Cincinnati and concomitant marital difficulties, Jones hypothesized that the design of the personalized chair as an enclosure was an unconscious desire to "isolate himself from others and to control what went on around him … These chairs could offer Chester control and protection, security and power, because they are very large, they elevate the sitter above others, and they surround the person using them" (1989, 186). I found a similar pattern

Figure 3.6 Bricoleur Clarence Yingst constructing structures in front of his house in Harrisburg, Pennsylvania

Source: Photograph by Simon J. Bronner.

with aging bricoleur Clarence Yingst, who in a gentrifying urban neighborhood, replaced his open frontscape that invited visitors to mingle with an enclosure that excluded passersby and emphasized his alienation (Figure 3.6). This pattern became important in bringing out class-based conflicts that were not projected until young urban professionals moving into the neighborhood put pressure on residents to conform to a model of social as well as expressive restraint (Bronner 1986b, 62–86).

Another psychological perspective is that folklore therapeutically deals with gaps in scientific knowledge or unusual physiological experiences. One can solicit many folk remedies for hiccups, common cold, warts, and headaches because they are viewed as lacking scientific cures. By this thinking, many farmers relied on traditional weather prognosticators before weather prediction became more reliable. Yet many uncertainties exist and traditional knowledge gives people a sense of control over nature and their bodies. In this context, the abundance of folklore concerning bodily flatulence and odor can be explained by the taboo placed upon bodily emissions in childhood. Folklorist Trevor Blank points out:

> Whether it is due to social taboos about bodily functions or sheer ingenuity, *flatulence* has well over a dozen common terms associated with its occurrence: passing gas, breaking wind, letting one rip (or go), cutting the cheese, busting ass, pooting, tooting, foofing, fluffing, puffing; folk retorts that mask the anxieties caused by flatulence through euphemistic annotations also exist, such as "dropping a bomb," "making a stinker," "cooking some eggs," "baking brownies," "making an air biscuit," "stepping on a duck," "cracking a boom-boom," or "rolling out some thunder."
>
> (Blank 2010, 61)

Responses to, and references to "farting," as the presumably "offensive" natural act is most commonly known in English, uses the mode of humor to defuse the embarrassing social situation, although no folklore need be invoked if passing gas alone. Blank also hypothesizes that men more than women engage in fartlore to reinforce cultural expectations of manly behavior, and G. Legman goes further in his psychoanalytic comment that jokes about farting constitute "an evasive form of scatological abuse of women" because of the use of emissions as a manly weapon that redirects concern about men's odor to women who are supposedly overly concerned about their appearance and smell" (1968, 858).

One symbolic interpretation is that flatulence attracts projection into folklore because in addition to being a societal taboo, it symbolically is liminal; it is uncomfortably "betwixt and between" the feeling of relief and constipation and in this gray area folklore kicks in to clarify status, if not ritually alleviate the predicament (see Turner, V. 1969). The need to project liminality is indicated in countless bathroom stalls containing the highly variable folk poetry of "Here I sit, broken hearted, Tried to shit, but only farted, Later on I took a chance, Went to fart but shit my pants" (Dundes 1966c, 99–100; Blank 2010, 69). Underlying these expressions is a notion that much of folklore embodies a conflict between the socialized (the need to please others) and natural (or uncaring childish) figure because of discomposure produced by social constructions or idealizations of the denaturalized body.

Some folklorists prefer to explain folkloric reactions to uncertainty and ambiguity in terms of "associations" that are more context-sensitive than projective processes. In such "experience-centered" approaches, analysts seek psychological associations that people make based upon prior experiences and assess the influence of traditional knowledge on the way these associations are narrated or materialized. Folklorist David Hufford (1982), who worked in a teaching hospital, analyzed, for example, a mysterious experience that patients described as being "ridden by a hag (witch)," "held down by a ghost," and "being pressed" in a nightmare. Individuals from different ethnic backgrounds reported a nightmarish phenomenon of feeling the presence of a scary creature often by sitting on their chest and immobilizing the sleeper. The folklore of these incubus and succubus figures have long been chronicled as night-demons who force sex on sleepers (see Genesis 6:1–2). Hufford connected the rise of the belief complex as a folk response to sleep paralysis with a particular kind of hypnagogic hallucination and points out that cultural factors determined the ways in which the experience was described and interpreted by patients as "supernatural."

An example of the influence of traditional knowledge on an emerging folk practice is the ritualization of turning forty years of age in North America. Stanley Brandes (1985) traced the folk practice of having a mock funerary party and pranks concerning the end of youth at age forty to the rise of a youth-oriented service and information economy more so than the extension of the life span. He drew connections that people made to forty as a specific quantity in the life span to religious reinforcement in biblical references to forty (forty years of wandering in the desert, forty days of the flood, forty days on the mount). Although the mock parties and popular beliefs indicate that people decline physically at forty years of age, medical evidence, Brandes found, did not lead to the conclusion that forty represented a point of decline. He explained the rise of the parties by positing that because of the symbolism attached to number 40 as a demarcation of life "ending," Americans expected trouble and devised a ritual, often jocular, transition to compensate for anxiety in a youth-oriented society.

By contrast, in Japan, turning sixty holds a special association with rebirth. In a *kanreki* ceremony men and women celebrate living through the sixty-year cycle of the tradition *eto* (ten stems and twelve branches) calendar and returning to the horoscope sign in which they were born. Instead of decorations in black marking decline, in Japan, honor is accorded for entering revered elderhood or *geju*. Rebirth is symbolically marked with red attire associated with birth: red cap, red seat cushion, and a *chanchanko* vest. In a hierarchical social structure in which seniority is accorded deference, the celebrant looks ahead to the middle stage of elderhood at eighty years old, or *chūju*, and the last stage beginning at 100, or *jōju*.

In various sports, organizers invoke folklore to connote meanings to events beyond being contests of athletic prowess. In the twenty-first century, for example, strongman and strongwoman competitions featured tests of strength with the mythological labels of Atlas (Manhood) Stones, Hercules Hold, Viking Press, and Fingal's Fingers. The associations with classical figures raised the images of the contestants not just as athletes but as legendary heroes or demigods and connected the modern organized events to ancient customs and narratives of social dominance. Contests declaring "The World's Strongest Man," for example, become ritualized as global settings for hypermasculine, superhuman, and supernatural, power. The logo of the World's Strongest Man showed the mythic Atlas lifting the globe on his shoulders. In regional contests, organizers of modern contests introduce local traditions representing mythic traditions to provide a cultural aura such as Samurai stone lifting in Japan (Figure 3.7), pig-carrying in China, Basque stone lifting in Europe and America (Figure 3.8), and Husafell Shield lifting in Iceland. Beyond the symbolism of the heavy, hard stone associated with outdoor manly endeavor within these cultures, the act, or praxis, of lifting is associated with triumph as the full extension of the body, or reaching a goal, despite "carrying a burden." It therefore suggests a "metaphorical literalization" of triumphant, forward (or upward) aspiration.

Many behaviors considered risky such as gambling, romance, business, and hunting raise questions of how folklore contributes to the repetition of ritual behaviors even in the face of negative reinforcement. Lucky numbers used in losing lottery ticket choices

Figure 3.7 A 99-year-old man describes the custom of lifting Samurai stones as a test of manhood in Fukuoka, Japan, 2010

Source: Photograph by Simon J. Bronner.

might be explained, for example, by the idea of intermittent rein-forcement of success that might be gained through narrative about others as well as experience. Failure to win might not stop the per-son from using that number because he or she remembers a previous success, even if infrequent. One might also continue to bury a statue of St. Joseph upside down in the yard to sell a home or pray to St. Anthony to find a lost object because others have narrated expe-riences of their effectiveness. The practices might be characterized as "folklore" and this rhetoric raises a fundamental cognitive asso-ciation of tradition as something unofficial, connected to ordinary people probably, and based upon collective wisdom, even if it is suspect scientifically. Folklorists might have a broader, more elastic view, but when considering the impact of folklore within commu-nities, folklorists often refer to associative perceptions of folklore as explanations for attitudes toward tradition.

Figure 3.8 British strongman champion Mark Felix competes on the "Atlas
        Stones" in the Arnold Strongman Classic in Columbus, Ohio, 2011

Source: Photograph by Simon J. Bronner.

Although folklorists often rely on fieldwork to identify cultural
associations to folklore (such as saint figurine, rabbit foot, clover, and
penny as good luck symbols), a few scholars have conducted experiments to verify associative behavior. Often the procedures involve
the observation of deviations of text as a planted narrative is transmitted through various chains of people. Most clinical examinations of
this sort verify that the oral process results in variation of content, and
relative stability of the form, but less clear are the associations to the
content made by participants (see Anderson 1951; 1956; Bachrach
1962; Bartlett 1920; Goldstein 1967; Oring 1978). With the basis
of proverbs encompassing the collective wisdom of a society, some
researchers have created experiments to analyze the most frequent
proverbs that come to mind in a set time within a sample group
at a point in time. Wolfgang Mieder (1992) summarized such tests

among Russian, German, and American students, Swedish villagers, and African-American youth. The goal was to establish a "paremiological minimum," that is, the proverbs that are most frequently known among a group. Suggestions have been made for this kind of associative data for beliefs, names, and slang that can be analyzed for themes or "folk ideas" that constitute a group's "worldview."

Mieder commented, for example, on the associative implications of folklore based on "life" as the most popular word in modern American proverbs. This information supports the proposition that folklore in an individualistic society helps provide guidance on the uncertainty of social situations. Alan Dundes (1969b) thematized popular American proverbs such as "the early bird catches the worm" in contrast to Japanese proverbs of "the nail that sticks up gets nailed down" to suggest that folklore not only reflects, but also inculcates, the importance of initiative and a future-orientation in an individualistic American society. Although a causal link between folklore and worldview is not easily demonstrated, the quantitative and qualitative study of projection and association is intended to find explanation for expressive behavior in the symbol-making capacities of humans.

QUESTIONS OF PERFORMANCE AND COMMUNICATION

When someone engages in a ritual, sings a folk song, or tells a joke, people might comment that they are performing or enacting folklore. Questions arise whether other expressive actions for which persons are not as aware of themselves as actors such as speech and craft constitute performance. Even if literally not on a stage, the tradition-bearer might infuse meaning into his or her rendition with the way the lore is expressed in various situations and with different audiences. The description of folklore as a performance suggests other dramaturgical metaphors for analyzing the communication of folklore between people: stage, audience, actors, cues, props. One of the implications of using this thespian rhetoric is that folklore draws attention to itself as artistic expression in the course of often mundane everyday life. As in a theater, people might expect a certain artistic license in the use of language and images; they might even look for messages beneath the scripts and body language drawn from tradition that would not be directly uttered in conversation.

Given that some forms of folklore can be recognized as performances, what does the strategy of enactment explain? Often there is the suggestion that the use of style in an expression establishes the agency of an individual in persuading his or her audience of values or identity. It differentiates the kind of utterance given as artistic and perhaps folkloric by drawing attention to it with various cues understood by the listeners and viewers. If not intentional, the person's use of performance cues to announce traditional knowledge might in the final analysis be viewed as a special use of folkloric performance, consciously or unconsciously, not just to draw attention but also to resolve tension or negotiate meanings in situations of ambiguity, tension, or even threat (Abrahams 1977).

Based in sociolinguistic theory, Dell Hymes's formulation of "The Ethnography of Speaking" informed much of performance analysis in folkloristics (Bauman and Sherzer 1975; Hymes 1962; 1971; 1972). In Hymes's view, both folkloristics and linguistics used speech for cultural patterns and grammar and therefore could be combined. He called for folklorists to uncover cognitive patterns that control speech, functions that are served by speech in specific situations, effects that situational context has on speech, and dynamics of performance. In this model, speech as meaningful expression arose from social interaction; in the process of communication, folklore plays, according to Hymes, a critical role. The frequent usage of *interact* (and later *enactment*) implied the alternating roles of performance and audience among people. With the recognition that communication among people involved more than speech—gestures, dress, setting, for instance—Hymes later changed the label of his proposed combined study to the "ethnography of communication" (Hymes 1964).

Methods that are involved in the ethnography of communication included close scrutiny of specific situations as they naturally developed. Texts were still essential to the ethnography, but additional information concerning surroundings, actions, and biographies was collected and incorporated into renderings of performances on paper and in media. The kind of explanation for these special states in which folklore is invoked or created is typically situationally specific.

It is focused on folklore as a process in which the individual rather than following tradition manipulates the situation for his or her own purposes (see Cashman *et al.* 2011; Jones, M. 2000; McDonald 1997; Mechling 2006). The action of performance as well as the content might be viewed as folkloric because the message is artistically expressed, probably with reference to precedent. The actor is aware of the particular setting, audience, and conditions and varies his or her performance accordingly. In theory, dramaturgical considerations might explain changes in content and development of performance, but typically will not account for the origin or persistence of traditional knowledge.

Questioning performance often leads to a microfunctionalism of the situation with the understanding of function interpreted as reasons for engaging verbal artistry to serve the needs of performer, audience, and the needs of the occasion (Bauman, R. 2012; Kapchan 2003). Folklorist W.F.H. Nicolaisen elaborates that the message-sender in a communication frame in these situations evinces a folk cultural register to set up his or her "creative risk-taking and fulfillment" (1984, 268). The audience does not expect a monotonous, mechanical recitation, but rather an artful rendering of a story or song, even if the material is familiar. Nicolaisen elaborated that storytelling, especially,

> [as] audible actualization depends completely on the performer's skill and inclination to create a text that channels the story's potential in performer- and audience-friendly forms, made for the occasion. Like all expressive manifestations of folklore, it derives its very existence from the tension between repetition and variability.
>
> (1990, 7)

By analyzing these often spontaneous situations, folklorists conceive folklore as arising out of social interaction and seek to explain the motivations for participants acting the way they do at these events.

An occasion that I observed that brought performance issues to the surface was the regular summer gathering of male cronies in front of laborer Eugene Powell's house in the African–American section of Greenville, Mississippi (Figure 3.9). Eugene Powell's house became a backdrop for convivial exchange because of his reputation as a creative man of words: in blues song and edgy story, he entertained a throng daily and drew African-American neighbors together while cognizant of racial divides in the region. His son, growing up in the midst of the civil rights movement, was also part of the group, and he also cultivated a reputation as a storyteller in settings such as the prisons and streets in which he often dwelled. Around Eugene's house, I found that storytelling, usually in the form of jokes told by men, invited competition. As one joke led to another, a discourse formed in a register apart from the everyday. Men were prime characters in the guise of tricksters and heroes who mocked the (white) Man and the Reverend, and they demonstrated sexual bravado, at least on the fictive plane of oral narration. In the performative frame of story, these men, who in real life were repressed by whites and dominated by women, could shine. Eugene was at the center of attention in his living room and out on the yard among his friends in their sixties. Eugene's son Ernest recognized and admired that quality in his father. He also wanted to be known as a good talker, and he tried to develop the talent of being ready with a joke or a rhyme whenever the occasion arose.

Figure 3.9 A social gathering of African-American men in Greenville, Mississippi, featuring joke and legend telling, 1976

Source: Photograph by Simon J. Bronner.

To get at the meaning placed in performance among this group on these occasions, I strove to comprehend the strategies underlying Eugene's storytelling and to see what would happen when joking as perceived in this particular situation was adapted from father to son (Figure 3.10). Whereas Eugene needed prodding from an attentive face to tell his jokes, Ernest told stories as if delivering a soliloquy. They were often more personal and independent, even bordering on the limits of the usual social standards of performance. For Ernest, engaging folklore in performance was more than sharing a story. In their themes of badmen, violence, and misogyny, the jokes told others who he was, without giving his autobiography. His folklore informed others how he wanted to be treated and what the consequences might be if they failed to treat him correctly. Folklore was a way to gain prestige and convey his emotional state. Eugene's performance style invited others to laugh with him; Ernest, even when he told the same jokes, told his audience to fear him.

Ernest had learned folk forms from Eugene, but the two men's individual personalities led them to select different tones and textures

Figure 3.10 Raconteur and blues singer Eugene Powell (left) with his son Ernest Powell (right), Greenville, Mississippi, 1976

Source: Photograph by Simon J. Bronner.

for their jokes. When Eugene and Ernest told the same narratives, it dramatized their differences. Both of them had a special fondness, for example, for a story Eugene called "Oink is Ugly" and passed on to his son (see Dance 1978, 199–200; Dorson 1967, 184; Roberts, L. 1955, 132–5; Jemie 2003, 278; Motif K406, "Stolen animal disguised as person so that thief may escape detection"; Aarne-Thompson Type 152H★, "Stolen sheep dressed as person sitting at helm of boat"). It is commonly reported in collections of African-American folklore and was known by others in Eugene's circle. Nonetheless, friends frequently asked Eugene to tell it, even though they knew the punch line. In their view, it was "a good one" that was worth hearing again as Eugene performed it. Without Ernest around, Eugene told his story in an easy-going manner:

> Some black folk went in the country and stole a hog. When they was going out there, one of 'em said, "Now we don't want to go out there and get no shoke [portmanteau of "shit" and "smoke"]. We gonna go out there and get a big hog, 'cause we got to eat." He went out there and got a hog and he caught the wrong one. He caught a big old bull hog. He wanted to turn him loose. His buddy said don't turn him loose. He said, "He's meat too, man. We can eat him." So he got him and put him in the car. They let out [highway] number one with him. They got to the red light. The police was behind them. They was running red lights, kinda scared. They stopped. The policeman come up and asked them, "What y'all running that red light for? What's the matter here?" [said in an official sounding voice in imitation of a white southern dialect]. They said, "I'll tell you what. This man is so sick in here we was trying to get him to the doctor" [said nervously]. So the other boy pulled off his coat right quick and slipped it on the hog and slid his hat up on his head. The policeman come over and looked at him and mumbled and then said, "That man is *sick* [elongates the sound of word]. We'll try and make it to the hospital with him quick." The policeman said, "You go on 'cause, damn he don't look like he's gonna be here much longer. He's the ugliest son of a bitch I ever seen in my life. He needs a shave, he needs his teeth fixed; he's in *bad* shape" [said assertively]. One of the fellas said, "His name is Oink." The policeman said, "I don't give a damn who them other people was but that god damn Oink sitting there in the back, that's one ugly son of a bitch!" [last part said loudly and with emphasis].

In the process of learning and personalizing the story, Ernest had become protective of his repertoire, or jealous of the honor accorded Eugene's rendition. Joining the gathering on his father's front yard under the cooling shade of a tree, Ernest wanted the spotlight. On his first day out of jail, Ernest had talked about the police not being able to "break him" by putting him in prison. Ernest acknowledged that the group knew the story of "Oink is Ugly" but he was going to differentiate himself from his father who he characterized as old-fashioned (and without saying it associated him with the Jim Crow South) by telling it his youthful way. To rivet attention among the gathered friends, his narration used names of people in his audience for the characters in the story.

These three guys went out and stole this hog and they was on their way back, and the road man was stopping everybody and checking for licenses and things [uses hands to imitated looking at documents]. One guy said, "What we gonna do y'all?" [exaggerates southern drawl]. The second guy said, "I'm gonna put my coat on him." The third guy said, "I'll give him my hat." The other guy said, "Well I'll tell you what I'm gonna do. I'll give him my shade glasses" [said excitedly]. So they did. They pulled up the road and the man said, "Hey, hold up there." He went over to the car and said, "What's your name?" The first guy said, "My name is Simon." He asked "What's your name?" The second guy said, "Old Joe." He asked again, "And what's your name?" The third guy said, "Tom." The road man said, "Who's that you got there in the back with you?" One of the guys said, "Oh that's a friend of ours." The roadman said, "By the way buddy, what's your name?" He was talking to the hog. The hog didn't answer. He said, "Man, don't you hear me talking to you? I said what's your name" [raising voice]. The one guy sitting beside the hog nudged him in the side and the hog said, "Oink Wig." The road man said, "Oh your name's Oink Wig huh? Where you on your way to?" [said skeptically]. One guy said, "Well, we taking Oink Wig to the doctor" [said nervously]. The road man said, "Well you mostly got to go to the dentist. You ain't got to tell me no more. I can see you got to the dentist, the way his teeth look in that mouth. Them teeth real bad. Y'all rush him on to the doctor 'cause he need them teeth pulled bad. He looks rough." They pulled away and said, "Boy we sure was lucky." The roadman went on back to his car and said to the other guy, "You know what man? You know I pulled them guys over and checked them out? They had a guy in that car they called Oink Wig. That son of a bitch looked just like a hog."

The effect of the story in this African-American section of Greenville came from the black characters outsmarting whitey. The African-American narrator knew the absurdity of disguising a hog as a person, but to the white person in a position of authority, the teller underscored, all the blacks were metaphorically in the same category. If that is a harsh message, the humorous cast derived from the blacks fooling the roadman. But unlike other jokes, this narrative lacked a clear, striking punchline. Instead, it depended on a comic delivery to emphasize, on the one hand, the ludicrousness of the ruse, and on the other, the roadman's folly. The audience on the lawn laughed at the creation of a comic situation and Ernest's boastful delivery of a scene where the rebels "got away with it." For Ernest, the story was told as if he was the one being stopped by the "man" and was explaining what he was doing.

In performance, Ernest's narration effused hostility. The roadman and the car passengers had little regard for each other. The theft of the hog was deliberate and defiant. Eugene used the detail of a search for food as justification for the act. Eugene's story used misunderstanding and duping for its dramatic impact. Eugene did not change expression after his story, as if he did not want to let on that he was laughing at the officer's stupidity. Ernest smiled broadly and reveled in the deception. He had bested his father, he thought, not necessarily by telling the more creative joke, but by effecting the stronger reaction. Ernest's jokes, like his presence, were stronger, cruder, and angrier. As good joketellers Ernest and Eugene knew the structure to use for spinning out humorous narratives, but they displayed strong differences in delivery. Ernest's rapid-fire style and tendency to look away from his audience sometimes shut people out from his narratives. He stressed deviance and aggressiveness in sexual relations, violence as an everyday occurrence, and manliness as a basic value of dominance that had to be constantly proven. Ernest also had a striking concern for persecution in his jokes. His protagonists hurled abuse to others in reaction to an overwhelming prejudice, and sometimes directed that antipathy at themselves. In real life, Ernest felt hounded too—by his father, his common-law wife, the police. Ernest's jokes became platforms to beat back the hounds and scoundrels.

Ernest delighted in subterfuge to foil the powerful and violence to smash antagonists and used a more demonstrative performance style to reflect this attitude. In real life, he was more often locked up in jail than triumphant on the street. The analysis of their different performances and strategies or purposes in interaction with an audience in a folkloric frame revealed much about their relationship and the use of folklore to relate their lives. While it did not explain the source or distribution of folkloric content, it suggested a process shaped by the particular backgrounds and location of the participants that can demonstrate, if not define, the ways that people in certain situations respond folklorically.

Because much of digital communication is not "face-to-face interaction" characteristic of what analog folklorists referred to as a performative frame of folklore, many analysts reserved performance analysis for communication of "verbal art" in small group situations. Folklorist Anthony Bak Buccitelli (2012), however, has suggested that Internet threads should be analyzed as communicative events, culminating in the performance of material that could be considered traditional. This inquiry has led to considerations of differences between "virtual" and "actual" performances. Although simulating audience reactions in face-to-face settings, digital communication is not bound by time and place in the same way. Buccitelli claimed that digital environments should be considered locations of performance on its own terms (with references to "forwarding," "posting," "blogging," and "spamming" as distinctive digital practices). Although the emphasis in this communicative analysis is on the identification of digital culture, Buccitelli sounded familiar analytic perspectives of locating agency and accounting for the forces that mediate expressions in "digital environments." In addition to finding unique manifestations of folk behavior in cyber-environments such as hackers injecting legendary characters (e.g., "The White Lady of Perion" in MapleStory video games based upon "White Lady" lovers' lane legends), "creepypastas" and collective creations (horror-related legends posted around the Internet such as the Slender Man and Ted the Caver), virus hoaxes (e.g., Goodtimes, Dance of the Pope, and An Internet Flower for You), viral "memes" (Grumpy Cat, U Mad Bro, But That's None of My Business), the comparative microfunctions of communicative topics in analog and digital culture provide material for analysis of joking, legend tripping, and ritualizing off- and on-line (see Chess and Newsom 2015; Ellis 2012; Frank, R. 2011; Gurak 2001, 82–109; Kinsella 2011; Oring 2014).

QUESTIONS OF POWER AND CONFLICT

A key phrase of folkloristic analysis that emerged in the late twen- tieth century is "cultural hegemony," suggesting usage of folk as a social category of marginalized, colonized, feminized, infantilized, orientalized, and minority groups who are often in conflict with the prevailing power structure. Partly in response to functional perspectives that emphasized the social bonding and stabilizing effects of folklore, approaches concentrating on the uses of folk- lore in power struggles were applied at the micro level in situated practice and performance as well as the macro level of nations, societies, and institutions. In addition to explaining the use of folklore as a tool of resistance to, or at least insulation from, ruling powers, analysts also noted manipulation or invention of tradi- tions by societal factions to effect control. Yet another point of analysis concerned contentious situations within communities in which issues of tradition arise. Folklorists working with folk soci- eties such as the Amish and Hasidim, for example, often sought to explain the propensity for schism in folk societies that strive for harmony among its members (Cong 1992; Heilman 1992; Kraybill 1989; Mintz, J. 1992).

Central to the idea of cultural hegemony is the discussion of folk- lore as part of a philosophy of reversing oppression of an underclass by Italian Marxist thinker, Antonio Gramsci (1891–1937). Gramsci characterized the folk—constituting in his view a rural peasant and urban proletariat class—as fundamentally subaltern, that is, a group kept in a lower status by the "hegemony," or imposed authority, of the ruling class (Gramsci 1999; Lears 1985). Questioning why the underclass does not more actively resist this hegemony, he theorized that it is not fully aware of its situation because the vernacular cul- ture in which they might take pride and probably take for granted is an instrument of their subjection. Gramsci observed that culturally, the lower rungs of society were associated with folklore, but elites claimed genteel refinement in the form of fine arts as the culture that spoke for them. This aesthetic of refinement, although it represented a minority of the population, became the standard of the society through educational, economic, and political institutions shaped by aspirations to become part of a dominant power structure. Folklore as the "voice of the people" was left unappreciated or derided as backward, ephemeral, marginal, and crude (Gibson 2015, 77–114).

According to Gramsci, the elites had a problem, however, if they were going to maintain control over the society characterized by folklore among the masses. Not only was the ruling class a minority of the population in the midst of modern democratizing movements, but elites could also be stigmatized for being monarchical if they become too visible in their forceful imposition of dominion by fiat. He claimed that in reaction to these possible threats on their control, the gentry exerted a political strategy to impose hegemony through culture by organizing and even inventing traditions that appealed to the masses but ultimately served the interests of the elite to remain economically, socially, and politically superordinate. The strategy had the effect of displacing the folk culture that could undermine the hierarchical social structure and aesthetic system.

Gramsci thus revised the strict Marxist view that elites consciously eliminated folklore to keep lower classes subordinate (Gencarella 2010; Gibson 2015, 77–114; Hawley 1980; Limón 1983; 2010). He held that elites with the authority of the "state" embraced peasants' folklore (or a sanitized, coopted version of it) for a small stratum of society to maintain control over the masses. Elites appeared benevolent by supporting certain kinds of folklore associated with the proletariat that held "mass appeal." Part of the reason that folklore was so critical in the control of culture, according to Gramsci, was that it contained a "conception of the world," that some observers might call "worldview" (Gramsci 1999, 133).

Sociologist Pierre Bourdieu later adapted this idea into a notion of "habitus," a system of "principles which generate and organize practices and representations" (1990, 52–65; see also Ben-Amos 2010a; Cantwell 1999; Tschofen 1999). Folklore, Bourdieu elaborated, constituted habits that had been developed through time, and have been unconsciously embodied into their physical and psychological disposition through repetition. The relation to Gramsci is that these practices depend on subordinating social structures for their viability and meaning, and superordinate elites work to dictate the prevailing social structure as hierarchical with subaltern groups beneath them.

More than engaging in folkloric performances, subaltern groups by invoking folklore as "traditional" inculcated this "conception" as a set of values and outlooks that informed their daily actions. To be sure, folklore, because it was a "reflection of the conditions of life of the people," according to Gramsci, might be trivialized and belittled in favor of science and business that favored the state (1999, 135). The state might insist on folklore being taught and celebrated as children's material—entertaining, but ultimately inconsequential—and recast it to emphasize the conservative, nationalist "conception of life" the state as the extension of elites wants. Gramsci as an activist thought that an analyst could challenge this elitist imposition of culture by explaining "what other conceptions are at work in the moral and intellectual formation of the young generations," and pointing out those perspectives or forms of habitus which by being authentically "folk" exist outside of institutional control. "Folklore must not be conceived as an oddity, a strange, ridiculous or, at best, a picturesque thing," Gramsci declared (1999, 135). He viewed a manipulation of folklore to get young minds to conform to a hierarchical social structure (1999, 135–36; see also Oinas 1975; Ortiz 1999). Folklore, Gramsci demanded, "must be conceived as something very serious and to be taken seriously" in a larger scheme of political change (1999, 136). The trouble, according to this theory, is that analysts as instruments of the state, as well as the masses, were often unaware of their own oppression because they thought they still held on to, or thought they could raise, their voice, their folklore, their tradition. Invented traditions of counter-hegemonic organizations, however, such as unions, cultural revitalization agencies, and social movements serve to represent folklore in the form of songs, rituals, and chants as a force of persuasion, often against the foil of "corporate culture" (Dorst 1990; Gencarella 2009; Rudd 2002; Samper 2002).

The explanation of folk revival movements usually associated with social reform is an example that has aroused argument over whether they have effected political change by drawing attention to the artistry of poor, disenfranchised, racialized folk, or in Gramscian terms, entrenched the cultural hegemony of the establishment.

Robert Cantwell's critique of American folk music revivals was that the forces that put vernacular voices in the limelight were ultimately controlled by commercial interests and the lofty intellectuals who wanted to liberalize society reflected their own elite educations and affluent socioeconomic backgrounds rather than changing the social structure (1996, 13–48). That is not to say they were not earnest in their reformist intentions by drawing out the communitarian, egalitarian ethos they associated with folklore, but according to Cantwell, the result was to designate folks at the grassroots as othered (often rooted in Deep South black and Appalachian Scots-Irish cultures) and anachronistic (preindustrial) rather than culturally integrated and empowered in mass society. This Gramscian view is disputed by those who see folklore revitalization movements as "cultural democracy" campaigns that validate diversity and reorder aesthetic assumptions about worthiness of various subaltern groups (Graves 2005; Hufford, M. 2002; Kurin 2002; Zuidervaart and Luttikhuizen 2000). Indeed, establishing the folk cultural basis of groups such as gays, lesbians, students, and people with disabilities who were thought to be culture-less has been presented in public discourse to heighten their democratic participation and credibility in the marketplace.

Some analysts might provide an alternative scenario in which technology-driven popular culture is more likely to be manipulated by elites to effect cultural hegemony than folkloristic movements. For example, renowned folk song collector Alan Lomax made the claim that in the mid-twentieth century the folk music revival could not be sustained because corporate elites in the name of maximizing profit controlled the radio airwaves and promoted more easily commodified musical forms (2003, 116–19). Others will dispute the conspiratorial assumption of hegemonic control by elites maintained through culture. They might also question the ineluctable conflict of class, particularly in societies marked by social and geographical mobility. Alan Dundes, in his Introduction to Gramsci's "Observations on Folklore" thought that Gramsci set up a false dichotomy between an underclass possessing folklore and elites who do not. He doubted the assumption that elites need to manipulate someone else's folklore for their own advantage (1999, 132–33). Bringing into question the function of folklore as an instrument of resistance limited to oppressed groups, Dundes referred to the folklore of lawyers, computer engineers, physicians, and mathematicians, although in his analyses he pointed out power relations of these occupations within a professional class. Another contentious point is the presumption of collusion between elites and intellectuals to maintain the status quo or to "colonize" the folk, especially when historiography shows many folklorists as agents of social change in their advocacy for marginalized groups and democratizing arts (Garlough 2008; Gencarella 2009; Kodish 2011; Shuldiner 1998; Westerman 2006).

For many theorists, social structures that maintain inequities of race, gender, and sexuality explain uses of folklore that bring to the fore power relations and negotiate norms in a plural culture. One distinction that analysts make is between folklore that is "esoteric," that is, generated within a group and about that group, and "exoteric," also referring to material about the community but emanating outside the group and often with the intention of depreciating it (Fine, G. 1987a; Jansen 1959; Tokofsky 2000). A comparison of these vantages, such as the ethnic joke told within a group to express lessons of social solidarity and outside the group to express prejudice, often suggests the idea that within a complex culture, a public contestation occurs for the standards of appropriateness in the language and representations used to describe groups. Of folkloristic significance, narrated depictions, even if based in fantasy, can become perceived as reality, such as the visual culture dubbed Oriental in a binary with the Occident that Asian men are effeminate, animalized (usually in the form of a monkey or snake), and racialized as "yellow" (Lee 1999; Said 1978). Narrated and visualized representations might be enculturated through immersion in folklore and thereby they normalize or naturalize a state of being. For instance, in feminist theory, there is often an explanation of constructed binaries that apparently privilege male dominance through lore that emphasizes the naturalness of patriarchy—a social structure in which the father or male elders hold primary power in family, polity, and work (Bourdieu 2001; Hollis, Pershing, and Young 1993; Radner 1993). The binary of male and female in society appears biologically equal, according to this theory, but cultural reinforcement of ideas about women as a "weaker (fairer, pursued, attractive, objectified, animalized) sex," biologically hampered by bodily differences (menstruation, smaller stature, protruding breasts), oriented toward domestic activities, and obsessed about appearance naturalize the superiority of men.

Some analysts have put forward a masculinist perspective that identifies the expectations of masculinity in society that are imposed in matrifocal institutions of school, home, and leisure and led to confusion for boys about their identities in a world they perceive as increasingly feminized (Bronner 2005b; Kimmel 2000; Mechling 2005). As part of "transgender" approaches, it also considers performance of masculinities and femininities as situated practices rather than naturalized categories. This is evident in constructions of identities such as "demiguys/demigirls" describing individuals who partially identify with a gender and folk events such as "raves" that invite transcending gender identifications (Avery 2005; Winter 2010).

In my study of naval equator-crossing initiation rituals in European and American navies, sailors, most of whom are male, engaged in practices to take them from being called lowly, slimy, feminized "pollywogs" to hard-shelled, manly "shellbacks." The sailors compensate with hypermasculine display for a perception that on board ship many of them engage in supposedly feminine activities such as cooking, laundering, and cleaning. Yet in the frame of the ritual, traditional events are a beauty contest with cross-dressed males and inclusion in the "royal court" of King Neptune and his queen Aphrodite with other maidens (Figure 3.11). Some ethnographers explain these events in the "ritual reversal" of social hierarchies (naval master-servant, male-female) allowed in the liminal space of the equator at 0 degrees latitude (viewed as betwixt and between north and south) within the vast Pacific Ocean (Richardson 1977; Podruchny 2006, 78–80; see also Babcock 1978). They also can be viewed as creating a play frame that highlights the absurdity of females in this environment, or as some have claimed, exhibits homoerotic tendencies in an all-male situation evident in traditional rituals such as "Kissing the Royal Baby" (putting the initiate's face from a kneeling position into a man's protruding belly covered with mayonnaise, oil, and other muculents, or as the sailors often call it "scummy" (Bronner 2007; see also Zeeland 1995). As more women enter into long-voyage ship service, the cross-dressing events have

Figure 3.11 Members of the "Royal Court" in a naval "crossing the line" ceremony on the *USS Oxford*, 1966: (l to r) Royal Baby, King Neptune, Davy Jones, Queen Aphrodite, Royal Sheriff

Source: Photograph by Perry Christensen.

dropped away because they make the men feel vulnerable, but the women still engage voluntarily in the hazing rituals (Bronner 2006; see also Fine, G. 2005; Henningsen 1961).

One gendered cultural mechanism that has drawn attention in courts as well as ethnographies, for example, is the "joking relationship" at work and home in which teasing is allowable within a play frame among men and women familiar to one another (Spradley and Mann 2008, 87–100; see also Alford 1981; Brant 1948; Radcliffe-Brown 1940). According to social theory, people feel obliged to participate in these relationships because not doing so would suggest being unfriendly, although the relationships often reinforce the marginalization of subordinates or in the relationship. Ethnographers have noticed, however, that men tend to initiate this teasing, often with insinuations about bodily appearance that for many observers constitutes sexual harassment (Mechling and Mechling 1985; Marsh, M. 2015, 129–33; Smith, M. 1995). Folklorists might point out that "dumb blonde jokes" (Why don't blondes get coffee breaks? It takes too long to retrain them) mocking the ignorance of blondes whose main asset is their sexual attractiveness to men creates a feminine ideal that questions the competence of women in corporate positions (Meder 2008, 179; Thomas 1997; Oring 2003, 58–70). Attention can be given to esoteric women's lore (transmitted by women) rather than this "folklore of women" (exoteric) to see if different values are expressed (see Mitchell 1977; Mitchell 1978).

Questioning the popular belief that women do not tell folk jokes, folklorist Carol Mitchell compared male and female tellers and found that indeed women have humorous repertoires but they tend to be more about congeniality and appearance rather than ethnic slurs and sex. She also found performative patterns of women using humor with one another to create emotional bonds, whereas men often use insult humor among their "buddies" to create distance from one another through the performative strategy of indirection. In the final analysis, the critical point is that gender and sexuality, whether biologically inherited or cultural constructed is understood as fundamental to lived experience and used to explain the projection of anxieties about gender roles and sexual orientation in folklore. One might notice, and explain, folklore that could be called "discursive practices" in which joking by and about men and women are presented with values that comment on the regulation of a cultural standard for gendered and sexual relations (Ana 2009; Finkin 2009; Lewin 1991). In this theory, joking as a "praxis" of social engagement commonly uses a play frame to test, and culturally negotiate power relations represented by the fundamental biological realities of gender and sexuality that would be difficult to broach outside of that frame.

Other culturally constructed, unbalanced binaries that arise in questions of embodied power and authority in folklore are white-black, old-young, thin-fat, abled-disabled, and Occidental-Oriental. For many analysts following from the philosophy of W. E. B. DuBois, the physical skin "color line" is especially important as a culturally reinforced standard in which whiteness is politically privileged. Discursive practices in speech, song, and story, he claimed, often identify cognitive binaries that treat blackness—and later in critical racial analysis, brownness and redness—as the foil for endangered whiteness, and resulting in whiteness being treated as in need of protection (Bosse 2007; Du Bois 2004; Moody-Turner 2013; Prashad 2000; Roediger 2001). In comparative folklore, "dirty" is often attached to ethnic slurs and implies a binary opposition between dirty-clean that is analogous to black-white, sexual-controlled, backward-learned, and them-us (see Douglas 1966). The discursive practice of *smearing* or *blackening* the reputation of a group as smelly, dark, sexualized, and dirty enters into English folklore about the Irish, European folklore about Jews and Roma, and American humor about African Americans, Native Americans, and Mexicans (Dundes 1997b, 92–119).

Power relations within occupational groups, especially those that have institutional contexts, often raise relational questions. Prominent in the folklore of hospital nurses, for example, is a traditional practice they call "eating their young." It does not entail a story type, ritual structure, or hospital slang, as much as it identifies an attitude and demeanor that outsiders might categorize as bullying. Ethnographies have noted verbal abuse, belittling gestures, physical threats, and "freezing out" (excluding a junior co-worker from activities and conversation) that is sociologically described as "horizontal violence" rather than vertical hierarchies of clients, families, or physicians perceived as oppressive. Such reports of aggression of nurses toward one another usually come as a surprise to outsiders because of the image of the nurturing, and indeed frequently maternal nurse. The phrase used by nurses of "eating their young" comes from the observation of infanticide in the animal kingdom such as prairie dogs. The metaphor implies the actions of the cannibalism of mothers eating their offspring, which appears horrifying from a human perspective. Thus the rough treatment of new nurses by their seniors is contextualized as routine and distinctive to this group working in a high-stress, high-stakes environment. "Nurses eat their young" has emerged as a proverbial saying among nurses to represent the expected initiatory experience in the modern hospital. Writing an exposé in the *New York Times*, Theresa Brown reported, "The expression is standard lore among nurses, and it means bullying, harassment, whatever you want to call it. It's that harsh, sometimes abusive treatment of new nurses that is entrenched on some hospital floors and schools of nursing" (Brown, T. 2010).

So if nurses themselves are offended, why does it continue? Examining nurses as a folk group in relation to the community of physicians in a hospital setting, Marshelle Thobaben (2007) theorized that nursing is an oppressed occupation, and feeling inferior and powerless, nurses behave aggressively toward subordinates to relieve tension that has accumulated because they cannot fight back against their oppressors (see also Dunn 2003). Other observers noted that senior staff, skeptical of the educational backgrounds of young nurses, impose harsh practices to convey the message that the real-world of the hospital is different from the classroom, the young initiates are subject to a higher standard, and the senior nurses are in charge. By treating this occupation as hard to enter and succeed, senior nurses believe that they are raising the professionalism, and status, of the group within the institutional hierarchy. Some nursing texts have suggested that senior staff are taking upon themselves the cultural responsibility for weeding out weaker workers in another animal-kingdom metaphor of the survival of the fittest. Although the phrase usually refers to female nurses, similar kinds of initiatory practices, and horizontal violence, have been reported among recruits coming through the ranks in occupational cultures of police, marching bands, athletic teams, and teachers.

At a national level, insecurities about power are often expressed in nicknames, chants, sayings, and visual depictions of people as animals that fall under the heading of *blason populaire*, translated as proclamations of popular reputations. The term comprises rivalry put-downs of many sorts—between professions, sports teams, neighboring universities, cities regions, and states—but is often associated with joking slurs between neighboring or competing countries. The term drew book-length attention as early as 1884 from French folklorists Henri Gaidoz and Paul Sébillot (2010 [1884]) who collected multiple slurs in folklore of the French about the Belgians and conversely, the Belgians about the French. In French and Dutch lore, Belgians appear stupid and speak with a strange accent (Meder 2008, 177–78). Belgian lore depicts the French as rude and arrogant belying a lack of good hygiene. Gaidoz and Sébillot attributed the emergence of the *blason populaire* to the rise of nationalism in Europe, but did not address the question of why many of the rivalries were of similar linguistic-cultural groups. Sigmund Freud in *Group Psychology and the Analysis of the Ego* (1922) presented examples of folklore involving ridicule of a similar group such as North Germans and South Germans, English and Scots, and Spaniards and Portuguese (Freud 1959, 42). Freud explained the tendency toward what he called a "narcissism of minor differences" by noting that in exaggerating "antipathies and aversions," groups exhibit "self-love–of narcissism" (Freud 1959, 42–43). In other words, in the face of a similar traits by a group that goes by a different identity, the folklore of national put-down raises the reputation of the speaker's national home and questions why the group does not convert to his or her identity. This situation might become exacerbated in situations where some social mixing in borderlands occur as happened in northern France where a wave of Belgians came to the area to find factory work. Post-Freudian analyst Heather Sykes finds political implications in the narcissism of minor differences of "a wish for sameness" that unable to be fulfilled is projected through national slurs (2001: 208; see also Britzman 1998: 97–112).

The inequity of broad, rather than minor, constructed differences is the concern of Edward Said's theory of Orientalism. He posited that global differences can be exaggerated in cultural constructions to emphasize domination of the West over the East, and if this argument is extended it can also affect a perception of things Oriental as folk or ancient and Occidental as modern or progressive. According to Said, this binary helped rationalize the cultural superiority of Europeans, especially when faced with peoples in the close proximity to them in North Africa and the Middle East. Within the countries of Europe, Jews, Roma, and Muslims were also ostracized, and exoticized, as Oriental. According to Said, Oriental also implied that they eschewed future-oriented change and the free will of individualism, unlike the Occident, and therefore were stuck in a subordinate folk stage of development.

In a folkloristic study comparing the representations of separate groups in the American Midwest performing Middle Eastern and Latino salsa dances, Sheila Bock and Katherine Borland (2011) asked whether the kind of Oriental representation in belly dancing by Americans outside of the donor country can be discerned in other forms of traditional embodiment practices. Several of the women in the belly- dance group who were interviewed drew a distinction between ballet and belly dances as two types of dances in opposition to one another—the former representing Western ideals and the latter signifying non-Western ideals. They were drawn to belly dance to allow the body more freedom; although not fully aware of the culture from whence it came, the dancers, according to the folklorists, used the cultural frame of the dance to transform how they viewed themselves and their bodies by distancing themselves from Western standards of beauty and movement. Thus, a paradox arose in which the tradition of the Oriental East was othered and exoticized, raising imperialist concerns, but at the same time allowed them to contest what they viewed as a denial of the female body in their own culture.

Bock and Borland found that salsa dancers described the expressive freedom of their tradition in much the same way that belly dancers described theirs: "salsa dance taps into a natural sensuality that exists prior to culturally imposed inhibitions on women's self-expression." (2011, 17). In addition, blackness as a source of vitality in contrast to the West was at play, according to the researchers, because of their connection of the dancing to Afro-Cuban rumba and its supposed pronounced sensuality. The dancing defied the embodied aesthetic of the long, thin woman; the women appreciated the sexual allure of the dance, but perceived it as an expression of female autonomy that differentiated it from a Western attitude. Problematizing the power relations suggested by the theory of Orientalism, the folklorists found that engagement with, or at least invocation of folk practices associated with an othered culture, disrupted disciplinary ideals of one kind of binary—Western/Eastern femininity—while reinforcing another—mainstream/exotic culture. According to the researchers,

> The resistance embodied by these dancers is based on extant dichotomies; invoking romanticized notions of women in other places as free and unconstrained, the discourse of belly dance among interlocutors in Ohio flattened the specificity of Middle Eastern women's identities into generalized portraits of otherness.
>
> (2011, 25)

They offer the integration of dichotomies between Occidental and Oriental into cultural embodiment practices, often outside the awareness of the participants, as explanation for the expressive choices that some women make. In the process, the traditions in the Western host nation are likely to be different from the donor country and raise the question of whether the cultural embodiment practices simultaneously liberate and reinforce imperialist power structures.

Scholarly concern for questions of power and authority has led to a reversal of the ethnographic lens back on researchers to consider connections of their political ideology to the subjects they analyzed and the forms of, as well as audiences for, their presentation. Many critical historiographies applying theories of Orientalism have taken British as well as other European agents to task for their ulterior motives in collecting folklore in Asia and Africa during periods of colonization. Even afterward, some theorists offer, the effects of colonialist legacy are evident in approaches that researchers take viewing traditions as pre-modern or exoticized. For example, Sadhana Naithani in a historical examination of British scholar-administrator Richard Carnac Temple (1850–1931), renowned author of *The Legends of the Panjâb* (1977 [1884–1900]), finds contradictory impulses in his work:

> The wealth, richness, and complexity of the folklore was emphasized simultaneously with the "poverty of imagination," primitiveness, and unculturedness of the narrators. This contradiction fit into the contemporary logic, justification, and reasoning of the colonial empire ... India became, in a sense, a "raw material supplier of folkloristics,"' as it was of cotton for the British textile industry.
>
> (Naithani 1997, 12; see also Naithani 2002)

Folklorists often distinguish their fieldwork from that of anthropology by studying their "own people/locale," which raises questions of objectivity in addition to the ideological perspective or racial, sexual, and cultural divides in cases of non-participant fieldwork (Behar 2008; Bronner 1980; Nájera-Ramírez 1999; Russell 2006; Scheiberg 1990). They frequently have a field strategy of building rapport with communities by having insider knowledge or status while also stepping back to assess traditions in light of comparative scholarship (Jackson 1987; Jackson and Ives 1996). Zora Neale Hurston (1891–1960) as an African-American folklorist and renowned novelist, for example, has received analysis from biographers such as Linda

Watts, who view Hurston's folklore fieldwork among southern and Caribbean blacks in the context of a "white-dominated society and university system" (2006, 210). Watts described Hurston's recording of "authentic" folklore in the South in works such as *Mules and Men* (Hurston 1935) as acts of resistance because they countered the impressions created of plantation-rooted culture by Joel Chandler Harris and on a political level debunked the "tragic black" as a stereotypical figure so as to stop being victimized. Some critics have objected to Hurston phoneticizing black dialect as undermining such an effort by making artful tradition-bearers sound primitive while others have viewed it as her giving African Americans their own "voice" toward the goal of cultural regeneration (Holloway 1987; Jones, G. 1991, 125–39). Questions have swirled about Hurston as well as other folklorists into the present not only about how their ideological or cultural background affect their explanations of cultural phenomena they observe, but also how their selective presentations and transcriptions of folklore, or as some scholars refer to it, "textualization," in print, oration, and media colors the perception of the cultures they describe (Bronner 1992e; 1998, 184–236; Brown, M.E. 2011; Honko 2000; McCarthy 2000; Miller 2010; Mullen 2008; Zipes 1988, 10–15).

As historian Michael Frisch (1990), working with oral materials, suggested the concept of "shared authority" for interpretative institutions, such as museums, historical societies, and cultural agencies to remove the hierarchy of observer and subject by involving non-professionals in exhibited/studied groups in the analysis and presentation of their material, so folklorists such as American Southerner William Ferris, presenting what he calls the "storied South," intentionally organized presentations of people ordinary and famous, but all of whom shared a creative drive, as if on a stage. After a brief introduction to each artist, "the speaker's voice follows uninterrupted" (2013, 20). The practice he instituted, as he did in films without a narrator giving a voice-over, was to let tradition-bearers explain themselves. In a reversal of the usual analysis, he concludes that "These stories shaped me and helped me understand my own life" (2013, 20). Although used to being behind the camera and microphone, he reflected on how the lens unwittingly had been turned back on him.

Arguably, issues of power and authority factor in most approaches to folklore as a product of human relations. Even if analysts are working historically with dead people and their dusty artifacts, they nonetheless are often in the position of evaluating the group or their artistry in relation to prevailing norms or the experiences of the analyzer. Thus, when offering explanation in answer to the basic question of why people repeat and express themselves, whether in historic-geographic, functionalist, psychoanalytic, feminist, or diffusionist terms, analysts in the research process often are pressed to evaluate the ideological as well as teleological implications of their position in relation to the material or people being studied. Some approaches ask special questions such as why folklore originates and spreads in a particular way, or why we think with, as well as about, folklore, but crucial to the explanation is the notion that whether as analysts or participants, individuals "put their heads"— and "get their act"—together to construe the sources, contexts, uses, meanings, connotations, and consequences of traditional knowledge.

WHAT IS FOLKLORE'S RELEVANCE?

IMPLICATIONS AND APPLICATIONS

Even if folklore research typically dwells on the way that people act, it ultimately returns in the final analysis to the way they think. Mindful of folklore, analysts frequently confront the idea of tradition and culture—as a philosophical concept, cognitive process, sociohistorical condition, behavioral response, and as I will emphasize in this concluding chapter, a pragmatic enterprise. A broad implication of folklore research is that practices drawing upon traditional knowledge are omnipresent, changeful, and instrumental. That does not mean specific traditions remain in perpetuity, and accordingly a task of folklore research is to determine reasons for the often winding, manifold paths that people take with their lore in the past and present. Even if transitory, folklore produces lasting effects, and can have a tremendous impact on politics, society, and environment at the macro level. In the micro situations of "cultural scenes," folklore additionally has a profound influence on the way that people lead lives, engage communication strategically, and perceive and narrate experiences. If folklore draws attention because of its expressive qualities within the ground-shifting march of modern history, or its quick rise into prominence in technological contexts, its absence, decline, and struggle to function because of social, geographical, economic, and political change also gain notice. As a result, projects and movements to display, preserve, and promote the use of traditional knowledge arise.

After the analysis of cultural scenes in which folklore plays a part, the big picture of folklore representing cultural expressiveness as well as tradition often comes to the fore and is related to issues such as the implications for folklore of (1) the supposed decline of community and rise of individualism; (2) the breakdown of regional and ethnic isolation with the advent of social, technological, and physical mobility; and (3) the perceived identity politics and need for subcultural belonging within a global economy and mass society purportedly moving away from a producer, communitarian, and spiritual ethos. The wording of the American Folklife Preservation Act (Public Law 94-201, 1976) in the United States, for example, tried to sum up the relevance of traditional knowledge in a modernizing mass society when it stated "that American folklife has a fundamental influence on the desires, beliefs, values, and character of the American people" (see Hufford, M. 2002). Although this statement sounds nationalistic, the declarations in the act also included references to the "diversity inherent in American folklife" and the sense of "individuality and identity" that traditions imparted for people. In many countries the role of governments and communities to address "the complex problems" suggested by the investigation of folklore sparks debate on the appropriate ways to apply traditional knowledge and the study of that process for what the law called "the general welfare" of the people.

Facilitating global communication on the issues and applications of traditional knowledge, the United Nations has actively engaged representatives of countries around the world to consider the implications of traditional knowledge as intellectual property and its connection to the sustainability of natural as well as cultural milieus. The United Nations Education, Scientific and Cultural Organization (UNESCO) warns that traditional knowledge and folklore should not be simplistically conceived as a pale reflection of mainstream knowledge but rather as critical "innovations and practices of indigenous and local communities embodying traditional lifestyles relevant for the conservation and sustainable use of biological diversity" (Nakashima and Roué 2002, 314). It defines traditional knowledge within a receding ecological context by noting its reference to "the cumulative and dynamic body of knowledge, know-how and representations possessed by peoples with long histories of interaction with their natural milieu" (UNESCO 2006). Many folklorists would question whether this definition limits such knowledge to rural environs, and historically defined groups, whereas it can also be observed in urbanized, industrialized, and complex societies in addition to being relevant to emergent, mobile, and temporary groups and individuals (American Folklore Society 2004; Foster 2015; Rikoon 2004). Nonetheless, as an international body, UNESCO is significant for recognizing traditional knowledge and folklore as importantly "tied to language, social relations, spirituality and worldview" tangibly and intangibly on a global scale (UNESCO 2006, 1).

UNESCO thus notes the policy making in which folklore is at issue because of its embodiment of collective identities, customary modes of transmission, and subaltern histories. Among these debates that have been mentioned are racial, gender, and ethnic equity, natural disaster, poverty eradication, biodiversity management, educational and economic opportunity, and human development. In this closing chapter, I examine the applications, and implications, in endeavors as well as occupations devoted to work with traditional knowledge expressed in folklore, proceeding from (1) publicizing folklore and (2) purposing folklore to (3) politicizing folklore and (4) legalizing folklore.

PUBLICIZING FOLKLORE

Groundbreaking in the preservation and display of regional folk culture is the transfer of several traditional farm buildings by King Oscar II of Norway and Sweden onto his estate near Oslo in 1867. Concerned for his reception as a Swedish monarch over independent-minded Norwegians, King Oscar in 1881, on the advice of his Norwegian agent, at the royal summer residence invited the public to view the buildings. The rural buildings were reminders to viewers, many from the nearby city, of the changes wrought by urbanization, immigration, and industrialization to the landscape. The king's cultural interests subsequently moved to Swedish music and theater, but Norwegian librarian Hans Aall, stirred by strong nationalist fervor and his experience in public exhibitions, hatched a plan to use the buildings to educate Norwegians about their folklife that he felt was threatened by these deep social and economic changes. In 1894, Aall received permission to use the collection to form the *Norsk Folkemuseum* (Norwegian Folk Museum) near the metropolis of Oslo, and thus advance the "folk museum" movement that quickly spread throughout the world (Aall 1920; Allan 1956; Bøe 2008, 113–15; Marshall 1977; Michelsen 1966; Norsk Folkemuseum 1929).

A boon to the movement was the creation of the folk, or "open-air" museum Skansen in Stockholm by Artur Hazelius in 1891 (Alexander 1983, 239–76). King Oscar's collection of buildings near Oslo had influenced Hazelius to expand the vision of a folklife museum he called Skansen outside of Stockholm to move beyond presenting buildings to the crafts and round of life in the Swedish countryside. He had earlier organized in 1872 the Scandinavian Ethnographic Collection (the Nordic Museum after 1880) to preserve the crafts and customs of regional folk cultures in Sweden. The museum featured demonstrators dressed in regional clothing pursuing the traditional round of daily life in sections of the country. Visitors did not have labels to read or guides to point out "masterpiece" objects to admire. Curators worked to immerse visitors in a village setting, and appreciate the productivity and communitarian spirit of regional folk cultures. Later variations on the Skansen concept included *Den Gamle By* (The Old Town) in Aarhus, Denmark, opened to the public in 1914 to show town and urban life in buildings spanning the eighteenth to the twentieth centuries rather than rural villages as a locus of folk culture. The Tenement Museum on the Lower East Side of New York City, a dense hub of immigrants during the Great Wave of Immigration from 1880 to 1920, features costumed interpreters representing different ethnic groups in restored apartments and businesses (Figure 4.1). They discuss the struggles of immigrants in the new land and their negotiation of Old World traditions with the new urban environment.

Visitors to Plimoth Plantation, the site of the Puritans' first settlement in America, come to view a reconstruction, rather than original buildings. They encounter costumed staff members who engage in "first person interpretation" dramatizing the role of seventeenth-century settlers (Figure 4.2). Visitors ask questions as they stroll through the settlement, but the staff do not go out of

Figure 4.1 Craig Edwards and Geoff Kaufman perform sea chanteys at Mystic
Seaport for the Sea Music Festival, 2014

Courtesy Mystic Seaport: The Museum of America and the Sea.

their roles, and insist that they are working the community in the
1620s (Snow 1993). To effect this performance, interpreters study
the dialect, customs, and foodways of the period with material provided by research departments that include folkloristic as well as
historical archives. Conner Prairie in Indianapolis, Indiana, another
museum with first-person interpretation and a research department
that provides folkloristic information, goes one step further by having guests take on historic roles. In an educational program called
"Follow the North Star," visitors "become actors on a 200-acre
stage, running from slave hunters and working together to navigate
the Underground Railroad to freedom," according to the museum's
website (Conner Prairie 2015). At the end of the program that
typically shakes youth to their core, participants draw correlations
between slavery in 1836 and contemporary human trafficking, bullying, and equal rights struggles. Whereas museums were often viewed
as providing a sanitized, romanticized view of the past, Conner Prairie
endeavors to confront hard realities of traditional life.

Figure 4.2 The Lower East Side Tenement Museum restored apartments at 97
            Orchard Street, New York City, 2015

Source: Photograph by Simon J. Bronner.

At the Netherlands Open-Air Museum, established in 1918 in
Arnhem, the past of ordinary residents is related to contemporary
issues with themes that are explored through exhibitions and events
through the site. Especially with many visitors more removed from
the traditional pre-industrial occupations and buildings preserved in
the museums, curators work to bring more educational programming into the site and reconceptualize the folk museum from its
nationalistic, preservationist roots to a location for public dialogue
on social and political issues and advocacy for cultural perspectives (De Jong 2010). The museum has refocused its mission, in

keeping with the changing view within folkloristic theory of the "folk" from rural life to everyday culture nationally and in the Dutch diaspora. Themes in the museum, amid concerns for a diversifying religious and ethnic Dutch population, have included "religion" and "migration." Behind the scenes, researchers work on documenting traditional life and mapping folk cultural traits that demonstrate the ethnic, regional, linguistic, and occupational diversity of a country as small as the Netherlands.

Although folklorists have had a hand in developing the folk museum concept primarily on land, a few locations embrace traditions of shore and sea, summarized as maritime folklife. The largest in the world is Mystic Seaport in Mystic, Connecticut, which contains re-creations of a nineteenth-century seafaring village with more than sixty historic buildings and a collection of sailing ships. In addition to developing research on material culture, a niche of the seaport museum has been the musical folklore of sailors (Figure 4.3) with academic symposia and concerts on music of the sea (Frank, S. 1980; Grasso 1998). Other maritime museums represent contemporary traditions so as not to give the impression that maritime folk culture is past and gone. The Chesapeake Bay Maritime Museum in St. Michaels on the eastern shore of Maryland, for example, has a floating fleet and is a center for a log canoe racing tradition (see Glassie 1972–1973; Williams, J. 2013, 177–79). Curators have designed an apprentice program to allow visitors to construct a wooden skiff under the guidance of traditional craftsworkers.

Folklorists working with collections and drawing patterns from the comparison of forms and their cultural contexts apply a curatorial function. Although the folk museum movement has been associated with the representation of historic settlements in outdoor sites, folklorists since the late twentieth century have expanded the concept to represent contemporary communities, use locations for conserving ethnic life and traditions, particularly folk arts, into the future, and to extend education and research of timely social issues. Often these extensions include fieldwork and civic engagement that had not been typical of the museum associated with a historic preservationist function (Dewhurst 2014). Outside of the museum borders, folklorists have initiated folk heritage trails with street markers, live events and schools with living folk artists in residence, and virtual

Figure 4.3 Visitors at Plimoth Plantation, Plymouth, Massachusetts, USA, go
inside a reconstructed thatched house representative of the Puritan
settlement on Cape Cod in 1627

Source: Photograph by Simon J. Bronner.

exhibitions of folk practices in the context of daily rounds of life. For
folklorist Howard Marshall in his assessment of the last century of
folk museums, these efforts suggest the distinctive curatorial function
for folklorists of relating historic sites to contemporary folk practices
and communities, and advancing cultural criticism and advocacy
(1977, 413).

A common kind of public programming for museums and other
cultural agencies is the folk festival. The staged festival of folk arts
and music evokes the socioeconomic centrality and buoyant vitality
of fairs in market towns in pre-industrial Europe. Besides attracting
a varied lot of craftsworkers and food vendors, they often featured
entertainment from street singers and musicians in a crowded central square. During the 1920s and 1930s, as many communities in
rural areas witnessed migration to industrialized cities and disruption
of traditional regional–ethnic life, civic leaders organized festivals to

promote local identification with folk traditions, attract tourism to their areas, and signal cultural resistance to socioeconomic trends of massification (Cantwell 1992; Cohen 2008, 1–30). The folk festival created a concentrated site for immersion, even if temporarily, in folklife as something current, lively, and relevant. Although intended to show the prevalence of traditional life, the folk festival as an occasional, intensive event to compete with more popular concerts could send a message of folk cultural weakening. One of the first staged folk festivals in North America, for example, was the Mountain Dance and Folk Festival begun in 1928 in Asheville, North Carolina, in the heart of Appalachia that had become depressed and was depicted in the media as culturally backward compared to the progress of American society (Cohen 2008, 5–7). Initiated by the Asheville Chamber of Commerce to promote visitation to the mountains, and regional pride by mountaineers, organizers created stages for performance of local "old-time" string-band musicians and square dance and clogging groups. Striking a theme of this music and its performers as the authentic, endangered roots of American culture, organizers strove to turn the stigma of crude "hillbillies" into an honored cultural place as America's pioneer ancestors with a romantic nationalist message.

The romanticism was also evident over in the mountains of eastern Kentucky to the west of Asheville, where Jean Bell Thomas who was born in Ashland, Kentucky, and sought a business career in New York City, was inspired by the Festival of the English Folk Song and Dance Society in London to organize the American Folk Song Festival. Her driving motivation was to promote the persistence of speech, song, and traditions that in England were considered defunct. She remembered traditional "singin' gatherins" in the mountains, and beginning in 1931 re-created them by staging acts who learned their music by oral tradition against the backdrop of a log cabin (Cohen 2008, 7–9). Meanwhile in Pennsylvania, which is known as America's industrial belt, journalist George Korson during the 1930s notably presented coal miners representing industrial folk cultures at the Pennsylvania Folk Festival held on the grounds of Bucknell University in Lewisburg, Pennsylvania (Cohen 2008, 19–23; Gillespie 1980, 41–55). The Great Depression put a halt to the festival but after World War II, folklorists at Franklin and Marshall

College created the Kutztown Folk Festival to feature Pennsylvania German folk culture with a folklife approach emphasizing crafts, foods, and farm practices (Bronner 1998, 278–304; Yoder 1974). Another distinctive feature of the festival was educational seminars at the festival to contextualize the traditions on display. Yet the festival as it came under commercial management also drew criticism in its later years because of amusement-park attractions such as carousel rides, an oversized "Dutchy" chair, the staging of an Amish wedding, and the re-enactment of a historic hanging. Held on fair grounds over a nine-day period, the festival became a national tourist destination and claimed to be America's largest paid-admission folk festival (Gillespie 2006, 397).

Aware of the festivals in Pennsylvania, North Carolina, and Kentucky, Sarah Gertrude Knott, who had been involved in staging historical pageants, had the idea of a larger festival during the Depression "era of the common man" featuring representatives of various cultures to showcase crafts and cookery as well as folk song in a gesture of national unity (Cohen 2008, 13–19; Williams, M. 2006). She organized the first National Folk Festival in St Louis in 1934, and she brought in prominent folklorists to advise the project. The festival came under the auspices of the National Council for the Traditional Arts, which reconfigured its mission to promoting a democratic society by the festival's representation of diverse communities as part of "America's multicultural, living heritage." (NCTA 2015). Sharing this goal in the symbolically important location and date of the National Mall in the United States capital over the Independence Day holiday is the Smithsonian Folklife Festival organized as a free public event since 1967 by the Center for Folklife and Cultural Heritage in the Smithsonian Institution. Begun as the Festival of American Folklife, the festival was globalized in the 1980s with the addition of cultural performances and displays from Korea, France, Soviet Union, and Senegal, and broad themes such as energy and community, folklore and aging, and cultural conservation (Kurin 1998).

In the twenty-first century, the Smithsonian Folklife Festival has confronted sociopolitical issues in presentations of "creativity and crisis" with the AIDS Memorial Quilt, urban folklore (New York City; Washington, D.C.), food cultures, urban decay, indigenous rights, and endangered languages. Many of these presentations including narrative-taking from visitors by Smithsonian folklorists in areas such as family and occupational folklore (see Groce 2010; McCarl 1985; Zeitlin *et al.* 1982). In addition to staged concerts, the festival featured craftsworkers and food preparers with whom visitors could engage on the grounds. Visitors could also try their hand at various traditional skills such as drop-spindle weaving and graffiti. At the 2015 festival, the presentation of Peruvian folklife included events that organizers hoped would spark thinking about sociopolitical issues. Masked dancers, for example, reenacted La Fiesta de la Virgen del Carmen de Paucartambo, a tradition of Paucartambo, Peru, every July to honor the town's patron's saint, the Virgin Mamacha Carmen (Figure 4.4). Folkloristic interpreters pointed out that the captain of the costumed participants, Víctor Germán Boluarte Medina, wore a mask with an exaggerated nose, poking fun at European colonial leaders.

Hailed by advocates as an important enterprise for presenting often overlooked or culturally threatened communities and traditions, sustaining traditional knowledge, and promoting multicultural respect and cultural equity, festivals have also attracted criticism for staging artists as entertaining acts in an unnatural performative context and therefore misrepresenting folk cultures, if not perpetuating stereotypes (Bauman 1992; Cantwell 1991; Diamond 2008; Diamond and Trimillos 2008; Satterwhite 2005; Sommers 1996). Especially in the absence of a culture of local festivals such as has been attributed to Japan, China, and India, the staged folk festival is sometimes analyzed as an artifact of "invented tradition" or "folklorism" (Bendix 1988; Ceribašić 1998; Hobsbawm and Ranger 1983; Šmidchens 1999; Sommers 1994; Thornbury 1995). Social historian Eric Hobsbawm claimed that public ceremonial events such as staged festivals, fairs, and pageants are products of the late nineteenth and twentieth centuries that seek to "inculcate certain values and norms of behavior by repetition, which automatically implies continuity with the past" (1983, 1). The advantage of creating continuity into the present, often with inauthentic rituals and performances, analysts with this view contend, is to claim cultural equity of a subordinated group that is often presumed to have become less modern, mainstream, or progressive. On other

Figure 4.4 Peruvian participants re-enact dances of the Fiesta de la Virgen del
Carmen de Paucartambo at the 49th annual Smithsonian Folklife
Festival held on the National Mall in Washington, DC, July 2015

Source: Photograph by Lei Cai.

occasions, such as nationalistic events, critics might view ulterior
motives of building patriotism or reinforcing cultural hegemony
behind staged folk celebrations, while defenders cite their usefulness
for building acceptance and community empowerment through
appreciation for traditional artistry of diverse groups (see Adelt
2008; Cantwell 1992; Graham 2000; Handler 1988; Roginsky
2007; Seitel 1991; Whisnant 1983, 181–52).

The labeling of "folklorism" particularly focuses on the issue of
authenticity because of the presentation of folk practices removed in
time and place from their original locations and purposes and performed by individuals whose traditional knowledge does not come
from participation in the cultures of origin. The question for many

folklorists is the role of folklorism in the perception, perpetuation, and revitalization of folkloric forms as well as the communities from which they came. Rather than dismissing this material as "fakelore," many folklorists insist that folklorism movements need analysis as part of larger cultural processes (Dorson 1976; Doyle 2009; Dundes 1985). One such folklorist, Guntis Šmidchens, suggests that rather than being an folkloristic application, folklorism is actually a subcategory of folklore, in which folk tradition is consciously recognized and repeated "as a symbol of ethnic, regional, or national culture" (1999, 56). Often in the rise and spread of festivals and media presentations, Šmidchens hypothesizes, the nostalgic feeling of historical continuity with past generations evident in folklorism is a consequence of events "bringing an impression of unchanging, stable tradition into the present" and represents a simpler "counterworld" to the "hectic, chaotic life of the modern world." (1999, 56).

Some folklorists would add that folklorism is organized with the idea of presenting traditions on stage as authentic or at least rhetorically invoking them as significant to the larger society. They might differentiate these events from the sense of the "folkloresque," following the terminology of carnivalesque by Russian literary theorist Mikhail Bakhtin to refer to literary modes that use humor and chaos to subvert dominant styles (Foster and Tolbert 2015; see also Lindahl 1996; Santino 2009). Folklorists using "folkloresque" consider products and events appropriated or reinvented by popular culture to appear frivolous, even meaningless, and yet suggest rhetorical uses of folklore to comment on social and political issues. St Patrick's Day is a holiday festival in the United States, for example, that is used to celebrate Irishness with parades, musical and dance performances, and wearing of green clothing, but analysts also note the appropriation of festivities in popular culture as social sanctioning of drunkenness (Adair and Cronin 2002). Critics worry that in its carnival atmosphere it undermines the cultural basis of ethnicity and trivializes Irishness as an easily wearable, and satirized, identity. This pattern especially came out in controversy over the folkloresque State Patty's Day in State College, Pennsylvania. Led by students concerned that St Patrick's Day fell when they were away from campus on spring break, State Patty's Day held on March 2 instead of March 17 featured revelry that spilled out onto the streets. In subsequent discourse through the media, issues of binge drinking and student behavior in a "college town" rose to the surface (Szkaradnik 2015). Part of the concern was recognition of students in their temporary stay in college representing a culture with their own traditions outside of the eye of the administration and professors (Bronner 2012a, 202–3).

Libraries, centers, and archives of folklore, once hidden in sequestered libraries and populated by monkish scholars, have become more public spaces with civically engaged scholars, and participants in tradition, who have made their materials more widely accessible through digital media. Even when connected to universities, they typically have an outreach function (Georgitis 2015; Gilmore 2015). Many are regional and national centers supported by governmental agencies or non-profit organizations devoted to sustaining ethnic, urban, and community cultural heritage. In addition to encouraging longitudinal studies of folk practices, they frequently reach out to the public to contribute folkloric material concerning contemporary events. The American Folklife Center at the Library of Congress, for example, in 2005 launched the first large-scale project in which the survivors of a major disaster took the lead in documentation when it collected first-person accounts from people who lived through Katrina and Rita hurricanes and followed with a public program that received wide media attention (American Folklife Center 2009).

The National Cowboy Poetry Gathering, begun in 1994, sponsored by the Western Folklife Center in Elko, Nevada, is another renowned example of a documentary center integrating research with public outreach. Folklorists advertise that visitors "can learn a traditional skill, dance the two-step, plan for the West's future with ranchers and conservationists, watch home-made films of rural life, meet new friends over a Buckaroo Brew, enjoy Basque food, listen to tall tales, dispel myths, build bridges and be inspired" (Western Folklife Center 2015). Probably its most popular program is the annual National Cowboy Poetry Gathering with performances of poetry, music, and storytelling expressing "the beauty and challenges of a life deeply connected to the earth and its bounty" (Western Folklife Center 2015). Once devoted to disseminating the results of fieldwork in print, folklore centers work in multimedia formats to capture, and spread, folklore for public and scholarly consumption.

PURPOSING FOLKLORE

When folklorist Michael Owen Jones gathered professionals to relate their experiences of "putting folklore to use" (1994), he expanded the idea of applied folklore from use in education, medicine, and creative industries to new occupations in organizational behavior, economic development, law and governmental agencies, regional planning, and social work. Twenty-three years before, debate had ensued on whether folklore should be applied at all (Sweterlitsch 1971). Robert Byington, who held a university position and specialized in occupational folklore, convened a special meeting in 1971 at Point Park College in Pittsburgh, Pennsylvania, to take up the question (Byington 1989). At the time, applications outside of academe primarily involved museums, schools, and festivals. A sea-change occurred, however, with the establishment of governmental "state folklorist" positions first in Pennsylvania, Maryland, and Florida, followed by most other states to century's end (Bronner 1998, 330–48; Camp 1977; Carey 1976; Loomis 1983, 42–48). In addition, a campaign to legislate a federally funded national folk-life center in the United States on the model of European cultural institutes in addition to a global "folk revival" sparked a discourse on the utility outside of academe of folklore in modern life (Loomis 1983, 7–26). Questions arose from the recognition of folklorists in the "public sector" in relation to academic work: Could folk-loristic work inform service professionals to better provide help to their clientele? Who would guide this application and for what objectives? For officially appointed folklorists in governmental and cultural agencies assigned to create public programming and admin-ister policy, what would they do for the public good?

Most of the discussion at Point Park College in 1971 was on applications of folklore by folklorists whereas later discourse moved to uses by service professionals who borrow folkloristic perspectives or utilize folklore materials. Some writers noted the stigma on applied folklore because of the lingering specter of Nazi propaganda manipulating folklore to show racial superiority and militarism (Jones, M. 1997b, 30). David Hufford, who went on to use folk-lore research in his groundbreaking position in a medical teaching hospital (Hershey Medical Center, Pennsylvania State University), argued that because folklore had been used badly did not mean that it could not be applied well (1971, 6). In the middle of an area where patients came from the background of Amish, Asian, Slavic, and African communities, he created medical ethnography programs to help doctors become aware of traditional health systems involving herbs and foods, faith healing, ritual, and massage therapies (Hufford, D. 1998).

Celebrated poets, novelists, playwrights, and artists acknowledged their debt to folklore for their creative work and many engaged in collecting the material. Early in the twentieth century, social reformers such as Allen Eaton proposed the formation of handicraft guilds and "folk schools" to improve the prospects of rural and mountainous regions suffering as a result of urbanization and industrialization (Eaton 1937). The first curator and early president of the American Folklore Society Stewart Culin worked with the garment industry in New York City to develop popular fashions based upon the collections of folk patterns in his museum (Exhibition of the Blouse 1922). The youth scouting movement applied folkloristic work on animal and Native American lore into its activities and featured a "folklore" badge for children to earn (Mechling 1989c). In the schools, pragmatic advocacy for "active," experiential learning created interest in applying ideas of social learning and storytelling to enhance student participation (Asimeng-Boahene and Baffoe 2014; Bowman and Hamer 2011; Grider 1995; Starnes 1999). In Georgia, the Foxfire program of cultural journalism by students interviewing elders in the community on their "old-time" traditions caught on in many schools across the country (Puckett 1989).

The Foxfire movement was not without criticism, however, as folklorists questioned the standards by which people and their traditional knowledge were documented (Dorson 1973b; Dorson and Carpenter 1978; Wigginton 1974). Some educators and organizational behaviorists went a step further than Foxfire by proposing that the learning and sharing of experiences characteristic of folkloric situations should be structured into "communities of practice" by teachers and even corporate managers to foster a collaborative environment (Jones *et al.* 1988; Jordan-Smith and Horton 2001; Raspa 2006, 924; Wenger 1998). These were the kind of applications that folklorists at the Point Park conference had in mind when they drafted a definition of applied folklore as "the utilization of the theoretical concepts, factual knowledge, and research methodologies of folklorists in activities or programs meant to ameliorate contemporary social, economic, and technological problems" (Jones, M. 1994, 11). Acknowledging that this definition sounded interventionist, David Hufford proposed a process-oriented rather than activist definition by stating that the application of academic folklore knowledge solves "practical problems" (Hufford 1971, 6).

Head of the degree-granting program in folklore at Indiana University, Richard Dorson objected to this redefinition of folklorists as reformers, preferring for folklorists to produce research rather than distilling, or feared, sanitizing or exploiting, it for public consumption. That is not to say that folklore has not been applied for the public good, he argued. He boasted that "Folklore studies in the nineteenth and twentieth centuries have done more than any other field of learning to bring attention to the culture of the overlooked sectors of the population" (Dorson 1971, 41). He worried that committing the end goal of folklore to an interventionist role of reforming society, folklorists "will succeed neither as a scholar nor as a philanthropist" (1971, 41). He feared that governmental officials would impose bowdlerized and politicized versions of folklore. In response to the lobbying to create an American Folklife Center, he protested that it would be an agency to crank out rather than study folklife and its tendency would be to romanticize and expurgate the gritty stuff of folklore. He pointedly asked, "And whose folklore will the foundation [Center] be thrusting upon the people? If the richest folklore is scatological, will the foundation [Center] exhibit latrinalia at its annual festival on the Mall?" (Dorson 1971, 41). Folklorists, Dorson insisted, needed to stay independent and objective by resisting what he called "the twinge of social conscience" and the desire to see one's work pervade "in the sophisticated culture" (1971, 40). The debate continued, although Dorson's admonitions did not stem the tide of folklorists entering the public sector for employment (Abrahams 1999; Baron 1999; Ben-Amos 1998; Kirshenblatt-Gimblett 1988; Payne 1998; Siporin 2000; Toelken 1996, 389–432).

For Jones and his colleagues in *Putting Folklore to Use*, the issues linking research to application went beyond whether folklorists were equipped to reshape society. Implied in folkloristic work with traditional knowledge is that it might be returned to the communities from whence they came as well as relativizing, and improving, modern science and technology (Wells 1994). Applied folklore in the public sector consequently is not just done by folklorists. It can refer to drawing insights by laypeople and various practitioners from academic folklore studies to benefit their lives (Bard 1994; Howell 1994; Congdon 1994). It can also mean folklorists collaborating with tradition-bearers, or acting as cultural brokers to perpetuate traditions in their communities and in cyberspace (Bendix and Welz 1999; Hansen 2009; Jacobs, M. 2014; Jacobs *et al*. 2014; Kurin 1997; Njoku 2012). Folklorists often view themselves, or are viewed, outside of the commercial sphere, but part of cultural sustainability is showing the economic viability of traditional knowledge. In hard numbers, economic impact studies consistently show that governmental spending in industrialized countries on folk arts results in a significant return on investment with production of jobs and revenues (Peterson 1996, 11). An argument can be made that the proportion for funding on folk cultural sustainability should be increased to better reach a number of population sectors engaged in artisan, heritage, and ethnic maintenance activity as a compelling interest of governmental cultural policy. But that argument has been difficult to make without recognition that folk culture and arts constitutes an "industry," or at least is engaged in corporate activity.

Many advocates for economic policies on folk cultural support look to federal "New Deal" programs in the United States during the 1930s as one model for governmental support and economic incentives to maintain traditions. In agencies of the New Deal, such as the Federal Writers' Project (FWP) of the Works Progress Administration (WPA), folklore was a keyword used to designate a populist response to the Great Depression that involved documenting and adapting folk culture. According to B.A. Botkin, who headed the Folklore Division of the FWP,

> In its belief in the public support of art and art for the public, in research not for research's sake but for use and enjoyment by the many, the WPA is attempting to assimilate folklore to the local and national life by understanding, in the first place, the relation between the lore and the life out of which it springs; and by translating the lore back into terms of daily living

and leisure-time activity. In other words, the WPA looks upon folklore research not as a private but as a public function and folklore as public, not private property.

(Botkin 1988 [1939], 261; see Graves 2005; Ivey 2008)

In Japan, the 1950 Law for Protection of Cultural Properties established a category of "living national treasures" that has encouraged maintenance and apprenticeship of folk crafts. Some locations such as Miyajima Island near Hiroshima around the Itsukushima Shrine (on UNESCO's World Heritage List) have been developed as folk craft centers where tourists flock to purchase as well as view traditional practices. In the public discourse about the site, visitors and government officials rarely voice a conflict between commercialization and tradition (see Foster 2011; Thornbury 1994). Based on these kinds of experiences, former chair of the National Endowment for the Humanities, William Ferris advocated for a cabinet-level department of cultural resources in the Executive Branch of the American government on the model of official bureaus and ministries in other countries to coordinate many agencies involved in folkloristic and cultural heritage programs in addition to forming a national cultural policy (Ferris 2008).

Overall, advocates of governmental involvement in folk cultural conservation argue on the theoretical basis that the social massification that coincides with modernization challenges the integration of tradition in everyday life, which people need for a sense of well-being. In this view, mass media and corporate social structures endanger the continuation of traditions that are important to a sense of social belonging associated with community and group bonding. Intervention is therefore necessary at several levels. One is in basic education involving multicultural appreciation that builds coincident values of embracing cultural difference, promoting democratic participation, and encouraging vernacular expressiveness (Asimeng-Boahene and Baffoe 2014; Bowman and Hamer 2011; Grider 1995; Jackson 1984; Stekert 1989). Another is in public culture that highlights in festivals, museums, and centers the contributions of traditions to the artistic life of society and encourages individuals and groups to cultivate folk practices for the continuation of their subcultural connection. Economic and ecological justifications are also made for public funding to support uses of traditional knowledge in a progressive society because it provides occupations, environmental consciousness, and services that are essential to cultural maintenance.

POLITICIZING FOLKLORE

In the nineteenth century, movements to declare national identities with a claim to a unified folklore were categorized as "romantic" ideals. In the twenty-first century, debates over national sovereignty take on post-colonial discourse involving the communitarian rights of citizens affected by dominant states. A complication for many communities is the role of migration and the formation of republics in the face of an ethnic group's diasporization. Kurds, among the largest language groups not to have their own country (estimated as high as 37 million), have religious and social distinctions among settlements in Turkey, Iran, Iraq, and Syria. Kurdish activists rallying support under a proposed flag for an ethnic nation of Kurdistan use the cultural icon of the fox, weaving traditions, and what they consider a unique oral tradition involving mythological creatures to show a cultural difference that requires separation from their host countries (Blum and Hassanpou 1996; Edmonds 1971; Hannum 1990, 178–202). The fall of the former Soviet Union also fostered folkloristic documentation projects with nationalistic overtones, such as Tajikistan with the Tajik ethnic group and neighboring Uzbekistan primarily populated by Uzbeks (Abdullaev and Ganiev 2006; Rahmonov and Rakhimov 2006). Yet some politicized folkloristic movements have not resulted in cultural nations. In the United States, the issue of a cultural connection to politics has been a part of the Puerto Rican independence movement that has struggled because, according to many observers, Puerto Ricans are cultural nationalists with an ethnic bond called *puertorriqueñismo* (based on the theory of creolization of Spanish, African, and English influences creating a new distinct identity). They resist Americanization folklorically, but the island's economic dependence on the United States has influenced a lack of electoral support for political independence (Negrón-Muntaner and Grosfoguel 1997).

Evident in many public folklore projects in the twenty-first century is application of cultural pluralism (sometimes referred to as cultural democracy or equity) more than state patriotism (Wells 2006). A landmark, highly publicized program that bought out the tension between national and local culturalism, especially with the issue of Muslim and North African migration to Western Europe, is the creation of a "Year of Folklore" by the *Nederlands Centrum voor Volkscultuur* (the Netherlands Center for Folk Culture) in 2004. It opened with a festival in Terneuzen featuring an array of traditional regional dress and other festivals followed at Arnhem showcasing *folkloristische groepen* (folk groups), and a festival of giant puppetry in Oisterwijk. Displaying the application of folklore to public issues, the living heritage festival in Utrecht in July focused on the connection of traditional knowledge to health care. A number of exhibitions on folklore were installed in libraries and museums throughout the country. Posters, postcards, websites, and magazines abounded with depictions of folk traditions, packaged gaily in national colors of red, white, and blue. Alongside the typical casual reading fare of tabloids for celebrity gossip and entertainment at train and bus stations, slick publications blaring "tradition" were avidly purchased. The government set aside October 22 on the national calendar to celebrate folklore and organized a folklore symposium and informational fair in Utrecht. Books on living traditions in the country published by the center sold widely. The head of state blessed the whole campaign and it led to planning for specific traditions to be featured in subsequent years. Folklore as a term, a form of study, and an event, could be seen and heard widely in the country. The structure of the campaign, however, separated its applied aspects from the goals of government-sponsored research.

The *Nederlands Centrum voor Volkscultuur* is in Utrecht to the east, and defined as a public heritage center, while the Meertens is a research institute within the Netherlands Royal Academy of Arts and Sciences in Amsterdam. They had different missions, although they joined together in a "heritage" conference intended for professional ethnologists and folklorists. In their separation is an important first lesson of Dutch cultural work: differences between public and academic work are highly structured. Indeed, applying Barbara Kirshenblatt-Gimblett's concept of "mistaken dichotomies" (1988) regarding the growing convergence of public and academic endeavor in American folkloristics, in the Netherlands dichotomies are unmistakably clear, unabashedly maintained, and unequivocally embraced. For the Dutch, the dichotomy drives the success of the folkloristic enterprise because of its clear delineation of responsibility and advocacy (Van der Zeijden 2004). By comparison, Americans appear to fuse public and academic work in a set of common ethnographic approaches, if not products, and deliberate more extensively, and emotionally, on the functions and borders of professional folkloristic work in an organizational landscape without a central authority (Abrahams 1999; Briggs 2008; Georges 1991; Ellis 1992).

The differences between American and Dutch patterns of organizing public folklore projects attitude raise the question of the appeal from a Dutch perspective of a "Year of Folklore" at a particular historical juncture in the multicultural Netherlands. Official responses to the question refer to the heightened importance of traditional culture to Dutch identity as well as to tourism in the new century. These perspectives could easily be applied to many other countries facing social change as a result of new ethnic configurations. For the Netherlands there was recognition that modernization and the European Union have undermined the traditional occupations and landscape of seafaring and fishing, farming, and dairying—indeed of community life generally. Related to tourism, a desire is frequently expressed to present more facets to Dutch culture than the commercialized trinity of windmills, tulips, and wooden shoes. To folklorists, such reductionist touristic images obscure the great complexity and diversity of Dutch traditions, and the populace also reacts negatively to the romantic portrayal of Dutch as quaint and cute, and even pre-modern.

Beneath the surface, one detects a political context for the "Year of Folklore" campaign. The Dutch have for centuries cultivated a value of tolerance toward minorities, dissidents, and refugees. The Dutch have long lived with the idea of a plural, multiracial, and multireligious society, and sought in the twentieth century to absorb Indonesians, Moluccans, Surinamese, and others from their former colonial empire into Dutch life. This globalist posture was shaken, however, with the influx of Muslim Moroccans and Turks, who were attracted to the Netherlands to work during the boom economy from the 1960s to the 1980s, and in the twenty-first century, refugees from the war-torn Middle East. Many politicians had the expectation that the workers would return to their homelands when the economy soured, and if they stayed, they would more readily assimilate into Dutch life. Neither happened, and some vocal politicians have advocated for exclusionary immigrant policies. One such activist, Pim Fortuyn, sent shockwaves through Dutch liberal society by declaring Islam to be a backward culture that would threaten Dutch civilization if not curbed (Lunsing 2003; Margry 2003). Part of the public discourse he opened was the question of what constituted Dutch society, since arguably, the historical experience of the Low Countries as a confederation of regional-ethnic cultures, has been less nationalistic, or at least concerned about a unified cultural core in the way that Romantic nationalism shaped German, Italian, Finnish, and French folkloristics. Fortuyn's stance was that the sovereignty of Dutch culture should be cultivated as a way to maintain its nationhood (Van Holsteyn and Irwin 2003).

The *Centrum voor Volkscultuur* confronted the guest worker issue directly in an exhibition and publication in 2004 entitled *Werken, werken, werken: De geschiedenis van de gastarbeiders in Tilburg en omstreken 1963–1975*. Its strategy was to put a human face on minorities by giving photographic and life story profiles of immigrants from an array of cultural backgrounds who came during the 1960s and 1970s. Countering Fortuyn, organizations mounted political campaigns for a *kleurrijk Nederland* (colorful Netherlands) or *multiculturele stad* (multicultural state) and denounced Fortuyn's racism (Buruma 2006; Van Schaik 2004). Folklorists contributed research questioning the tradition of Dutch tolerance by pointing out the entrenchment of "exoteric" ethnic humor told by autochthonous Dutch about the otherness and backwardness of recent immigrants (Meder 2001; see also Meder 2009).

The "Year of Folklore" appeared to work for both national and multicultural political goals. Looking at the postcards issued for the year, one notices that most of them made a linkage between the present and the country's "Golden Age," its heyday as a mercantile and artistic center (1584–1702). Dancers, craftsworkers, and singers were dressed in costumes of the period against the backdrop of contemporary life. The slogan for the year was "Folklore is onvoltooid verleden tijd" translated as "Folklore is the unfinished past," and the book produced with the same title features a picture of sailors

re-enacting seafaring traditions of the Golden Age (Stads *et al.* 2004).
The icon for the year was a female figure in national colors with a
torso shaped into the outline of the country. Her cap was a peasant
cap and her footwear consisted of a wooden shoe.

In contrast to many cards featuring racially white figures enacting national traditions and wearing costumes associated with the
Golden Age, the "multicultural" postcard showed dark-faced men
and women, representing, if not overtly stating, Muslim and Turkish
identities (Figure 4.5). The figures were shown amiably embracing
each other, with a traditionally clad Dutch character in the middle.
Two of the figures waved greetings to the viewer, as if to convey

Figure 4.5 Postcard commissioned by the Dutch Centre for Folk Culture for the
"Year of Folklore" (2005), illustration by Studio BLiQ

Source: Courtesy Albert van Zeijden.

to that they are "at home," not foreign, standing on a green carpet in the shape of the Netherlands. Contemporary multiculturalism as a component of overall Dutch identity was also shown in the representation on one postcard of the headgear of various cultures, including Asian (in a conical hat), Muslim (in a *khimar*), Turkish (in a fez), and American (in a baseball cap). Overall, though, images of Dutch Golden Age traditions predominated: dancers in peasant costume, blacksmithing, Carnival, shoemaking, foodways, archery, games, and music.

This high-context environment in Dutch life may explain why the Dutch do not proclaim the inclusiveness that American public folklorists frequently strived to achieve. American folklorists, their vision colored by resistance to "official language" and culture political movements, misperceived the "Year of Folklore" as an exclusionary, Romantic nationalistic exercise, while the Dutch often misinterpret the fragmentary localistic programming of American public folklore institutions as counter-productive. Both public heritage trajectories have similar goals of creating cultural understanding, and indeed, acceptance for diverse cultures as well as appreciation for national traditions. But central to the difference in applied folklore is the perceived relation of the public and private realms and its translation into organizational, social, and intellectual structures. In the Netherlands, dichotomy is a social value, with instrumental purpose, while in the United States, it is viewed as a counter-democratic, even hegemonic, tool of exclusion.

LEGALIZING FOLKLORE

The appeal to communitarianism in public folklore projects is a response to the perceived decline of group-belonging as a result of massification and individualism in modern nation-states. Folklorists document traditional arts to show the vitality of cultural practices as well as to recover historic legacies that have been dissolved in modern life. Often this enterprise suggests that despite not being visible in dress, language, and settlement, various groups nonetheless have a strong connection to a traditional knowledge that can benefit the whole of society. During the 1930s and the era of New Deal folklore projects through the end of the twentieth century with the creation of national and state folk arts agencies, the groups of concern were primarily regional, ethnic, racial, and occupational. The possibility remained for folklore to identify as cultural additional groups less visible as rooted "communities." These include gay, lesbian, and transgender orientations; deaf and blind persons; and special interest, often connected by the Internet, such as people identifying as neo-pagans and gamers.

The basic idea of enculturation, sometimes presented in contrast to assimilation in which values of the dominant society displaces communitarian values, concerns the acquisition of distinct values and practices by individuals as result of their upbringing and later social experiences in the community. This pattern suggests that individuals are socialized to hold distinctive values and beliefs through folk practices and create cultural continuity through time by trying to maintain a totalizing environment. Most public folklore projects are occasional events involving spectatorship rather than immersion in a total environment. Some ethnic, religious, and special-interest organizations can be said to apply folklore in a total environment by immersing participants in summer camps, retreats, and roots tours. Some pietistic groups even look to establish separate settlements where they can exclusively maintain their traditions. An example is the all-Hasidic village of New Square in Rockland County, New York, created in 1954 with the purchase of a 130-acre dairy farm for construction of single-family homes around a synagogue. The settlement became formally incorporated as a village in 1961, which allowed Hasidic leaders to set zoning and building codes to support an insular religious community. For the Amish, the landmark Supreme Court case of *Wisconsin v. Yoder* (406 U.S. 205, 1972) was instrumental in establishing that the "traditional interest of parents with respect to the religious upbringing of their children" outweighed the state's interest in universal education. The court upheld the claim of the Amish defendant that "the traditional way of life of the Amish" would be endangered by enforcement of compulsory education laws. Yet a conflict erupted between the state and a religious group when New York State turned down requests of Hasidic parents of disabled children, unable to receive support within the district, to private Yiddish-language schools that follow Orthodox customs.

In Europe, traditional dress worn to public schools became a focus when the French government in 2004 passed a law prohibiting the wearing of conspicuous religious symbols in public, including Muslim veils, Sikh turbans, and Jewish skullcaps. Citing security concerns, in 2010, additional legislation prohibited "concealment of the face in public space," such as Muslim *burqa* and *niqāb* in shops, buses, parks, and streets. Facing an outcry of Islamophobia, the French government stood trial in the European Court of Human Rights in 2014 after a woman brought suit. The court upheld the ban because it claimed that the law "was not expressly based on the religious connotation of the clothing in question but solely on the fact that it concealed the face." It also commented on the precedence of the majority culture by citing problems of "open interpersonal relationships, which, by virtue of *an established consensus*, formed an indispensable element of community life within the society in question" (BBC 2014; emphasis added). A related battlefront for folk practices in Europe is on traditional ritual slaughtering of animals according to religious law, such as the Islamic *dhabiha* for halal meat and Jewish *shechita* for Koshering. In the United States, courts have exempted such slaughtering from animal welfare laws, and in a case of ritual slaughter not intended for food consumption, the Supreme Court in *Church of Lukumi Babalu Aye v. City of Hialeah (1993)* ruled unconstitutional a Florida ban on Santeria ritual animal sacrifice.

The balance between a religious or folk group's rights to maintain traditions that potentially run counter to the state's broader interests is constantly in dispute. Controversial traditions that test laws expressing the majority culture's norms to minorities include attire, use of animals, and ritual practices including marriage and burial in addition to education. The issue bubbled to the surface in the United States when some states proposed a version of the federal Religious Freedom Restoration Act (RFRA) of 1993 that prevented government from "burden[ing] a person's exercise of religion." While appearing to confirm the importance of preserving minority religious traditions and values, opponents warned that it could allow individuals to deny services to gays and lesbians because their religions do not condone homosexuality (Dacey and Koproske 2011; Sullivan 2009, 1188–192). Using *Wisconsin v. Yoder* as a precedent, state RFRAs question whether extension of open-access, anti-discrimination laws work to limit expression of religious values by members of some groups. A landmark case testing the RFRA principle was *Burwell v. Hobby Lobby Stores (2014)* that recognized the claim of a for-profit corporation owned by a Southern Baptist family to deny health coverage for contraceptives because doing so conflicted with its religious beliefs. The court ruled in favor of the corporation on statutory grounds and warned courts not to answer religious questions because that would entail judging the relative legitimacy of folk beliefs. But dissenting opinions held that the ruling allowed for discriminatory, even repressive, actions by corporations on members of groups following different traditions (Epps 2014, 123–38).

The political debate over these court decisions and laws center on the legitimacy of individuals to maintain a group's folk practices, and indeed the traditional knowledge or beliefs that drive them, within a pluralistic society that implies a person's rights to hold onto his or her heritage. Alison Dundes Renteln (2004) refers to the "cultural defense" as a use of cultural background in legal decisions. She theorizes the kinds of traditions that are legally protected by the right to culture which might be different from those considered ethnographically significant such as the cockfight or drug taking (2004, 73–113). From a legal viewpoint, she finds prevalent a philosophical position that cultural traditions that violate a human right are not protected, but often defendants present claims that their cultural rights hold priority over others, such as Sikhs arrested for violating student safety rules when they wore a ceremonial sword to school. In cases where harm is allegedly psychological such as exposure to offensive jokes or objectionable gestures, defendants typically dispute the injurious intention and context of the practice as a misunderstanding of the cultural setting (Beiner 2005; Tinkler 2008). A counter-argument might be made for folklore as freedom of speech or freedom of expression, especially when the praxis is anti-authoritarian "play" and parody (Oring 2004).

Renteln suggests a no-harm principle in determining whether a tradition of a segment of society, even if it offends majority values, threatens physical and emotional trauma (2004, 217). Her principle would preclude, for example, female genital cutting practiced among Somalis as a rite of passage to ensure the marriageability of girls. The principle can apply to non-ethnic organizations that presumably justify traditions for their social bonding, values education, and legacy-maintenance functions. For example, non-ethnic organizations such as fraternities and sororities have faced criminal charges for hazing rituals that resulted in bodily injury (Jones, R. 2015; Mechling 2009; Nuwer 2004). While they agree to work toward prevent abuses, they argue that hazing should be regulated rather than banned, because it is central to initiating members into an organization that takes on the attributes of a culture. An initiatory tradition called a "rat line" in which upper classmen order freshmen to perform rigorous physical exercises was at the heart of a controversy on the entrance of women into military schools. Virginia Military Institute (VMI) was the last military college in the United States to admit women. It argued in *United States v. Virginia (1996)* that keeping its exclusionist policy was necessary because of the grueling traditions of the rat experience, but after the Supreme Court forced VMI to open its doors to women, the rat lines indeed continued with female participants. The women would not become "sister rats"; they were equally "brother rats" who endured the traditional fifteen-mile forced march together with the men, culminating according to tradition with a punishing crawl up a mud-covered hill (Bronner 2012a, 150; Strum 2002, 315).

The "folk law" of institutions such as VMI—a set of obligations and prohibitions that are understood and passed on, and transgressions that are punished, within a group—extend to a number of cultures and sometimes run into conflict with governmental rule of law (Renteln and Dundes 1995). The Amish, for example, in their *Ordnung* (literally "order" but idiomatically an unwritten code of conduct placing emphasis on values of community and religion) consider birth a natural process that should occur in the home with a midwife. In Pennsylvania, the state's policy is that birth is a medical procedure requiring a nurse or doctor. Many non-nurse midwives continued their practice based upon a long tradition in the Amish community, but after the death of an Amish baby in 2005 (the coroner had determined that the midwife was not at fault), the state cracked down on non-nurse midwives and issued cease-and-desist orders. Ten Amish families filed an amicus brief in the case of Diane Goslin, one of the non-nurse midwives affected by the orders, to claim that the policy was a "serious threat" to their way of life and their right to the free exercise of religion (*Goslin v. State Board of Medicine, 2007*). The Commonwealth Court recognized the "conflict between the interests of the Commonwealth in seeking to ensure the health and safety of both women and their children and the interest of Goslin's clients [Amish] to direct the manner of delivery of pre- and post-natal care, as well as the actual delivery of their child" (*Goslin v. State Board of Medicine 2007*). The court ruled, however, against Goslin claiming that the state has a paramount interest in ensuring the lives of the unborn over the impingement of parental choice based upon religious or folk belief.

Folkloristic perspectives became crucial to the defense of the traditional Pigeon Shoot in Hegins, Pennsylvania. The defendant, the Labor Day Committee mounted a defense based upon the event being a folkloristically recognized, "time-honored" Pennsylvania German tradition that also served the public good by eliminating birds that they considered deleterious "pests" associated with urban blight. Witnesses called by the defense resented the imposition of urban values on their traditional rural lifestyles that they viewed as endangered while activists proclaimed that the abolition of animal exploitation is necessary to create a civil society. Since animals do not have legal status as persons, animal rights advocates claimed to be moral agents for them, much as children might be protected from abusive parents. One cultural definition of cruelty from the American Veterinary Medical Association that was introduced into the court proceedings (18 Pa.C.S. 5511[c]) referred to criminalized spectator events that have the intention of causing injury or death to animals. Folk practices such as cockfighting and dogfighting fall under this category. Supporters answered that a pigeon shoot was not set up for spectators but was a sportsmen's event, although onlookers watched the event at a fundraising picnic (Bronner 2008, 138–39). The judge ruled that the pigeon shoots were legal under the law, but tradition as a basis of knowledge to care for animals instead of animal welfare authorities was illegitimate.

The court sidestepped the cultural defense and verified the role of the ASPCA to provide injunctive relief, therefore shutting down the public shoot. The tradition continues in private clubs, however, and like other "blood sports" has gone underground. Although the decision was based on a legalistic issue, it was clearly influenced by the worldview of the dominant culture that the event was a sign of a backward rural, or folk, culture. The case affirmed the conclusion of Renteln that judges often "discount arguments about the importance of the animals to minority groups" (2004, 112). The supporters' customary or folk laws of animal hierarchy, based on a biblical idea of dominion, and its experience in animal husbandry were viewed as contrary to scientific authority (Bronner 2008, 130–43).

Beyond legal issues arising when the practice of folk traditions violates state codes is the cultural credibility of a group that shows it has living traditions. A group of persons claims social standing as well as rights when it demonstrates it possesses folklore. Lawyers, as well as folklorists, argue that the practices attributed to the community are comparable to ethnic, regional, and religious groups because they provide benchmarks of what the dominant society considers a valid cultural heritage. The questioning of Bruce E. Nickerson and Richard M. Dorson, for example, in titles of studies, "Is There a Folk in the Factory?" and "Is There a Folk in the City?," suggested that industrial workers and urban dwellers were legitimate cultures despite their lack of recognition in pastorally oriented scholarship (Dorson 1970; Nickerson 1974). One result of this conceptualization of cultural construction is the investigation of organizations as generating folklore. Thus groups that had been viewed as too formal and corporate such as students, soldiers, lawyers, hospital workers, business managers, and Boy Scouts all had cases made for them as folk cultures in response to the conservative view that non-intellectual, pastoral settings foster folklore.

More politically charged was the designation of sexual orientation as the basis of a culture. Folklorists Mickey Weems, Polly Stewart, and Joseph P. Goodwin (2012) stated that the "loose LGBTQ [Lesbian, Gay, Bisexual, Transgender, Queer] collective as a folk … may be framed as if its members functioned as an ethnic group." Nonetheless they realized that to many observers, "such a richly diverse population may appear to have very little in common other than a shared history of oppression." They made the case, however, that despite a variety of identities under the initialism of LGBTQ, a raft of "celebratory, sensual, and spiritual folkways" represents the expression of gay culture—and a set of values that could be called traditional knowledge (2012). Toward that end they created an encyclopedia of LGBTQ folklore (Weems *et al.* 2012). As a culture, the people sharing folklore identify with one or more of the sexual identities and are therefore entitled to protection of their rights (see Mechling 1993; Poindexter 1997). The irony is that much of the folklore under the rubric is a response to oppression to create signals that those outside of the group would not recognize. In the process of legitimizing, and legalizing, their practices, LGBTQ activists publicize their esoteric lore (Goodwin 1989; Newall 1986; Weems 2008). In addition, customs such as weddings are constructed to make the statement that they are part of the normative culture and at the same time create traditions signaling a LGBTQ cultural identity (Ochs 2011).

Some of the animal rights activists mentioned earlier also claim protection for animals because they purportedly engaged in repeatable play and social learning, and in many forms express sounds that human observers interpret as songs and narratives (Fagen 1981; Sanders 1999, 111–48; Thompson, T. 2010). Even if the formation of culture is behaviorally not unique to humans, people can be heard explaining certain culturally shared practices as distinctively folkloric because they evoke a sense of tradition. They might share games and gestures with an anthropomorphized animal given a human name, call these activities part of their family folklore, and at the end of life provide the pet a burial plot with a traditional headstone in a cemetery (Grier 2006; Irvine 2004; Mechling 1989b).

Folk practices often suggest to people ideas, beliefs, values, and legacies that carry meaning as well as connect identities. Whether athletes looking for an edge or spectators rooting them on at an event, individuals might ritualize gestures and narrate personal experiences as their "own" folklore. In the cradle or crib, babies first encounter tradition as play and in the grave, adults have been marked and transitioned by ritual to the hereafter, but not before expressing and passing on a wealth of folklore. Throughout the course of human lives, whether people are aware of it or not, folklore is a consequential, if not always apparent, wellspring of connotative traditional knowledge and action. Its implications and applications for young and old in the past and present in time, and here and there in space, compel identification, annotation, analysis, and explanation.

REFERENCES

Aall, Hans. 1920. *Norsk Folkemuseum, 1894–1919: Trek av dets Histori*. Kristiana: Kirstes Boktrykkeri.

Aarne, Antti, and Stith Thompson. 1961. *The Types of the Folktale: A Classification and Bibliography.* Helsinki: Academia Scientiarum Fennica.

Abdullaev, Rustambek, and Ulugbek Ganiev. 2006. "Uzbek." In *The Greenwood Encyclopedia of World Folklore and Folklife*, 4 vols., ed. William M. Clements, vol. 2: 348–55. Westport, CT: Greenwood.

Abello, James, Peter Broadwell, and Timothy R. Tangherlini. 2012. "Computational Folkloristics." *Communications of the Association for Computing Machinery* 55: 60–70.

Aboujaoude, Elias. 2008. *Compulsive Acts: A Psychiatrist's Tale of Ritual and Obsession*. Berkeley, CA: University of California Press.

Abrahams, Roger D. 1969. *Jump-Rope Rhymes: A Dictionary*. Austin, TX: University of Texas Press.

——. 1970. *Deep Down in the Jungle…: Negro Narrative Folklore from the Streets of Philadelphia*. Chicago: Aldine.

——. 1977. "Toward an Enactment-Centered Theory of Folklore." In *Frontiers of Folklore*, ed. William R. Bascom, 79–120. Boulder, CO: Westview Press.

——. 1982. "Storytelling Events: Wake Amusements and the Structure of Nonsense on St. Vincent." *Journal of American Folklore* 95: 389–414.

——. 1999. "American Academic and Public Folklore: Late-Twentieth Century Musings." *Journal of Folklore Research* 36: 127–37.

———. 2005. *Everyday Life: A Poetics of Vernacular Practices*. Philadelphia: University of Pennsylvania Press.

———, and Lois Rankin, eds. *Counting-Out Rhymes: A Dictionary*. Austin: University of Texas Press.

Adair, Daryl, and Mike Cronin. 2002. *The Wearing of the Green: A History of St. Patrick's Day*. London: Routledge.

Adam, Leonhard. 1946. "Functionalism and Neo-Functionalism." *Oceania* 17: 1–25.

Adelt, Ulrich. 2008. "Germany Gets the Blues: Negotiations of 'Race' and Nation at the American Folk Blues Festival." *American Quarterly* 60: 951–74.

Adler, Thomas A. 2011. *Bean Blossom: The Brown County Jamboree and Bill Monroe's Bluegrass Festivals*. Urbana: University of Illinois Press.

Adorno, Theodor W. 1993. "On Tradition." *Telos* 94: 75–82.

Adrados, Francisco Rodríguez. 1999. *History of the Graeco-Latin Fable I: Introduction and From the Origins to the Hellenistic Age*, trans. Leslie A. Ray. Leiden: Brill.

Alexander, Edward P. 1983. *Museum Masters: Their Museums and Their Influence*. Nashville, TN: American Association for State and Local History.

Alford, Finnegan. 1981. "The Joking Relationship in American Society." *American Humor* 8: 1–8.

Allan, Douglas A. 1956. "Folk Museums at Home and Abroad." *Proceedings of the Scottish Anthropological and Folklore Society* 5: 91–121.

American Folklife Center. 2009. "Surviving Katrina and Rita in Houston." *American Folklife Center* website. Available at: www.loc.gov/folklife/events/BotkinArchives/2009htmlflyers/LindahlandJasperFlyer.html.

American Folklore Society. 2004. "American Folklore Society Recommendations to the WIPO Intergovernmental Committee on Intellectual Property and Genetic Resources, Traditional Knowledge, and Folklore." *Journal of American Folklore* 117: 296–9.

———. 2015. *American Folklore Society Ethnographic Thesaurus*. Available at: http://id.loc.gov/vocabulary/ethnographicTerms.html

Ana, Otto Santa. 2009. "Did You Call in Mexican? The Racial Politics of Jay Leno Immigrant Jokes." *Language in Society* 38: 23–45.

Ancelet, Barry Jean. 2001. "Falling Apart to Stay Together: Deep Play in the Grand Marais Mardi Gras." *Journal of American Folklore* 114: 144–53.

Anderson, Walter. 1951. *Ein volkskundliches Experiment*. Helsinki: Suomalainen Tiedeakatemia.

———. 1956. *Eine neue Arbeit zur experimentellen Volkskunde*. Helsinki: Suomalainen Tiedeakatemia.

Asimeng-Boahene, Lewis, and Michael Baffoe, eds. 2014. *African Traditional and Oral Literature as Pedagogical Tools in Content Area Classrooms K-12*. Charlotte, NC: Information Age.

Augusto, David. 1970. "Network Analysis: A Contribution to the Theory of Folklore Transmission." *Folklore Forum* 3: 78–90.

Austin, J. L. 1961. *Philosophical Papers*. Oxford: Clarendon Press.

——. 1968. *How to Do Things with Words*. New York: Oxford University Press.

Avery, Anthony P. 2005. "'I Feel That I'm Freer to Show My Feminine Side': Folklore and Alternative Masculinities in a Rave Scene." In *Manly Traditions: The Folk Roots of American Masculinities*, ed. Simon J. Bronner, 157–70. Bloomington: Indiana University Press.

Azadovskii, Mark. 1974. *A Siberian Tale Teller*, trans. James R. Dow. Austin: Center for Intercultural Studies in Folklore and Ethnomusicology, University of Texas.

Azuonye, Chucwuma. 1990. "Morphology of the Igbo Folktale: Its Ethnographic, Historiographic and Aesthetic Implications." *Folklore* 101: 36–46.

Azzolina, David S. 1987. *Tale Type- and Motif-Indexes: An Annotated Bibliography*. New York: Garland.

Babcock, Barbara A., ed. 1978. *The Reversible World: Symbolic Inversion in Art and Society*. Ithaca, NY: Cornell University Press.

——, Guy Monthan, and Doris Monthan. 1986. *The Pueblo Storyteller: Development of a Figurative Ceramic Tradition*. Tucson: University of Arizona Press.

Bachrach, Arthur J. 1962. "An Experimental Approach to Superstitious Behavior." *Journal of American Folklore* 75: 1–9.

Baker, Ronald L. 1980. "Some Contributions of Native Americans to American Material Culture."*Mississippi Folklore Register* 14: 3–12.

——. 1986. *Jokelore: Humorous Folktales from Indiana*. Bloomington: Indiana University Press.

——, and Simon J. Bronner. 2005. "'Letting Out Jack': Sex and Aggression in Manly Recitations." In *Manly Traditions: The Folk Roots of American Masculinities*, ed. Simon J. Bronner, 315–50. Bloomington: Indiana University Press.

Bard, Marjorie. 1994. "Aiding the Homeless: The Use of Narratives in Diagnosis and Intervention." In *Putting Folklore to Use*, ed. Michael Owen Jones, 76–93. Lexington: University Press of Kentucky.

Bar-Itzhak, Haya. 2005. *Israeli Folk Narratives: Settlement, Immigration, Ethnicity*. Detroit: Wayne State University Press.

——. ed. 2010. *Pioneers of Jewish Ethnography and Folkloristics in Eastern Europe*. Ljubljana: Scientific Research Centre of the Slovenian Academy of Science and Arts.

Barnes, Barry. 1995. *The Elements of Social Theory*. Princeton, NJ: Princeton University Press.

Baron, Robert. 1999. "Theorizing Public Folklore Practice: Documentation, Genres of Representation, and Everyday Competencies." *Journal of Folklore Research* 36: 185–201.

Barret, Le Roy C. 1948. "Fables from India." *Classical Weekly* 42: 66–73.

Barry, Phillips, and Fannie Hardy Eckstorm. 1930. "What Is Tradition?" *Bulletin of the Folk-Song Society of the Northeast* 1: 2–3.

Bartlett, F. C. 1920. "Some Experiments on the Reproduction of Folk-Stories." *Folklore* 31: 30–47.

Basanavičius, Jonas. 1993–2004. *Jono Basanavičiaus Tautosakos Biblioteka* [Jonas Basanavičius Folklore Library], 15 vols., ed. Kostas Aleksynas and Leonardas Sauka. Vilnius: Vaga.

Bascom, William R. 1954. "Four Functions of Folklore." *Journal of American Folklore* 67: 333–49.

——. 1955. "Verbal Art." *Journal of American Folklore* 68: 245–52.

Baughman, Ernest W. 1966. *Type and Motif-Index of the Folktales of England and North America.* The Hague: Mouton.

Bauman, Richard. 1969. "Towards a Behavioral Theory of Folklore." *Journal of American Folklore* 82: 167–70.

——. 1977. *Verbal Art as Performance.* Rowley, MA: Newbury House.

——. 1992. "Folklore." In *Folklore, Cultural Performances, and Popular Entertainments: A Communications-Centered Handbook*, ed. Richard Bauman, 29–40. New York: Oxford University Press.

——. 2012. "Performance." In *A Companion to Folklore*, ed. Regina F. Bendix and Galit Hasan-Rokem, 94–118. Malden, MA: Wiley-Blackwell.

——, and Joel Sherzer. 1975. "The Ethnography of Speaking." *Annual Review of Anthropology* 4: 95–119.

——, Patricia Sawin, and Inta Gale Carpenter. 1992. *Reflections on the Folklife Festival: An Ethnography of Participant Experience.* Bloomington: Folklore Institute, Indiana University.

Bauman, Zygmunt. 1999. *Culture as Praxis.* Thousand Oaks, CA: Sage.

Bausinger, Hermann. 1990. *Folk Culture in a World of Technology*, trans. Elke Dettmer. Bloomington: Indiana University Press.

BBC. 2014. "European Court Upholds French Full Veil Ban." *BBC News* (July 1). Available at: www.bbc.com/news/world-europe-28106900.

Behar, Ruth. 2008. "Folklore and the Search for Home." *Journal of American Folklore* 122: 251–66.

Beiner, Theresa M. 2005. *Gender Myths v. Working Realities: Using Social Science to Reformulate Sexual Harassment Law.* New York: NYU Press.

Ben-Amos, Dan. 1972. "Toward a Definition of Folklore in Context." In *Toward New Perspectives in Folklore*, ed. Américo Paredes and Richard Bauman, 3–15. Austin: University of Texas Press.

——. 1976. "Analytical Categories and Ethnic Genres." In *Folklore Genres*, ed. Dan Ben-Amos, 215–42. Austin: University of Texas Press.

——. 1984. "The Seven Strands of *Tradition:* Varieties in Its Meaning in American Folklore Studies." *Journal of Folklore Research* 21: 97–131.

——. 1998. "The Name is the Thing." *Journal of American Folklore* 111: 257–80.

——. 2010a. "Dani Schrire, Raphael Patai, Pierre Bourdieu, and the Rest of Us." *Journal of Folklore Research* 47: 45–50.

——. 2010b. "Straparola: The Revolution that Was Not." *Journal of American Folklore* 123: 426–46.

——, and Kenneth S. Goldstein, eds. 1975. *Folklore: Performance and Communication*. The Hague: Mouton.

Bendix, Regina. 1988. "Folklorism: The Challenge of a Concept." *International Folklore Review* 6: 5–15.

——. 1997. *In Search for Authenticity: The Formation of Folklore Studies*. Madison: University of Wisconsin Press.

——. 2000. "The Pleasures of the Ear: Toward an Ethnography of Listening." *Cultural Analysis* 1. Available at: http://socrates.berkeley.edu/~caforum/volume1/vol1_article3.html

——, and Gisela Welz. 1999. "Introduction: 'Cultural Brokerage' and 'Public Folklore' within a German and American Field of Discourse." *Journal of Folklore Research* 36: 111–25.

Bernstein, Richard. 1971. *Praxis and Action: Contemporary Philosophies of Human Activity*. Philadelphia: University of Pennsylvania Press.

Blank, Trevor J. 2010. "'Cheeky Behavior': The Meaning and Function of 'Fartlore' in Childhood and Adolescence." *Children's Folklore Review* 32: 61–86.

——. 2012. "Introduction: Pattern in the Virtual Folk Culture of Computer-Mediated Communication." In *Folk Culture in the Digital Age: The Emergent Dynamics of Human Interaction*, ed. Trevor J. Blank, 1–24. Logan: Utah State University Press.

——. 2013a. "Hybridizing Folk Culture: Toward a Theory of New Media and Vernacular Discourse." *Western Folklore* 72: 105–30.

——. 2013b. *The Last Laugh: Folk Humor, Celebrity Culture, and Mass-Mediated Disasters in the Digital Age*. Madison: University of Wisconsin Press.

Bluestein, Gene. 1994. *Poplore: Folk and Pop in American Culture*. Amherst: University of Massachusetts Press.

Blum, Stephen, and Amir Hassanpour. 1996. "'The Morning of Freedom Rose Up': Kurdish Popular Song and the Exigencies of Cultural Survival." *Popular Music* 15: 325–43.

Blumenreich, Beth, and Bari Lynn Polonsky. 1974. "Re-evaluating the Concept of Group: ICEN as an Alternative." *Folklore Forum* (Bibliographic and Special Series No. 12): 12–18.

Bock, Sheila, and Katherine Borland. 2011. "Exotic Identities: Dance, Difference, and Self-Fashioning." *Journal of Folklore Research* 48: 1–36.

Bøe, Liv Hilde. 2008. "*Norwegian Yesterday, Today, Tomorrow?* A Joint Documentation Project." In *Scandinavian Museums and Cultural Diversity*, ed. Katherine Goodnow and Haci Akman, 113–23. New York: Berghahn.

Bogatyrev, Petr. 1971. *The Functions of Folk Costume in Moravian Slovakia,* trans. Richard G. Crum. The Hague: Mouton.

Bosse, Joanna. 2007. "Whiteness and the Performance of Race in American Ballroom Dance." *Journal of American Folklore* 120: 19–47.

Boström, Katarzyna Wolanik, and Magnus Öhlander. 2015. "Mobile Physicians Making Sense of Culture(s): On Mobile Everyday Ethnography." *Ethnologia Europaea* 45: 7–24.

Botkin, B.A. 1988 [1939]. "WPA and Folklore Research: 'Bread and Song.'" In *The Conservation of Culture: Folklorists and the Public Sector*, ed. Burt Feintuch, 258–63. Lexington: University Press of Kentucky.

Bottigheimer, Ruth B. 2002. *Fairy Godfather: Straparola, Venice, and the Fairy Tale Tradition*. Philadelphia: University of Pennsylvania Press.

———. 2010. *Fairy Godfather*, Fairy-Tale History, and Fairy-Tale Scholarship: A Response to Dan Ben-Amos, Jan M. Ziolkowski, and Francisco Vaz da Silva." *Journal of American Folklore* 123: 447–96.

Bourdieu, Pierre. 1990. *The Logic of Practice*, trans. Richard Nice. Stanford, CA: Stanford University Press.

———. 2001. *Masculine Domination*, trans. Richard Nice. Stanford, CA: Stanford University Press.

Bowman, Paddy, and Lynne M. Hamer, eds. 2011. *Through the Schoolhouse Door: Folklore, Community, Curriculum*. Logan: Utah State University Press.

Bradford, William. 1898. *Bradford's History "Of Plymouth Plantation."* Boston: Wright & Potter.

———. 2006. *Of Plymouth Plantation*. 1920 rpt., New York: Dover.

Brandes, Stanley. 1985. *Forty: The Age and the Symbol*. Knoxville: University of Tennessee Press.

Brant, Charles S. 1948. "On Joking Relationships." *American Anthropologist* 50: 160–2.

Bremmer, Jan, and Herman Roodenburg, eds. 1992. *A Cultural History of Gesture*. Ithaca, NY: Cornell University Press.

Brewster, Paul G. 1953. *American Nonsinging Games*. Norman: University of Oklahoma Press.

Briggs, Charles L. 2008. "Disciplining Folkloristics." *Journal of Folklore Research* 45: 91–105.

Briody, Mícheál. 2007. *The Irish Folklore Commission 1935–1970: History, Ideology, Methodology*. Helsinki: Finnish Literature Society.

Brisson, Luc. 2000. *Plato the Myth Maker*, trans. Gerard Naddaf. Chicago: University of Chicago Press.

Britzman, Deborah P. 1998. *Lost Subjects, Contested Objects: Toward a Psychoanalytic Inquiry of Learning*. Albany: State University of New York Press.

Broadwell, Peter, and Timothy R. Tangherlini. 2015. *The Danish Folklore Macroscope: Modeling Complexity in the Evald Tang Kristensen Collection*. Available at: http://etkspace.scandinavian.ucla.edu/macroscope.html

Bronner, Simon J. 1980. "Reflections on Field Research in the Folklife Sciences." *New York Folklore* 6: 151–60.

——. 1982. "Special Section: Historical Methodology in Folkloristics." *Western Folklore* 41: 28–29.

——. ed. 1986a. *American Folklore Studies: An Intellectual History*. Lawrence: University Press of Kansas.

——. 1986b. *Grasping Things: Folk Material Culture and Mass Society in America*. Lexington: University Press of Kentucky.

——. 1988. "Art, Performance, and Praxis: The Rhetoric of Contemporary Folklore Studies." *Western Folklore* 47: 75–102.

——. 1989. *American Children's Folklore: Annotated Edition*. Little Rock, KS: August House.

——. ed. 1992a. "Elaborating Tradition: A Pennsylvania-German Folk Artist Ministers to His Community." In *Creativity and Tradition in Folklore: New Directions*, ed. Simon J. Bronner, 277–326. Logan: Utah State University Press.

——. 1992b. *Creativity and Tradition in Folklore: New Directions*. Logan: Utah State University Press.

——. 1992c. "Cane Making as Symbol and Tradition." In *American Folk Art Canes: Personal Sculpture*, ed. George H. Meyer, 219–21. Bloomfield Hills, MI: Sandringham Press, 1992.

——. 1992d. "Introduction." In *Creativity and Tradition in Folklore: New Directions*, ed. Simon J. Bronner, 1–40. Logan: Utah State University Press.

——. 1992e. "James Maidment, Ballad Editor." *Midwestern Folklore* 18: 64–8.

——. 1996. *The Carver's Art: Crafting Meaning from Wood*. Lexington: University Press of Kentucky.

——. 1998. *Following Tradition: Folklore in the Discourse of American Culture*. Logan: Utah State University Press.

——. 2000. "The Meanings of Tradition: An Introduction." *Western Folklore* 59: 87–104.

——. 2005a. "Contesting Tradition: The Deep Play and Protest of Pigeon Shoots." *Journal of American Folklore* 118: 409–52.

——. 2005b. "Hidden Erections and Sexual Fabrications: Old Men Crafting Manliness." In *Manly Traditions: The Folk Roots of American Masculinities*, ed. Simon J. Bronner, 315–50. Bloomington: Indiana University Press.

——. 2005c. "Menfolk." In *Manly Traditions: The Folk Roots of American Masculinities*, ed. Simon J. Bronner, 1–60. Bloomington: Indiana University Press.

——. 2006. *Crossing the Line: Violence, Play, and Drama in Naval Equator Traditions*. Amsterdam: Amsterdam University Press.

——. 2007. "Sailor Men: Are Navy Rituals, Like Kissing the Royal Belly, Homophobic or Homoerotic?" *American Sexuality Magazine* (June 19, 2007). Available at: http://nsrc.sfsu.edu

——. 2008. *Killing Tradition: Inside Hunting and Animal Rights Controversies*. Lexington: University Press of Kentucky.

——. 2010. "Framing Folklore: An Introduction." *Western Folklore* 69: 5–27.

——. 2011. *Explaining Traditions: Folk Behavior in Modern Culture*. Lexington: University Press of Kentucky.

——. 2012a. *Campus Traditions: Folklore from the Old-Time College to the Modern Mega-University*. Jackson: University Press of Mississippi.

——. 2012b. "Practice Theory in Folklore and Folklife Studies." 123 (2012): 23–47.

——. 2012c. "The Jewish Joke Online: Framing and Symbolizing Humor in Analog and Digital Culture." In *Folk Culture in the Digital Age: The Emergent Dynamics of Human Interaction*, ed. Trevor J. Blank, 119–49. Logan: Utah State University Press.

——, and Lynn Gamwell. 2014. *Whirligigs: The Art of Peter Gelker*. Fullerton, CA: Grand Central Press.

Brown, Mary Ellen. 2011. *Child's Unfinished Masterpiece: The English and Scottish Popular Ballads*. Urbana: University of Illinois Press.

Brown, Melissa. 2008. "Introduction: Developing a Scientific Paradigm for Understanding Culture." In *Explaining Culture Scientifically*, ed. Melissa J. Brown, 3–16. Seattle: University of Washington Press.

Brown, Theresa. 2010. "When the Nurse is a Bully." *New York Times*, February 11. Available at: http://well.blogs.nytimes.com/2010/02/11/when-the-nurse-is-a-bully/?_r=0

Brunvand, Jan Harold. 1998. *The Study of American Folklore: An Introduction*. 4th ed. New York: W. W. Norton.

Buccitelli, Anthony Bak. 2012. "Performance 2.0: Observations toward a Theory of the Digital Performance of Folklore." In *Folk Culture in the Digital Age: The Emergent Dynamics of Human Interaction*, ed. Trevor J. Blank, 60–84. Logan: Utah State University Press.

Burns, Tom. 1969. "Involving the Introductory Student of Folklore in the Functional Analysis of the Material He Collects." In *Perspectives on Folklore and Education*, ed. Elliott Oring and James Durham, 13–27. Bloomington, IN: Folklore Forum Bibliographic and Special Series No. 2.

Burr, Elizabeth, trans. 1994. *The Chiron Dictionary of Greek and Roman Mythology: Gods and Goddesses, Heroes, Places, and Events of Antiquity.* Wilmette, IL: Chiron.

Burrison, John A. 1989. *Storytellers: Folktales and Legends from the South.* Athens: University of Georgia Press.

Buruma, Ian. 2006. *Murder in Amsterdam: The Death of Theo Van Gogh and the Limits of Tolerance.* New York: Penguin.

Byington, Robert H. 1989. "What Happened to Applied Folklore?" in *Time and Temperature*, ed. Charles Camp, 77–9. Washington, DC: American Folklore Society.

Camp, Charles. 1977. "State Folklorists and Folklife Programs: A Second Look." *Folklore Forum* 10: 26–9.

Cantwell, Robert S. 1991. "Conjuring Culture: Ideology and Magic in the Festival of American Folklife." *Journal of American Folklore* 104: 148–63.

——. 1992. "Feasts of Unnaming: Folk Festivals and the Representation of Folklife." In *Public Folklore*, ed. Robert Baron and Nicholas R. Spitzer, 263–305. Washington, DC: Smithsonian Institution Press.

——. 1993. *Ethnomimesis: Folklore and the Representation of Culture.* Chapel Hill: University of North Carolina Press.

——. 1996. *When We Were Good: The Folk Revival.* Cambridge, MA: Harvard University Press.

——. 1999. "Habitus, Ethnomimesis: A Note on the Logic of Practice." *Journal of Folklore Research* 36: 219–34.

Carey, George. 1976. "State Folklorists and State Arts Councils: The Maryland Pilot." *Folklore forum* 9: 1–8.

Carvalho-Neto, Paulo de. 1971. *The Concept of Folklore*, trans. Jacques M. P. Wilson. Coral Gables, FL: University of Miami Press.

Cashman, Ray, Tom Mould, and Pravina Shukla. 2011. *The Individual and Tradition: Folkloristic Perspectives*, ed., 93–112. Bloomington: Indiana University Press.

Caton, Steven C. 1993. "Icons of the Person: Lacan's 'Imago' in the Yemeni Male's Tribal Wedding." *Asian Folklore Studies* 52: 359–81.

Ceribašić, Naila. 1998. "Folklore Festivals in Croatia: Contemporary Controversies." *World of Music* 40: 25–49.

Chess, Shira, and Eric Newsom. 2015. *Folklore, Horror Stories, and the Slender Man: The Development of an Internet Mythology.* New York: Palgrave Macmillan.

Christy, Alan. 2012. *A Discipline on Foot: Inventing Japanese Native Ethnography, 1910–1945.* Lanham, MD: Rowman & Littlefield.

Christy, Robert. 1893. *Proverbs, Maxims and Phrases of All Ages.* New York: G. P. Putnam's Sons.

City Lore. 2008. *City of Memory.* Available at: www.cityofmemory.org/map/index.php

Clark, Michael D. 2005. *The American Discovery of Tradition, 1865–1942*. Baton Rouge: Louisiana State University Press.

Claus, Peter J., and Frank J. Korom. 1991. *Folkloristics and Indian Folklore*. Udupi, India: Regional Resources Centre for Folk Performing Arts, Mahatma Gandhi Memorial College.

Clements, William M. 1997. "Oikotype/Oicotype." In *Folklore: An Encyclopedia of Beliefs, Customs, Tales, Music, and Art*, 2 vols., ed. Thomas A. Green, vol. 2: 604–5. Santa Barbara, CA: ABC-CLIO.

Cocchiara, Giuseppe. 1981. *The History of Folklore in Europe*, trans. John N. McDaniel. Philadelphia: Institute for the Study of Human Issues.

Cochrane, Timothy. 1987. "The Concept of Ecotypes in American Folklore." *Journal of Folklore Research* 24: 33–55.

Cohen, Ronald D. 2008. *A History of Folk Music Festivals in the United States*. Lanham, MD: Scarecrow Press.

Cong, Dachang. 1992. "Amish Factionalism and Technological Change: A Case Study of Kerosene Refrigerators and Conservatism." *Ethnology* 31: 205–18.

Congar, Yves. 2004. *The Meaning of Tradition*, trans. A. N. Woodrow. San Francisco: Ignatius Press.

Congdon, Kristin G. 1994. "Democratizing Art Therapy." In *Putting Folklore to Use*, edited by Michael Owen Jones, 136–49. Lexington: University Press of Kentucky.

Congdon-Martin, Douglas. 1999. *Storytellers and other Figurative Pottery*, Revised 2nd ed. Atglen, PA: Schiffer.

Conner Prairie. 2015. "Follow the North Star: You'll Walk Away with a Lot to Think About." *Conner Prairie*. Available at: www.connerprairie.org/Things-To-Do/Events/2015/Follow-the-North-Star/.

Conway, Cecelia. 1995. *African Banjo Echoes in Appalachia: A Study of Folk Tradition*. Knoxville: University of Tennessee Press.

Cooper, Patricia Irvin. 1991. "Some Misconceptions in American Log-Building Studies." *Material Culture* 23: 43–61.

Cosquin, Emmanuel. 1892. "Quelques Observations sur les 'Incidents communs aux Contes Européens et aux Contes Orientaux.'" In *The International Folk-Lore Congress 1891: Papers and Transactions*, ed. Joseph Jacobs and Alfred Nutt, 67–75. London: David Nutt.

Cothran, Kay L. 1973. "Participation in Tradition." *Keystone Folklore* 18: 7–13.

Coupland, Justine, Nikolas Coupland, and Jeffrey D. Robinson. 1992. "'How Are You?': Negotiating Phatic Communion." *Language in Society* 21: 207–30.

——, Jeffrey D. Robinson, and Nikolas Coupland. 1994. "Frame Negotiation in Doctor-Elderly Patient Consultations." *Discourse & Society* 5: 89–124.

Craith, Máiréad Nic, Ullrich Kockel, and Reinhard Johler, eds. 2008. *Everyday Culture in Europe: Approaches and Methodologies*. Burlington, VT: Ashgate.

Creighton, Helen. 1950. *Folklore of Lunnenberg County, Novia Scotia*. Ottawa: National Museum of Canada.

Dacey, Austin, and Colin Koproske. 2011. "Against Religious Freedom." *Dissent* 58: 81–85.

Dance, Daryl Cumber. 1978. *Shuckin' and Jivin': Folklore from Contemporary Black Americans*. Bloomington: Indiana University Press.

D'Andrade, Roy. 2008. "Some Kinds of Causal Powers that Make up Culture." In *Explaining Culture Scientifically*, ed. Melissa J. Brown, 19–36. Seattle: University of Washington Press.

Da Silva, Francisco Vaz. 2010. "The Invention of Fairy Tales." *Journal of American Folklore* 123: 398–425.

Da Silva, Sara Graça, and Jamshid J. Tehrani. 2016. "Comparative Phylogenetic Analyses Uncover the Ancient Roots of Indo-European Folktales." *Royal Society Open Science* 3: 150645. http://dx.doi.org/10.1098/rsos.150645

Davidson, Cathy N. 1993. "Laughing in English." *Academe* 79: 18–22.

De Caro, Francis A. 1976. "Concepts of the Past in Folkloristics." *Western Folklore* 35: 3–22.

——, and Rosan Augusta Jordan. 2004. *Re-Situating Folklore: Folk Contexts and Twentieth-Century Literature and Art*. Knoxville: University of Tennessee Press.

De Certeau, Michel. 1984. *The Practice of Everyday Life*, trans. Steven Rendall. Berkeley: University of California Press.

Dégh, Linda. 1968. "The Hook." *Indiana Folklore* 1: 92–100.

——. 1971. "The 'Belief Legend' in Modern Society: Form, Function, and Relationship to Other Genres." In *American Folk Legend: A Symposium*, ed. Wayland D. Hand, 55–68. Berkeley: University of California Press.

——. 1988. "What Did the Grimm Brothers Give to and Take from the Folk?" In *The Brothers Grimm and Folktale*, ed. James M. McGlathery, 66–90. Urbana: University of Illinois Press.

——. 1994a. *American Folklore and the Mass Media*. Bloomington: Indiana University Press.

——. 1994b. "The Approach to Worldview in Folk Narrative Study." *Western Folklore* 53: 243–52.

——. 1997. "Conduit Theory/Multiconduit Theory." In *Folklore: An Encyclopedia of Beliefs, Customs, Tales, Music, and Art*, ed. Thomas A. Green, 142–44. Santa Barbara, CA: ABC-CLIO.

——, and Andrew Vázsonyi. 1975. "The Hypothesis of Multi-Conduit Transmission of Folklore." In *Folklore: Performance and Communication*, ed. Dan Ben-Amos, and Kenneth Goldstein, 207–52. The Hague: Mouton.

De Jong, Adriaan. 2010. "New Initiatives in the Netherlands Open Air Museum: How an Early Open Air Museum Keeps Up with the Times." *Acta Ethnographica Hungarica* 55: 333–56.

Demos, John. 2004. *Circles and Lines: The Shape of Life in Early America.* Cambridge, MA: Harvard University Press.

Dewhurst, C. Kurt. 2014. "Folklife and Museum Practice: An Intertwined History and Emerging Convergences." *Journal of American Folklore* 127: 247–63.

Diamond, Heather A. 2008. *American Aloha: Cultural Tourism and the Negotiation of Tradition.* Honolulu: University of Hawai'I Press.

——, and Ricardo D. Trimillos. 2008. "Introduction: Interdisciplinary Perspectives on the Smithsonian Folklife Festival." *Journal of American Folklore* 121: 3–9.

Dorson, Richard M. 1967. *American Negro Folktales.* Greenwich, CT: Fawcett.

——. 1968. *The British Folklorists: A History.* Chicago: University of Chicago Press.

——. 1970. "Is There a Folk in the City?" *Journal of American Folklore* 83: 185–216.

——. 1971. "Applied Folklore." In *Papers on Applied Folklore*, ed. Dick Sweterlitsch, 40–42. Bloomington, IN: Folklore Forum Bibliographic and Special Series, No. 8.

——, ed. 1973a. *Folklore Research Around the World: A North American Point of View.* Port Washington, NY: Kennikat Press.

——. 1973b. "The Lesson of Foxfire." *North Carolina Folklore Journal* 21: 157–59.

——. 1976. *Folklore and Fakelore: Essays toward a Discipline of Folk Studies.* Cambridge, MA: Harvard University Press.

——. 1978a. "Folklore in the Modern World." In *Folklore in the Modern World*, ed. Richard M. Dorson, 11–51. The Hague: Mouton.

——. 1978b. "We All Need the Folk." *Journal of the Folklore Institute* 15: 267–69.

——, and Inta Gale Carpenter. 1978. "Can Folklorists and Educators Work Together?" *North Carolina Folklore Journal* 26: 3–13.

Dorst, John. 1990. "Tags and Burners, Cycles and Networks: Folklore in the Telectronic Age." *Journal of Folklore Research* 27: 179–90.

Douglas, Mary. 1966. *Purity and Danger: An Analysis of Concepts of Pollution and Taboo.* New York: Praeger.

Doyle, Charles Clay. 2009. "Fakelore: Richard Dorson and His Coinage." *Folklore Historian* 26: 51–58.

Du Bois, W. E. B. 2004. *The Social Theory of W. E. B. Du Bois*, ed. Phil Zuckerman. Thousand Oaks, CA: Pine Forge Press.

Duhigg, Charles. 2012. *The Power of Habit: Why We Do What We Do in Life and in Business.* New York: Random House.

Duilearga, Séamus Ó. 1999. "Irish Tales and Story-Tellers." In *International Folkloristics: Classic Contributions by the Founders of Folklore*, ed. Alan Dundes, 153–76. Lanham, MD: Rowman & Littlefield.

Dundes, Alan. 1962a. "From Etic to Emic Units in the Structural Study of Folktales." *Journal of American Folklore* 75: 95–105.

——. 1962b. "Trends in Content Analysis: A Review Article." *Midwest Folklore* 12: 31–38.

——. 1964a. "On Game Morphology: A Study of the Structure of Non-Verbal Folklore." *New York Folklore Quarterly* 20: 276–88.

——. 1964b. "Texture, Text, and Context." *Southern Folklore Quarterly* 20: 251–65.

——. 1965a. "The Study of Folklore in Literature and Culture: Identification and Interpretation." *Journal of American Folklore* 78: 136–42.

——. 1965b. "What is Folklore?" In *The Study of Folklore*, ed. Alan Dundes, 1–3. Englewood Cliffs, NJ: Prentice-Hall.

——. 1966a. "The American Concept of Folklore." *Journal of the Folklore Institute* 3: 226–49.

——. 1966b. "Chain Letter: A Folk Geometric Progression." *Northwest Folklore* 1: 14–19.

——. 1966c. "Here I Sit—A Study of American Latrinalia." *Papers of the Kroeber Anthropological Society* 34: 91–105.

——. 1969a. "The Devolutionary Premise in Folklore Theory." *Journal of the Folklore Institute* 6: 5–19.

——. 1969b. "Thinking Ahead: A Folkloristic Reflection of the Future Orientation in American Worldview." *Anthropological Quarterly* 42: 53–72.

——. 1971a. "Folk Ideas as Units of Worldview." *Journal of American Folklore* 84: 93–103.

——. 1971b. "On the Psychology of Legend." In *American Folk Legend: A Symposium*, ed. Wayland D. Hand, 21–36. Berkeley: University of California Press.

——. 1975. "On the Structure of the Proverb." *Proverbium* 25: 961–73.

——. 1978. "Structuralism and Folklore." In *Essays in Folkloristics* by Alan Dundes, 178–206. Meerut, India: Folklore Institute.

——. 1980. *Interpreting Folklore*. Bloomington: Indiana University Press.

——. 1984. "Earth-Diver: Creation of the Mythopoeic Male." In *Sacred Narrative: Readings in the Theory of Myth*, ed. Alan Dundes, 270–94. Berkeley: University of California Press.

——. 1985. "Nationalistic Inferiority Complexes and the Fabrication of Fakelore: A Reconsideration of Ossian, the *Kinder-und Haumsmärchen*, the *Kalevala*, and Paul Bunyan." *Journal of Folklore Research* 22: 5–18.

——. 1987a. *Cracking Jokes: Studies of Sick Humor Cycles and Stereotypes*. Berkeley, Calif.: Ten Speed Press.

——. 1987b. *Parsing Through Customs: Essays by a Freudian Folklorist*. Madison: University of Wisconsin Press.

———. 1991. "The Ritual Murder or Blood Libel Legend: A Study of Anti-Semitic Victimization through Projective Inversion." In *The Blood Libel Legend: A Casebook in Anti-Semitic Folklore*, ed. Alan Dundes, 336–78. Madison: University of Wisconsin Press.

———. 1994. "Gallus as Phallus: A Psychoanalytic Cross-Cultural Consideration of the Cockfight as Fowl Play." In *The Cockfight: A Casebook*, ed. Alan Dundes, 241–84. Madison: University of Wisconsin Press.

———. 1995. "Worldview in Folk Narrative: An Addendum." *Western Folklore* 54: 229–32.

———. 1997a. "Binary Opposition in Myth: The Propp/Lévi-Strauss Debate in Retrospect." *Western Folklore* 56: 39–50.

———. 1997b. *From Game to War, and Other Psychoanalytic Essays on Folklore.* Lexington: University Press of Kentucky.

———. 1997c. "The Motif-Index and the Tale Type Index: A Critique." *Journal of Folklore Research* 34: 195–202.

———. 2002. *Bloody Mary in the Mirror: Essays in Psychoanalytic Folkloristics.* Jackson: University Press of Mississippi.

———. 2004. "As the Crow Flies: A Straightforward Study of Lineal Worldview in American Folk Speech." In *What Goes Around Comes Around: The Circulation of Proverbs in Contemporary Life*, ed. Kimberly J. Lau, Peter Tokofsky, and Stephen D. Winick, 171–87. Logan: Utah State University Press.

———. 2005. "Folkloristics in the Twenty-First Century." *Journal of American Folklore* 118: 385–408.

———. 2007 [1966]. "Metafolklore and Oral Literary Criticism." In *The Meaning of Folklore: The Analytical Essays of Alan Dundes,* ed. Simon J. Bronner, 80–87. Logan: Utah State University Press.

———, and Carl R. Pagter. 1975. *Urban Folklore from the Paperwork Empire.* Austin, TX: American Folklore Society.

———. 1991. "The Mobile SCUD Missile Launcher and Other Persian Gulf Warlore: An American Folk Image of Saddam Hussein's Iraq." *Western Folklore* 50: 303–22.

Dunn, Herbert. 2003. "Horizontal Violence among Nurses in the Operating Room." *AORN Journal* 78: 977–88.

Eaton, Allen H. 1937. *Handicrafts of the Southern Highlands, with an Account of the Rural Handicraft Movement in the United States and Suggestions for the Wider Use of Handicrafts in Adult Education and Recreation.* New York: Russell Sage Foundation.

Edmonds, C. J. 1971. "Kurdish Nationalism." *Journal of Contemporary History* 6: 87–107.

Edmonson, Munro S. 1971. *Lore: An Introduction to the Science of Folklore and Literature.* New York: Holt, Rinehart & Winston.

Ellis, Bill. 1982. "'Ralph and Rudy': The Audience's Role in Recreating a Camp Legend." *Western Folklore* 41: 169–91.

——. 1992. "The Self-Declared Folklorist: Howlings of a Lone Wolf." *Western Folklore*, 51: 179–86.

——. 1994. "'The Hook' Reconsidered: Problems in Classifying and Interpreting Adolescent Horror Legends." *Folklore* 105: 61–75.

——. 2012. "The E-Mail Virus Panic." In *The Martians Have Landed! A History of Media-Driven Panics and Hoaxes*, by Robert E. Bartholomew and Benjamin Radford, 123–30. Jefferson, NC: McFarland.

El-Shamy, Hasan M. 1995. *Folk Traditions of the Arab World: A Guide to Motif Classification*. Bloomington: Indiana University Press.

——. 2004. *Types of the Folktale in the Arab World: A Demographically Oriented Tale-Type Index*. Bloomington: Indiana University Press.

Elster, Jon. 2007. *Explaining Social Behavior: More Nuts and Bolts for the Social Sciences*. New York: Cambridge University Press.

Emrich, Duncan. 1946. "'Folk-Lore': William John Thoms." *California Folklore Quarterly* 5: 355–74.

Epps, Garrett. 2014. *American Justice 2014: Nine Clashing Visions on the Supreme Court*. Philadelphia: University of Pennsylvania Press.

Erixon, Sigurd. 1943. *Kulturart och folkliv*. Stockholm: Esseltie aktiebolag.

Evans, David. 1982. *Big Road Blues: Tradition and Creativity in the Folk Blues*. Berkeley: University of California Press.

Ewing, Tom, ed. 2006. *The Bill Monroe Reader*. Urbana: University of Illinois Press.

"Exhibition of the Blouse." 1922. *Better Waists* 8 (2): 13–15.

Fagen, Robert. 1981. *Animal Play Behavior*. New York: Oxford University Press.

Fanany, Rebecca, and Ismet Fanany. 2000. "Let Nature Be Your Teacher: Images of Nature in the Proverbs of the Minangkabau of West Sumatra, Indonesia." *Proverbium* 17: 101–20.

Feleppa, Robert. 1986. "Emics, Etics, and Social Objectivity." *Current Anthropology* 27: 243–55.

Felson, Richard B., and George Gmelch. 1979. "Uncertainty and the Use of Magic." *Current Anthropology* 20: 587–89.

Fenton, Alexander, general ed. 2013. *Scottish Life and Society: A Compendium of Scottish Ethnology*, 14 vols. Edinburgh: John Donald.

Ferris, William R. 2008. "Put Culture in the Cabinet." *New York Times* (December 26), A25.

——. 2013. *The Storied South: Voices of Writers and Artists*. Chapel Hill: University of North Carolina.

Fine, Elizabeth C. 1984. *The Folklore Text: From Performance to Print*. Bloomington: Indiana University Press.

Fine, Gary Alan. 1979a. "Cokelore and Coke Law: Urban Belief Tales and the Problem of Multiple Origins." *Journal of American Folklore* 92: 477–82.

———. 1979b. "Folklore Diffusion through Interactive Social Networks: Conduits in a Preadolescent Community." *New York Folklore* 5: 87–126.

———. 1980. "Multi-Conduit Transmission and Social Structure: Expanding a Folklore Classic." In *Folklore on Two Continents: Essays in Honor of Linda Dégh*, ed. Nikolai Burlakoff and Carl Lindahl, 300–309. Bloomington, IN: Trickster Press.

———. 1983. "Network and Meaning: An Interactionist Approach to Structure." *Symbolic Interaction* 6: 97–110.

———. 1984. "Evaluating Psychoanalytic Folklore: Are Freudians Ever Right?" *New York Folklore* 10: 5–20.

———. 1987a. "Community and Boundary: Personal Experience Stories of Mushroom Collectors." *Journal of Folklore Research* 24: 223–40.

———. 1987b. "Joseph Jacobs: A Sociological Folklorist." *Folklore* 98: 183–93.

———. 2005. "In the Company of Men: Female Accommodation and the Folk Culture of Male Groups." In *Manly Traditions: The Folk Roots of American Masculinities*, ed. Simon J. Bronner, 61–76. Bloomington: Indiana University Press.

———. 2012. *Tiny Publics: A Theory of Group Action and Culture.* New York: Russell Sage Foundation.

———, and Christine Wood. 2010. "Accounting for Jokes: Jocular Performance in a Critical Age." *Western Folklore* 69: 299–321.

Fineman, Mia. 2004. "Photography, Vernacular." In *Encyclopedia of American Folk Art*, ed. Gerard C. Wertkin, 384–87. New York: Routledge.

Finkin, Jordan. 2009. "Jewish Jokes, Yiddish Storytelling, and Sholem Aleichem: A Discursive Approach." *Jewish Social Studies* 16: 85–110.

Fischer, David Hackett. 1989. *Albion's Seed: Four British Folkways in America.* New York: Oxford University Press.

Foley, John Miles. 1985. *Oral-Formulaic Theory and Research: An Introduction and Annotated Bibliography.* New York: Garland.

———. 1988. *The Theory of Oral Composition: History and Methodology.* Bloomington: Indiana University Press.

———, ed. 1990. *Oral-Formulaic Theory: A Folklore Casebook.* New York: Garland.

———. 1995. *The Singer of Tales in Performance.* Bloomington: Indiana University Press.

———. 1999. *Homer's Traditional Art.* University Park: Pennsylvania State University Press.

Forrest, John, and Deborah Blincoe. 1995. *The Natural History of the Traditional Quilt.* Austin: University of Texas Press.

Fortes, Meyer. 1960. "Oedipus and Job in West African Religion." In *Anthropology of Folk Religion*, ed. Charles Leslie, 5–49. New York: Vintage Books.

Foster, Helen Bradley, and Donald Clay Johnson, eds. 2003. *Wedding Dress Across Cultures*. Oxford: Berg.

Foster, Michael Dylan. 2011. "The UNESCO Effect: Confidence, Defamiliarization, and a New Element in the Discourse on a Japanese Island." *Journal of Folklore Research* 48: 63–107.

———. 2015. "UNESCO on the Ground." *Journal of Folklore Research* 52: 143–56.

———, and Jeffrey A. Tolbert, eds. 2015. *The Folkloresque: Reframing Folklore in a Popular Culture World*. Logan: Utah State University Press.

Frank, Russell. 2011. *Newslore: Contemporary Folklore on the Internet*. Jackson: University Press of Mississippi.

Frank, Stuart M., ed. 1980. *Songs of the Sea: Proceedings of the First Annual Symposium on Traditional Music of the Sea, Mystic Seaport Museum*. Mystic, CT: Mystic Seaport Museum.

Freeman, Iam A. 2014. *Seeds of Revolution: A Collection of Axioms, Passages and Proverbs*, vol. 1. Bloomington, IN: iUniverse.

French, Richard Valpy. 1881. *The History of Toasting, or Drinking of Healths in England*. London: National Temperance Publication Depot.

Freud, Sigmund. 1959. *Group Psychology and the Analysis of the Ego*, trans. James Strachey. New York: W. W. Norton.

———. 1963 [1915]. "Symbolism in Dreams." In *The Standard Edition of the Complete Psychological Works of Sigmund Freud*, trans. and ed. James Strachey, 149–69. London: Hogarth.

———. 1999 [1900]. *The Interpretation of Dreams*. Oxford: Oxford University Press.

Frisch, Michael H. 1990. *A Shared Authority: Essays on the Craft and Meaning of Oral and Public History*. Albany: State University of New York Press.

Gaidoz, Henri, and Sébillot, Paul. 2010. 1884 rpt. *Blason Populaire de la France*. Charleston, SC: Nabu Press.

Gara, Larry. 1961. *The Liberty Line: The Legend of the Underground Railroad*. Lexington: University of Kentucky Press.

Garlough, Christine Lynn. 2008. "On the Political Uses of Folklore: Performance and Grassroots Feminist Activism in India." *Journal of American Folklore* 121: 167–91.

Garry, Jane, and Hasan El-Shamy, eds. 2005. *Archetypes and Motifs in Folklore and Literature: A Handbook*. Armonk, NY: M.E. Sharpe.

Gaster, Theodor. 1949. *Passover: Its History and Traditions*. New York: Schuman.

———. 1952. *The Oldest Stories in the World*. New York: Viking Press.

Gastil, Raymond D. 1975. *Cultural Regions of the United States*. Seattle: University of Washington Press.

Geertz, Clifford. 1972. "Deep Play: Notes on a Balinese Cockfight." *Daedalus* 134: 1–37.

——. 1973. "Thick Description: Toward an Interpretive Theory of Culture." In *The Interpretation of Cultures* by Clifford Geertz, 3–32. New York: Basic Books.

——. 2000. *Local Knowledge: Further Essays in Interpretive Anthropology*. New York: Basic Books.

Gencarella, Stephen Olbrys. 2009. "Constituting Folklore: A Case for Critical Folklore Studies." *Journal of American Folklore* 122: 172–96.

——. 2010. "Gramsci, Good Sense, and Critical Folklore Studies." *Journal of Folklore Research* 47: 221–52.

Georges, Robert A. 1969. "Toward an Understanding of Storytelling Events." *Journal of American Folklore* 82: 313–28.

——. 1986. "The Pervasiveness in Contemporary Folklore Studies of Assumptions, Concepts, and Constructs Usually Associated with the Historic-Geographic Method." *Journal of Folklore Research* 23: 87–103.

——. 1991. "Earning, Appropriating, Concealing, and Denying the Identity of Folklorist." *Western Folklore* 50: 3–12.

——. 1997. "The Centrality in Folkloristics of Motif and Tale Type." *Journal of Folklore Research* 34: 203–208

——, and Michael Owen Jones. 1995. *Folkloristics: An Introduction*. Bloomington: Indiana University Press.

Georgitis, Nathan. 2015. "A Case Study in Folklore Archives Management: The Randall V. Mills Archives of Northwest Folklore at the University of Oregon." *Journal of Folklore Research* 52: 85–98.

Gibbs, Raymond W., and Dinara Beitel. 1995. "What Proverb Understanding Reveals about How People Think." *Psychological Bulletin* 118: 133–54.

Gibson, Corey. 2015. *The Voice of the People: Hamish Henderson and Scottish Cultural Politics*. Edinburgh: Edinburgh University Press.

Giddens, Anthony. 1994. *The Consequences of Modernity*. Cambridge: Polity.

Gillespie, Angus K. 1980. *Folklorist of the Coal Fields: George Korson's Life and Work*. University Park: Pennsylvania State University Press.

——. 2006. "Folk Festivals." In *Encyclopedia of American Folklife*, ed. Simon J. Bronner, 395–98. Armonk, NY: M. E. Sharpe.

Gilmore, Janet C. 2015. "Filling 'An Immense Brain with Very Little in the Brain' for 'Perpetual Memory': Folklore Archiving New and Old." *Journal of Folklore Research* 52: 99–138.

Glassie, Henry. 1968. *Pattern in the Material Folk Culture of the Eastern United States*. Philadelphia: University of Pennsylvania Press.

——. 1972–1973. "The Nature of the New World Artifact: The Instance of the Dugout Canoe." *Schweizerisches Archiv für Volkskunde* 68–69: 153–70.

——. 1973. "Structure and Function, Folklore and the Artifact." *Semiotica* 7: 313–51.

——. 1974. "The Variation of Concepts within Tradition: Barn Building in Otsego County, New York." *Geoscience and Man* 5: 177–235.

——. 1975. *Folk Housing in Middle Virginia: A Structural Analysis of Historic Artifacts*. Knoxville: University of Tennessee Press.

——. 1983. "The Moral Lore of Folklore." *Folklore Forum* 16: 123–51.

——. 1992. "Artifact and Culture, Architecture and Society." In *American Material Culture and Folklife: A Prologue and Dialogue*, ed. Simon J. Bronner, 47–62. Logan: Utah State University Press.

——. 1995. "Tradition." *Journal of American Folklore* 108: 395–412.

Gmelch, George. 1971. "Baseball Magic." *Trans-action* 8 (8): 39–41.

——. 2006. *Inside Pitch: Life in Professional Baseball*. Lincoln: University of Nebraska Press.

Goethals, Gregor. 2003. "Myth and Ritual in Cyberspace." In *Mediating Religion: Conversations in Media, Religion and Culture*, ed. Jolyon Mitchell and Sophia Marriage, 257–70. London: T& T Clark.

Goffman, Erving. 1974. *Frame Analysis: An Essay on the Organization of Experience*. New York: Harper & Row.

Goldberg, Christine. 1984. "The Historic-Geographic Method: Past and Future." *Journal of Folklore Research* 21: 1–18.

Goldstein, Kenneth S. 1964. *A Guide for Field Workers in Folklore*. Hatboro, PA: Folklore Associates.

——. 1967. "Experimental Folklore: Laboratory vs. Field." In *Folklore International: Essays in Traditional Literature, Belief and Custom in Honor of Wayland Debs Hand*, ed. D.K. Wilgus, 71–82. Hatboro, PA: Folklore Associates.

Goodwin, Joseph P. 1989. *More Man Than You'll Ever Be: Gay Folklore and Acculturation in Middle America*. Bloomington: Indiana University Press.

Goslin v. State Board of Medicine. 2007. *FindLaw* (October 31). Available at: http://caselaw.findlaw.com/pa-commonwealth-court/1381290.html

Gottesman, Itzik Nakhmen. 2003. *Defining the Yiddish Nation: The Jewish Folklorists of Poland*. Detroit: Wayne State University Press.

Graham, Andrea. 2000. "The Up-Side of Folklife Festivals: Why We Keep Doing Them." *Folklore Forum* 31: 71–72.

Gramsci, Antonio. 1999. "Observations on Folklore." In *International Folkloristics: Classic Contributions by the Founders of Folklore*, ed. Alan Dundes, 131–36. Lanham, MD: Rowman & Littlefield.

Grasso, Glenn, ed. 1998. *Songs of the Sailor: Working Chanteys at Mystic Seaport*. Mystic, CT: Mystic Seaport.

Graves, James Bau. 2005. *Cultural Democracy: The Arts, Community, and the Public Purpose*. Urbana: University of Illinois Press.

Green, Thomas A., ed. 2006. *The Greenwood Library of American Folktales*, 4 vols. Westport, CT: Greenwood Press.

Greenhill, Pauline, and Kendra Magnusson. 2010. "'Your Presence at Our Wedding is Present Enough': Lies, Coding, Maintaining Personal Face, and the Cash Gift." *Journal of Folklore Research* 47: 307–33.

Gregory, George C. 1936. "Log Houses of Jamestown, 1607." *Virginia Magazine of History and Biography* 44: 287–95.

Grider, Sylvia. 1995. "Passed Down from Generation to Generation: Folklore and Teaching." *Journal of American Folklore* 108: 178–85.

Grier, Katherine C. 2006. *Pets in America: A History*. Chapel Hill: University of North Carolina Press.

Groce, Nancy. 2010. *Lox, Stocks, and Backstage Broadway: Iconic Trades of New York City*. Washington, DC: Smithsonian Institution Scholarly Press.

Groome, F. Hindes. 1892. "The Influence of the Gypsies on the Superstitions of the English Folk." In *The International Folk-Lore Congress 1891: Papers and Transactions*, ed. Joseph Jacobs and Alfred Nutt, 292–308. London: David Nutt.

Gross, David. 1992. *The Past in Ruins: Tradition and the Critique of Modernity*. Amherst: University of Massachusetts Press.

Gura, Philip F., and James F. Bollman. 1989. *America's Instrument: The Banjo in the Nineteenth Century*. Chapel Hill: University of North Carolina Press.

Gurak, Laura J. 2001. *Cyberliteracy: Navigating the Internet with Awareness*. New Haven, CT: Yale University Press.

Hallowell, A. Irving. 1965. "The Backwash of the Frontier: The Impact of the Indian on American Culture." In *The Frontier in Perspective*, ed. Walker D. Wyman and Clifton B. Kroeber, 229–58. Madison: University of Wisconsin Press.

Hamon, Raeann R., and Bron B. Ingoldsby, eds. 2003. *Mate Selection Across Cultures*. Thousand Oaks, CA: Sage.

Hand, Wayland D., ed. 1952. *The Frank C. Brown Collection of North Carolina Folklore. Volume VI and VII: Superstitions from North Carolina*. Durham, NC: Duke University Press.

Handler, Richard. 1988. *Nationalism and the Politics of Culture in Quebec*. Madison: University of Wisconsin Press.

Hannum, Hurst. 1990. *Autonomy, Sovereignty, and Self-Determination: The Accommodation of Conflicting Rights*. Philadelphia: University of Pennsylvania Press.

Hansen, Gregory. 2009. "Public Folklore in Cyberspace." In *Folklore and the Internet: Vernacular Expression in a Digital World*, ed. Trevor J. Blank, 194–212. Logan: Utah State University Press.

Harlow, Ilana. 1997. "Creating Situations: Practical Jokes and the Revival of the Dead in Irish Tradition." *Journal of American Folklore* 110: 140–68.

Harmon, Mamie. 1949. "Folklore." In *Funk & Wagnalls Standard Dictionary of Folklore, Mythology, and Legend*, 2 vols., ed. Maria Leach, 399–400. New York: Funk & Wagnalls.

Hartland, Edwin Sidney. 1885. "The Science of Folklore." *Folk-Lore Journal* 3: 115–21.

———. 1891. *The Science of Fairy Tales: An Inquiry into Fairy Mythology*. London: Walter Scott.

———. 1894–1896. *The Legend of Perseus: A Study of Tradition in Story, Custom, and Belief*. London: D. Nutt.

———. 1899. *Folklore: What Is It and What Is the Good of It?* London: David Nutt.

———. 1968 [1899]. "Folklore: What Is It and What Is the Good of It?" In *Peasant Customs and Savage Myths: Selections from the British Folklorists*, ed. Richard M. Dorson, vol. 1: 230–51. Chicago: University of Chicago Press.

Hawley, James P. 1980. "Antonio Gramsci's Marxism: Class, State and Work." *Social Problems* 27: 584–600.

Headland, Thomas N., Kenneth L. Pike, and Marvin Harris, eds. 1990. *Emics and Etics: The Insider/Outsider Debate*. Newbury Park, CA: Sage.

Hearne, Betsy. 1988. "Booking the Brothers Grimm: Art, Adaptations, and Economics." In *The Brothers Grimm and Folktale*, ed. James M. McGlathery, 220–34. Urbana: University of Illinois Press.

Heilman, Samuel C. 1992. *Defenders of the Faith: Inside Ultra-Orthodox Jewry*. New York: Schocken.

Henningsen, Henning. 1961. *Crossing the Equator: Sailors' Baptism and Other Initiation Rites*. Cophenhagen: Munksgaard.

Historical Society of Pennsylvania. 2009. *PhilaPlace*. Available at: www.philaplace.org/

Hobsbawm, Eric. 1983. "Introduction: Inventing Traditions." In *The Invention of Tradition*, ed. Eric Hobsbawm and Terence Ranger, 1–14. Cambridge: Cambridge University Press.

———, and Terence Ranger, eds. 1983. *The Invention of Tradition*. Cambridge: Cambridge University Press.

Hoffmann, Frank. 1973. *Analytical Survey of Anglo-American Traditional Erotica*. Bowling Green, OH: Bowling Green State University Popular Press.

Hollis, Susan T., Linda Pershing, and M. Jane Young, eds. 1993. *Feminist Theory and the Study of Folklore*. Urbana: University of Illinois Press.

Holloway, Karla F.C. 1987. *The Character of the Word: The Texts of Zora Neale Hurston*. Westport, CT: Greenwood.

Homans, George C. 1941. "Anxiety and Ritual: The Theories of Malinowski and Radcliffe-Brown." *American Anthropologist* 43: 164–72.

Honko, Lauri, ed. 2000. *Textualization of Oral Epics*. Berlin: Mouton de Gruyter.

——. 2013a. "Folkloristic Studies on Meaning: An Introduction." In *Theoretical Milestones: Selected Writings of Lauri Honko*, ed. Pekka Hakamies and Anneli Honko, 81–103. Helsinki: Suomalainen Tiedeakatemia, Academia Scientiarum Fennica.

——. 2013b. "The Folklore Process." In *Theoretical Milestones: Selected Writings of Lauri Honko*, ed. Pekka Hakamies and Anneli Honko, 29–54. Helsinki: Suomalainen Tiedeakatemia, Academia Scientiarum Fennica.

Horn, James. 2010. *A Kingdom Strange: The Brief and Tragic History of the Lost Colony of Roanoke*. New York: Basic Books.

Howard, Robert Glenn. 2005. "Toward a Theory of the World Wide Web Vernacular: The Case for Pet Cloning." *Journal of Folklore Research* 42: 323–60.

——. 2008. "Electronic Hybridity: The Persistent Processes of the Vernacular Web." *Journal of American Folklore* 121: 192–218.

——. 2015. "Why Digital Network Hybridity is the New Normal (Hey! Check This Stuff Out)." *Journal of American Folklore* 128: 247–59.

Howell, Benita J. 1994. "Folklife, Cultural Conservation, and Environmental Planning." In *Putting Folklore to Use*, ed. Michael Owen Jones, 94–114. Lexington: University Press of Kentucky.

Hufford, David. 1971. "Some Approaches to the Application of Folklore Studies." In *Papers on Applied Folklore*, Dick Sweterlitsch, 6–9. Bloomington, IN: Folklore Forum Bibliographic and Special Series No. 8.

——. 1982. *The Terror that Comes in the Night: An Experience-Centered Study of Supernatural Assault Traditions*. Philadelphia: University of Pennsylvania Press.

——. 1998. "Folklore Studies Applied to Health." *Journal of Folklore Research* 35: 295–313.

——. 1999. "Working in the Cracks: Public Space, Ecological Crisis, and the Folklorist." *Journal of Folklore Research* 36: 157–67.

Hufford, Mary. 2002. "American Folklife: A Commonwealth of Cultures." In *Folk Nation: Folklore in the Creation of American Tradition*, ed. Simon J. Bronner, 237–48. Wilmington, DE: SR Books.

——. 2003. "Context." In *Eight Words for the Study of Expressive Culture*, ed. Burt Feintuch, 146–75. Urbana: University of Illinois Press.

——, Marjorie Hunt, and Steven J. Zeitlin. *The Grand Generation: Memory, Mastery, Legacy*. Seattle: University of Washington Press.

Hurston, Zora Neale. 1935. *Mules and Men*. Philadelphia, PA: Lippincott.

Hutchings, Tim. 2007. "Creating Church Online: A Case-Study Approach to Religious Experience." *Studies in World Christianity* 13: 243–60.

Hymes, Dell. 1962. "The Ethnography of Speaking." In *Anthropology and Human Behavior*, ed. Thomas Gladwin and William C. Sturtevant, 13–53. Washington, DC: Anthropological Society of Washington.

——. 1964. "Introduction: Toward Ethnographies of Communication." *American Anthropologist* 66: 1–34.

———. 1971. "Sociolinguistics and Ethnography of Speaking." In *Social Anthropology and Language*, ed. Edwin Ardener, 41–93. London: Tavistock.

———. 1972. "The Contribution of Folklore to Sociolinguistic Research." In *Toward New Perspectives in Folklore*, ed. Américo Paredes and Richard Bauman, 42–50. Austin: University of Texas Press.

Irvine, Leslie. 2004. *If You Tame Me: Understanding Our Connection with Animals*. Philadelphia, PA: Temple University Press.

Ivey, Bill. 2008. *Arts, Inc.: How Greed and Neglect Have Destroyed Our Cultural Rights*. Berkeley: University of California Press.

Jackson, Bruce. 1974. *Get Your Ass in the Water and Swim Like Me: Narrative Poetry from Black Oral Tradition*. Cambridge, MA: Harvard University Press.

———, ed. 1984. *Teaching Folklore*. Buffalo, NY: Documentary Research.

———. 1987. *Fieldwork*. Urbana: University of Illinois Press.

———, and Edward Ives, eds. 1996. *The World Observed: Reflections on the Fieldwork Process*. Urbana: University of Illinois Press.

Jacobs, Joseph. 1892. "The Science of Folk-Tales and the Problem of Diffusion." In *The International Folk-Lore Congress 1891: Papers and Transactions*, ed. Joseph Jacobs and Alfred Nutt, 76–102. London: David Nutt.

———. 1893. "The Folk." *Folk-Lore* 4: 233–38.

———. 1896. *Jewish Ideals, and Other Essays*. London: David Nutt.

———, and Alfred Nutt, eds. 1892. *The International Folk-Lore Congress 1891: Papers and Transactions*. London: David Nutt.

Jacobs, Marc. 2014. "Cultural Brokerage: Addressing Boundaries and the New Paradigm of Safeguarding Intangible Cultural Heritage, Folklore Studies, Transdisciplinary Perspectives and UNESCO." *Volkskunde* 3: 265–91.

———, Jorijn Neyrinck, and Albert van der Zeijden. 2014. "UNESCO, Brokers and Critical Success (F)Actors in Safeguarding Intangible Cultural Heritage." *Volkskunde* 3: 249–56.

Jacobsen, Johanna Micaela. 2001. "Creating Disciplinary Identities: The Professionalization of Swedish Folklife Studies." *Folklore Historian* 18: 3–16.

Jansen, William Hugh. 1959. "The Esoteric-Exoteric Factor in Folklore." *Fabula* 2: 205–11.

Jason, Heda, and Dimitri Segal, eds. 1977. *Patterns in Oral Literature*. The Hague: Mouton.

Jemie, Onwuchekwa, ed. 2003. *Yo' Mama! New Raps, Toasts, Dozens, Jokes and Children's Rhymes from Urban Black America*. Philadelphia, PA: Temple University Press.

Jenkins, Henry. 2006. *Convergence Culture: Where Old and New Media Collide*. New York: New York University Press.

Jensen, Minna Skafte. 1980. *The Homeric Question and the Oral-Formulaic Theory*. Copenhagen: Museum Tusculanum Press.

Johnson, F. Roy, and Thomas C. Parramore. 1983. *The Lost Colony in Fact and Legend.* Murfreesboro, NC: Johnson.

Jones, Gayl. 1991. *Liberating Voices: Oral Tradition in African American Literature.* Cambridge, MA: Harvard University Press.

Jones, Michael Owen. 1989. *Craftsman of the Cumberlands: Tradition and Creativity.* Lexington: University Press of Kentucky.

———. 1994. "Applying Folklore Studies: An Introduction." In *Putting Folklore to Use,* ed. Michael Owen Jones, 1–44. Lexington: University Press of Kentucky.

———. 1995. "Why Make (Folk) Art?" *Western Folklore* 54: 253–76.

———. 1997a. "Applied Folklore/Folkloristics." In *Folklore: An Encyclopedia of Beliefs, Customs, Tales, Music, and Art,* ed. Thomas A. Green, 30–36. Santa Barbara: ABC-CLIO.

———. 1997b. "How Can We Apply Event Analysis to Material Behavior, and Why Should We?" *Western Folklore* 56: 199–214.

———. 2000. "'Tradition' in Identity Discourses and an Individual's Symbolic Construction of Self." *Western Folklore* 59: 115–42.

———, Michael Moore, and Richard Snyder, eds. 1988. *Inside Organizations: Understanding the Human Dimension.* Newbury Park, CA: Sage.

Jones, Ricky L. 2015. *Black Haze: Violence, Sacrifice, and Manhood in Black Greek-Letter Fraternities. Second Edition.* Albany: State University of New York Press.

Jones, Steven Swann. 1990. *The New Comparative Method: Structural and Symbolic Analysis of the Allomotifs of Snow White.* Helsinki: Suomalainen Tiedeakatemia, Academica Scientiarum Fennica.

Jordan, Terry G. 1985. *American Log Buildings: An Old World Heritage.* Chapel Hill: University of North Carolina Press.

Jordan-Smith, Paul, and Laurel Horton. 2001. "Guest Editors' Introduction: Communities of Practice: Traditional Music and Dance." *Western Folklore* 60: 103–9.

Kamenetsky, Christa. 1992. *The Brothers Grimm and Their Critics: Folktales and the Quest for Meaning.* Athens: Ohio University Press.

Kammen, Carol. 1999. "On Doing Local History: The Underground Railroad and Local History." *History News* 54 (2): 3–4.

Kapchan, Deborah. 1993. "Hybridization and the Marketplace: Emerging Paradigms in Folkloristics." *Western Folklore* 52: 303–26.

———. 2003. "Performance." In *Eight Words for the Study of Expressive Culture,* ed. Burt Feintuch, 121–45. Urbana: University of Illinois Press.

———, and Pauline Turner Strong. 1999. "Theorizing the Hybrid." *Journal of American Folklore* 112: 239–53.

Ketner, Kenneth Laine. 1971. "Superstitious Pigeons, Hydrophobia, and Conventional Wisdom." *Western Folklore* 30: 1–17.

——. 1973. "The Role of Hypotheses in Folkloristics." *Journal of American Folklore* 86: 114–30.

——. 1975. "Hypotheses Fingo." *Journal of American Folklore* 88: 411–17.

——. 1976. "Identity and Existence in the Study of Human Traditions." *Folklore* 87: 192–200.

Kim, Kwang-Ki. 2002. *Order and Agency in Modernity: Talcott Parsons, Erving Goffman, and Harold Garfinkel.* Albany: State University of New York Press.

Kimmel, Michael S. 2000. *The Gendered Society.* New York: Oxford University Press.

Kinsella, Michael. 2011. *Legend-Tripping Online: Supernatural Folklore and the Search for Ong's Hat.* Jackson: University Press of Mississippi.

Kirkland, Edwin C. 1973. "A Projected Bibliography of the Folklore of India." In *Folklore Research Around the World: A North American Point of View*, ed. Richard M. Dorson, 127–32. Port Washington, NY: Kennikat Press.

Kirshenblatt-Gimblett, Barbara. 1988. "Mistaken Dichotomies." *Journal of American Folklore* 101: 140–55.

Klotilatviešu Folkloras Krātuve. 2015. *Latviešu Folkloras Krātuves Digitālais Arhīvs* [Latvian Folklore Archives]. Available at: http://garamantas.lv/

Klotiņš, Arnolds. 2002. "The Latvian Neo-Folklore Movement and the Political Changes of the Late 20th Century." *World of Music* 44: 107–30.

Kluckhohn, Clyde. 1943. "Bronislaw Malinowski, 1884–1942." *Journal of American Folklore* 56: 208–19.

Knapp, Mary, and Herbert Knapp. 1978. *One Potato, Two Potato: The Folklore of American Children.* New York: W. W. Norton.

Kniffen, Fred B. 1965. "Folk Housing: Key to Diffusion." *Annals of the Association of American Geographers* 55: 549–77.

——, and Henry Glassie. 1966. "Building in Wood in the Eastern United States: A Time-Place Perspective." *Geographical Review* 56: 40–66.

Knight, Douglas A. 2006. *Rediscovering the Traditions of Israel.* 3rd ed. Atlanta, GA: Society of Biblical Literature.

Kodish, Debora. 2011. "Envisioning Folklore Activism." *Journal of American Folklore* 124: 31–60.

Köpping, Klaus-Peter. 1983. *Adolf Bastian and the Psychic Unity of Mankind: The Foundations of Anthropology in Nineteenth Century Germany.* St Lucia: University of Queensland Press.

Kotthoff, Helga. 2013. "Comparing Drinking Toasts—Comparing Contexts." In *Culinary Linguistics: The Chef's Special*, ed. Cornelia Gerhardt, Maximiliane Frobenius, and Susanne Ley, 211–40. Amsterdam: John Benjamins.

Kraybill, Donald B. 1989. *The Riddle of Amish Culture.* Baltimore. MD: Johns Hopkins University Press.

Kristeller, Paul Oskar. 1983. "'Creativity' and 'Tradition.'" *Journal of the History of Ideas* 44: 105–14.

Krohn, Kaarle. 1971. *Folklore Methodology*, trans. Roger L. Welsch. Austin: University of Texas Press.

Kurin, Richard. 1997. *Reflections of a Culture Broker: A View from the Smithsonian.* Washington, DC: Smithsonian Institution Press.

———. 1998. *Smithsonian Folklife Festival: Culture Of, By, and For the People.* Washington, D.C.: Smithsonian Institution.

———. 2002. "Folklife in Contemporary Multicultural Society." In *Folk Nation: Folklore in the Creation of American Tradition*, ed. Simon J. Bronner, 249–64. Wilmington, DE: SR Books.

Lach, Donald F. 1977. *Asia in the Making of Europe.* Vol. II, *A Century of Wonder. Book Two: The Literary Arts.* Chicago: University of Chicago Press.

Lang, Andrew. 1893. *Custom and Myth.* London: Longmans Green.

Latviešu Folkloras Krātuve 2015. "Digital Archives of Latvian Folklore." *Archives of Latvian Folklore* (ALF). Available at: http://folklore.lv/en.

Laver, John. 1975. "Communicative Functions of Phatic Communion." In *Organization of Behavior in Face-to-Face Interaction,* ed. Adam Kendon, Richard M. Harris, and Mary Ritchie Key, 215–40. The Hague: Mouton.

Lawless, Elaine J. 1997. Weaving Narrative Texts: The Artistry of Women's Sermons." *Journal of Folklore Research* 34: 15–43.

Leach, Edmund. 1968. "Myth as Justification for Faction and Social Change." In *Studies on Mythology*, ed. Robert Georges, 184–98. Homewood, IL: Dorsey Press.

Leach, MacEdward. 1966. "Folklore in American Regional Literature." *Journal of the Folklore Institute* 3: 376–97.

Leach, Maria, ed. 1949. *Funk & Wagnalls Standard Dictionary of Folklore, Mythology, and Legend.* New York: Funk & Wagnalls.

Lears, T. J. Jackson. 1985. "The Concept of Cultural Hegemony: Problems and Possibilities." *American Historical Review* 90: 567–93.

Lee, Robert G. 1999. *Orientals: Asian Americans in Popular Culture.* Philadelphia, PA: Temple University Press.

Legman, G. 1968. *Rationale of the Dirty Joke: An Analysis of Sexual Humor.* New York: Grove.

Lévi-Strauss, Claude. 1955. "The Structural Study of Myth." *Journal of American Folklore* 68: 428–44.

———. 1963. *Structural Anthropology*, trans. Claire Jacobson and Brooke Grundfest Schoepf. New York: Basic Books.

Lewin, Philip Michael. 1991. "Persons, Discursive Practices, Traditions." *Soundings* 74: 459–83.

Limón, José. 1983. "Western Marxism and Folklore: A Critical Introduction." *Journal of American Folklore* 96: 34–52.

———. 2010. "Breaking with Gramsci: Gencarella on Good Sense and Critical Folklore Studies." *Journal of Folklore Research* 47: 253–57.

Lindahl, Carl. 1996. "Bakhtin's Carnival Laughter and the Cajun Country Mardi Gras." *Folklore* 107: 57–70.

———, ed. 2004. *American Folktales from the Collections of the Library of Congress.* Armonk, NY: M.E. Sharpe.

———, Maida Owens, and C. Renée Harrison, eds. 1971. *Swapping Stories: Folktales from Louisiana.* Jackson: University Press of Mississippi.

Linn, Karen. 1991. *The Half-Barbaric Twang: The Banjo in American Popular Culture.* Urbana: University of Illinois Press.

Lockhart, Betty Ann. 2008. *Maple Sugarin' in Vermont: A Sweet History.* Charleston, VA: History Press.

Lomax, Alan. 2003. *Alan Lomax: Selected Writings, 1934–1997*, ed. Ronald D. Cohen. New York: Routledge.

Loomis, Ormond. 1983. *Cultural Conservation: The Protection of Cultural Heritage in the United States.* Washington, DC: Library of Congress.

Lord, Albert. 1960. *The Singer of Tales.* Cambridge, MA: Harvard University Press.

Lunsing, Wim. 2003. "Islam versus Homosexuality? Some Reflections on the Assassination of Pim Fortuyn." *Anthropology Today* 19: 19–21.

Lyons, John. 1968. *Introduction to Theoretical Linguistics.* Cambridge: Cambridge University Press.

Mahner, Martin, and Mario Bunge. 2001. "Function and Functionalism: A Synthetic Perspective." *Philosophy of Science* 68: 75–94.

Malinowski, Bronislaw. 1918. "Fishing and Fishing Magic in the Trobriand Islands." *Man* 18: 87–92.

———. 1926. "Anthropology." *Encyclopedia Britannica*, 13th ed., suppl. 1, pp. 131–40. London.

———. 2002. *A Scientific Theory of Culture, and Other Essays.* 1944 rpt. London: Routledge.

Maranda, Pierre, and Elli Köngäs Maranda, eds. 1971. *Structural Analysis of Oral Tradition.* Philadelphia: University of Pennsylvania Press.

Margry, Peter Jan. 2003. "The Murder of Pim Fortuyn and Collective Emotions: Hype, Hysteria and Holiness in The Netherlands?" *Etnofoor* 16: 106–31.

Marsh, Kathryn. 2008. *The Musical Playground: Global Tradition and Change in Children's Songs and Games.* Oxford: Oxford University Press.

Marsh, Moira. 2015. *Practically Joking.* Logan: Utah State University Press.

Marshall, Howard Wight. 1977. "Folklife and the Rise of American Folk Museums." *Journal of American Folklore* 90: 391–413.

Mazo, Jeffrey Alan. 1996. "A Good Saxon Compound." *Folklore* 107: 107–8.

McCarl, Robert. 1985. *The District of Columbia Fire Fighters' Project: A Case Study in Occupational Folklife.* Washington, DC: Smithsonian Institution Press.

McCarthy, William Bernard. 2000. "Richard Dorson in Upper Michigan." *Folklore Historian* 17: 23–33.

McDonald, Barry. 1997. "Tradition as Personal Relationship." *Journal of American Folklore* 110: 47–67.

McKenna, Robert. 2005. *Bottoms Up! Toasts, Tales and Traditions of Drinking's Long History as a Nautical Pastime.* Mystic, CT: Flat Hammock Press.

Mechling, Jay. 1983. "Mind, Messages, and Madness: Gregory Bateson Makes a Paradigm for American Culture Studies." In *Prospects 8: An Annual Review of American Cultural Studies*, ed. Jack Salzman, 11–30. New York: Cambridge University Press.

———. 1989a. "An American Culture Grid, with Texts." *American Studies International* 27: 2–12.

———. 1989b. "'Banana Cannon' and Other Folk Traditions between Human and Nonhuman Animals." *Western Folklore* 48: 312–23.

———. 1989c. "The Collecting Self and American Youth Movements." In *Consuming Visions: Accumulation and Display of Goods in America, 1880–1920*, ed. Simon J. Bronner, 255–85. New York: W. W. Norton.

———. 1993. "On Sharing Folklore and American Identity in a Multicultural Society." *Western Folklore* 52: 271–89.

———. 1999. "Children's Folklore in Residential Institutions: Summer Camps, Boarding Schools, Hospitals, and Custodial Facilities." In *Children's Folklore: A Source Book*, ed. Brian Sutton-Smith, Jay Mechling, Thomas W. Johnson, and Felicia R. McMahon, 273–92. Logan: Utah State University Press.

———. 2002. "Children and Colors: Folk and Popular Cultures in America's Future." In *Folk Nation: Folklore in the Creation of American Tradition*, ed. Simon J. Bronner, 265–83. Wilmington, DE: SR Books.

———. 2004. "Picturing Hunting." *Western Folklore* 63: 51–78.

———. 2005. "The Folklore of Mother-Raised Boys." In *Manly Traditions: The Folk Roots of American Masculinities*, ed. Simon J. Bronner, 211–27. Bloomington: Indiana University Press.

———. 2006. "Solo Folklore." *Western Folklore* 65: 435–54.

———. 2008. "Gun Play." *American Journal of Play* 1: 192–209.

———. 2009. "Is Hazing Play?" In *Transactions at Play*, ed. Cindy Dell Clark, 45–62. Lanham, MD: University Press of America.

———, and Elizabeth Mechling. 1985. "Shock Talk: From Consensual to Contractual Joking Relationships in the Bureaucratic Workplace." *Human Organization* 44: 339–43.

Meder, Theo, ed. 2001. *"Er waren een marokkaan, een Turk en een Nederlander…": Volkskundige en taalkundige opstellen over het vertellen van moppen in de multiculturele wijk Lombok.* Amsterdam: Stichting beheer IISG.

———. 2008. *The Flying Dutchman, and Other Folktales from the Netherlands*. Westport, CT: Libraries Unlimited.

———. 2009. "They Are Among Us and They Are Against Us: Contemporary Horror Stories about Muslims and Immigrants in the Netherlands." *Western Folklore* 68: 257–74.

Meyer, John C. 2015. *Understanding Humor Through Communication: Why Be Funny, Anyway?* Lanham, MD: Lexington Books.

Michelsen, Peter. 1966. "The Origin and Aim of the Open-Air Museum." In *Dansk Folkemuseum & Frilandsmuseet: History & Activities*, ed. Holger Rasmussen, 227–43. Copenhagen: Nationalmuseet.

Mieder, Wolfgang. 1986. *The Prentice-Hall Encyclopedia of World Proverbs*. New York: MJF Books.

———. 1989. *American Proverbs: A Study of Texts and Contexts*.

———. 1992. "Paremiological Minimum and Cultural Literacy." In *Creativity and Tradition in Folklore: New Directions*, ed. Simon J. Bronner, 185–204. Logan: Utah State University Press.

———. 1993. *Proverbs are Never Out of Season: Popular Wisdom in the Modern Age*. New York: Oxford University Press.

———. 2004. *Proverbs: A Handbook*. Westport, CT: Greenwood Press.

———. 2012. "'Think Outside the Box': Origin, Nature, and Meaning of Modern Anglo-American Proverbs." *Proverbium* 29: 137–96.

Miller, Karl Hagstrom. 2010. *Segregating Sound: Inventing Folk and Pop Music in the Age of Jim Crow*. Durham, NC: Duke University Press.

Milligan, Amy. 2010. "Prost! German Drinking Etiquette at an American *Stammtisch*." Unpublished manuscript (April 29). Simon Bronner Archives, Penn State Harrisburg, April 29.

Milner, G. G. 1969. "Quadripartite Structures." *Proverbium* 14: 379–83.

Mintz, Jerome R. 1992. *Hasidic People: A Place in the New World*. Cambridge, MA: Harvard University Press.

Mintz, Lawrence E. 1999. "American Humor as Unifying and Divisive." *Humor* 12: 237–52.

Mitchell, Carol. 1977. "The Sexual Perspective in the Appreciation of Jokes." *Western Folklore* 36: 303–29.

———. 1978. "Hostility and Aggression toward Males in Female Joke Telling." *Frontiers* 3: 19–23.

———. 1985. "Some Differences in Male and Female Joke-Telling." In *Women's Folklore, Women's Culture*, ed. Rosan A. Jordan and Susan J. Kalčik, 163–86. Philadelphia: University of Pennsylvania Press.

Moody-Turner, Shirley. 2013. *Black Folklore and the Politics of Racial Representation*. Jackson: University Press of Mississippi.

Morris, Henry. 1938. "Irish Wake Games." *Béaloideas* 8: 123–41.

Morse, Ronald A. 1990. *Yanagita Kunio and the Folklore Movement: The Search for Japan's National Character and Distinctiveness*. New York: Garland.

Mortensen, Camilla H. 2005. "(Eco)Mimesis and the Ethics of the Ethnographic Presentation." *Journal of American Folklore* 118: 105–20.

Mullen, Patrick B. 1969. "The Function of Magic Folk Belief among Texas Coastal Fishermen." *Journal of American Folklore* 82: 214–25.

———. 1992. *Listening to Old Voices: Folklore, Life Stories, and the Elderly*. Urbana: University of Illinois Press.

———. 2000. "Collaborative Research Reconsidered." *Journal of Folklore Research* 37: 207–14.

———. 2008. *The Man Who Adores the Negro: Race and American Folklore*. Urbana: University of Illinois Press.

Naithani, Sadhana. 1997. "The Colonizer-Folklorist." *Journal of Folklore Research* 34: 1–14.

———. 2002. "To Tell a Tale Untold: Two Folklorists in Colonial India." *Journal of Folklore Research* 39: 201–16.

———. 2004. "The Teacher and the Taught: Structures and Meaning in the 'Arabian Nights' and the 'Panchatantra.'" *Marvels & Tales* 18: 272–85.

Nájera-Ramírez, Olga. 1999. "Of Fieldwork, Folklore, and Festival: Personal Encounters." *Journal of American Folklore* 112: 183–99.

Nakashima, Douglas, and Marie Roué. 2002. "Indigenous Knowledge, Peoples and Sustainable Practice." In *Encyclopedia of Global Environmental Change: Vol. 5, Social and Economic Dimensions of Global Environmental Change*, ed. Peter Timmerman, 314–24. New York: John Wiley & Sons, Inc.

Narváez, Peter. 1994. "'Tricks and Fun': Subversive Pleasures at Newfoundland Wakes." *Western Folklore* 53: 263–93.

———, and Martin Laba, eds. 1986. *Media Sense: The Folklore-Popular Culture Continuum*. Bowling Green, OH: Bowling Green State University Popular Press.

Nas, Peter J. M., and Anja Roymans. 1998. "Reminiscences of the Relief of Leiden: A Total Ritual Event." *International Journal of Urban and Regional Research* 22: 550–64.

NCTA (National Council for the Traditional Arts). 2015. "Mission/Major Programs." *National Council for the Traditional Arts* website. Available at: http://ncta-usa.org/mission/

Negrón-Muntaner, Frances, and Ramón Grosfoguel. 1997. *Puerto Rican Jam: Rethinking Colonialism and Nationalism*. Minneapolis: University of Minnesota Press.

Neustadt, Kathy. 1992. *Clambake: A History and Celebration of an American Tradition*. Amherst: University of Massachusetts Press.

Newall, Venetia. 1986. "Folklore and Male Homosexuality." *Folklore* 97: 123–47.

Newell, W. W. 1895. "Theories of Diffusion of Folk-Tales." *Journal of American Folklore* 8: 7–18.

Nickerson, Bruce E. 1974. "Is There a Folk in the Factory?" *Journal of American Folklore* 87: 133–39.

Nicolaisen, W.F.H. 1980. "Variant, Dialect and Region: An Exploration in the Geography of Tradition." *New York Folklore* 6: 137–49.

———. 1984. "Names and Narratives." *Journal of American Folklore* 97: 259–72.

———. 1990. "Why Tell Stories?" *Fabula* 31: 5–10.

———. 2006. "Cultural Register." In *Encyclopedia of American Folklife*, ed. Simon J. Bronner, 255. Armonk, NY: M. E. Sharpe.

Niehaus, Isak, and Jonathan Stadler. 2004. "Muchongolo Dance Contests: Deep Play in the South African Lowveld." *Ethnology* 43: 363–80.

Niles, John D. 1999. *Homo Narrans: The Poetics and Anthropology of Oral Literature.* Philadelphia: University of Pennsylvania Press.

Njoku, J. Akuma-Kalu. 2012. "Establishing Igbo Community Tradition in the United States: Lessons from Folkloristics." *Journal of American Folklore* 125: 327–42.

Noble, Allen G. 1984. *Wood, Brick, and Stone: The North American Settlement Landscape.* Amherst: University of Massachusetts Press.

Norkunas, Martha. 2004. "Narratives of Resistance and the Consequences of Resistance." *Journal of Folklore Research* 41: 105–23.

Norrick, Neal R. 1985. *How Proverbs Mean: Semantic Studies in English Proverbs.* Berlin: Mouton.

Norsk Folkemuseum. 1929. *Norsk Folkemuseum: A Short Guide with Plan.* Oslo: Norsk Folkemuseum.

Noyes, Dorothy. 2003. "Group." In *Eight Words for the Study of Expressive Culture*, ed. Burt Feintuch, 7–41. Urbana: University of Illinois Press.

———. 2009. "Tradition: Three Traditions." *Journal of Folklore Research* 46: 233–68.

Nuwer, Hank, ed. 2004. *The Hazing Reader.* Bloomington: Indiana University Press.

Ochs, Vanessa. 2011. "Same-Sex Marriage Ceremonies in a Time of Coalescence." In *Revisioning Ritual: Traditions in Transition*, ed. Simon J. Bronner, 190–210. Oxford: Littman.

Oinas, Felix J. 1973. "Folklore Activities in Russia." In *Folklore Research Around the World: A North American Point of View.* Port Washington, NY: Kennikat Press.

———. 1975. "The Political Uses and Themes of Folklore in the Soviet Union." *Journal of the Folklore Institute* 12: 157–75.

———, and Stephen Soudakoff, eds. and trans. 1975. *The Study of Russian Folklore.* The Hague: Mouton.

Oliver, Paul. 1969. *The Story of the Blues.* Philadelphia, PA: Chilton.

Opie, Iona, and Peter Opie. 1969. *Children's Games in Street and Playground.* Oxford: Oxford University Press.

———. 1985. *The Singing Game.* Oxford: Oxford University Press.

Oring, Elliott. 1975. "Everything Is a Shade of Elephant: An Alternative to a Psychoanalysis of Humor." *New York Folklore* 1: 149–60.

———. 1976. "Three Functions of Folklore: Traditional Functionalism as Explanation in Folkloristics." *Journal of American Folklore* 89: 67–80.

———. 1978. "Transmission and Degeneration." *Fabula* 19: 193–210.

———. 1986. "On the Concepts of Folklore." In *Folk Groups and Folklore Genres,* ed. Elliott Oring, 1–22. Logan: Utah State University Press.

———. 1987. "Jokes and the Discourse on Disaster." *Journal of American Folklore* 100: 276–86.

———. 1989. "Documenting Folklore: The Annotation." In *Folk Groups and Folklore Genres: A Reader,* ed. Elliott Oring, 358–73. Logan: Utah State University Press.

———. 1992. *Jokes and Their Relations.* Lexington: University Press of Kentucky.

———. 1996. "Folklorizing Theory." *Folklore Historian* 13: 30–32.

———. 2003. *Engaging Humor.* Urbana: University of Illinois Press.

———. 2004. "Risky Business: Political Jokes Under Repressive Regimes." *Western Folklore* 63: 209–36.

———. 2006a. "Folk or Lore? The Stake in Dichotomies." *Journal of Folklore Research* 43: 205–18.

———. 2006b. "Missing Theory." *Western Folklore* 65: 455–65.

———. 2008. "Legendry and the Rhetoric of Truth." *Journal of American Folklore* 121: 127–66.

———. 2014. "Memetics and Folkloristics: The Theory." *Western Folklore* 73: 432–54.

Ortiz, Carmen. 1999. "The Uses of Folklore by the Franco Regime." *Journal of American Folklore* 112: 479–96.

Owen, Trefor M. 1991. *The Customs and Traditions of Wales.* Cardiff: University of Wales Press.

Packard, Vance. 1972. *A Nation of Strangers.* New York: David McKay.

Page, Ruth, and Bronwen Thomas, eds. 2011. *New Narratives: Stories and Storytelling in the Digital Age.* Lincoln: University of Nebraska Press.

Paredes, Américo, and Richard Bauman, eds. 1972. *Toward New Perspectives in Folklore.* Austin: University of Texas Press.

———, and Ellen Jane Stekert, eds. 1971. *The Urban Experience and Folk Tradition.* Austin: University of Texas Press.

Parochetti, JoAnn Stephens. 1965. "Scary Stories from Purdue." *Keystone Folklore Quarterly* 10: 49–57.

Parry, Milman. 1971. *The Making of Homeric Verse: The Collected Papers of Milman Parry,* ed. Adam Parry. Oxford: Clarendon Press.

Parsons, Gerald E. 1991. "How the Yellow Ribbon Became a National Folk Symbol." *Folklife Center News* 13(3): 9–11. Available at: www.loc.gov/folk life/ribbons/ribbons.html

Pass, Forrest D. 2015. "Research Note: Material Culture and the Meaning of Rough Sports in Nineteenth-Century Canada: The Case of 'Champion Hecter.'" *Journal of Sport History* 42: 220–26.

Payne, Jessica M. 1998. "The Politicization of Culture in Applied Folklore." *Journal of Folklore Research* 35: 251–77.

Peck, Andrew. 2015. "Tall, Dark, and Loathsome: The Emergence of a Legend Cycle in the Digital Age." *Journal of American Folklore* 128: 333–48.

Pelikan, Jaroslav. 1984. *The Vindication of Tradition*. New Haven, CT: Yale University Press.

Pershing, Linda, and Margaret R. Yocom. 1996. "The Yellow Ribboning of the USA: Contested Meanings in the Construction of a Political Symbol." *Western Folklore* 55: 41–85.

Peterson, Elizabeth. 1996. *The Changing Face of Tradition: A Report on the Folk and Traditional Arts in the United States*. Washington, D.C.: National Endowment for the Arts.

Pocius, Gerald L. 1979. "Hooked Rugs in Newfoundland: The Representation of Social Structure in Design." *Journal of American Folklore* 92: 273–84.

Podruchny, Carolyn. 2006. *Making the Voyageur World: Travelers and Traders in the North American Fur Trade*. Lincoln: University of Nebraska Press.

Poggie, John J., Jr., Richard B. Pollnac, and Carl Gersuny. 1976. "Risk as a Basis for Taboos among Fishermen in Southern New England." *Journal for the Scientific Study of Religion* 15: 257–62.

Poindexter, Cynthia Cannon. 1997. "Sociopolitical Antecedents to Stonewall: Analysis of the Origins of the Gay Rights Movement in the United States." *Social Work* 42: 607–15.

Porter, David, ed. 1996. *Internet Culture*. New York: Routledge.

Prashad, Vijay. 2000. *The Karma of Brown Folk*. Minneapolis: University of Minnesota Press.

Preston, Michael J. 1994. "Traditional Humor from the Fax Machine: 'All of a Kind.'" *Western Folklore* 53: 147–69.

Propp, Vladimir. 1968. *Morphology of the Folktale*, trans. Svatava Pirkova-Jakobson. Austin: University of Texas Press.

Puckett, John L. 1989. *Foxfire Reconsidered: A Twenty-Year Experiment in Progressive Education*. Urbana: University of Illinois Press.

Radcliffe-Brown, A. R. 1935. "On the Concept of Function in Social Science." *American Anthropologist* 37: 394–402.

———. 1940. "On Joking Relationships." *Africa: Journal of the International African Institute* 13: 195–210.

——. 1952. *Structure and Function in Primitive Society: Essays and Addresses*. Glencoe, IL: Free Press.

——. 1968. "The Interpretation of Andamese Customs and Beliefs: Myths and Legends." In *Studies on Mythology*, ed. Robert Georges, 46–71. Homewood, IL: Dorsey Press.

Radner, Joan Newlon, ed. 1993. *Feminist Messages: Coding in Women's Folk Culture*. Urbana: University of Illinois Press.

Rahmonov, Ravshan, and Dishod Rakhimov. 2006. "Tajik." In *The Greenwood Encyclopedia of World Folklore and Folklife*, 4 vols., ed. William M. Clements, 2: 325–35. Westport, CT: Greenwood.

Rajan, Chandra. 1993. "Introduction." In *The Pañcatantra* by Viṣṇu Śarma, xv–lv. London: Penguin.

Randolph, Vance. 1951. *We Always Lie to Strangers: Tall Tales from the Ozarks*. New York: Columbia University Press.

Raspa, Richard. 2006. "Organizations, Corporate and Work." In *Encyclopedia of American Folklife*, ed. Simon J. Bronner, 921–24. Armonk, NY: M. E. Sharpe.

Reaver, J. Russell. 1972. "From Reality to Fantasy: Opening-Closing Formulas in the Structures of American Tall Tales." *Southern Folklore Quarterly* 36: 369–82.

Reed, Thomas. 2005. "A Qualitative Approach to Boys Rough and Tumble Play: There is More than Meets the Eye." In *Play: An Interdisciplinary Synthesis*, ed. F.F. McMahon, Donald E. Lytle, and Brian Sutton-Smith, 53–71. Lanham, MD: University Press of America.

Renteln, Alison Dundes. 2004. *The Cultural Defense*. New York: Oxford University Press.

——, and Alan Dundes, eds. 1995. *Folk Law: Essays in the Theory and Practice of Lex Non Scripta*. Madison: University of Wisconsin Press.

Richardson, Keith P. 1977. "Polliwogs and Shellbacks: An Analysis of the Equator Crossing Ritual." *Western Folklore* 36: 154–59.

Richmond, W. Edson. 1973. "The Study of Folklore in Finland." In *Folklore Research Around the World: A North American Point of View*, ed. Richard M. Dorson, 39–49. Port Washington, NY: Kennikat Press.

Rikoon, J. Sanford. 2004. "On the Politics of Origins: Social (In)Justice and the International Agenda on Intellectual Property, Traditional Knowledge, and Folklore." *Journal of American Folklore* 117: 325–36.

Rings, Lana. 1994. "Beyond Grammar and Vocabulary: German and American Differences in Routine Formulae and Small Talk." *Die Unterrichtspraxis/ Teaching German* 27: 23–28.

Roberts, Leonard W. 1955. *South from Hell-fer-Sartin: Kentucky Mountain Folk Tales*. Lexington: University of Kentucky Press.

Roberts, Warren E. 1958. *The Tale of the Kind and the Unkind Girls: Aa-Th 480 and Related Tales*. Berlin: De Gruyter.

Roediger, David R. 2001. "Critical Studies of Whiteness, USA: Origins and Arguments." *Theoria* 98: 72–98.

Roemer, Danielle. 1994. "Photocopy Lore and the Naturalization of the Corporate Body." *Journal of American Folklore* 107: 121–38.

Roginsky, Dina. 2007. "Folklore, Folklorism, and Synchronization: Preserved-Created Folklore in Israel." *Journal of Folklore Research* 44: 41–66.

Rölleke, Heinz. 1988. "New Research on *Grimms' Fairy Tales*." In *The Brothers Grimm and Folktale*, ed. James M. McGlathery, 101–11. Urbana: University of Illinois Press.

Rosenberg, Bruce A. 1970. *The Art of the American Folk Preacher*. New York: Oxford University Press.

Rosenberg, Neil V., and Charles K. Wolfe. 2007. *The Music of Bill Monroe*. Urbana: University of Illinois Press.

Ross, Edward Alsworth. 1909. *Social Psychology: An Outline and Source Book*. New York: Macmillan.

Roud, Steve. 2010. *The Lore of the Playground: One Hundred Years of Children's Games, Rhymes & Traditions*. London: Random House.

——. 2015. "Folk Song Index." *Vaughan Williams Memorial Library* website. Available at: www.vwml.org/search/search-roud-indexes

Rudd, Sarah M. 2002. "Harmonizing Corrido and Union Song at the Ludlow Massacre." *Western Folklore* 61: 21–42.

Russell, Ian. 2006. "Working with Tradition: Towards a Partnership Model of Fieldwork." *Folklore* 117: 15–32.

Sackett, S.J., and William E. Koch, eds. 1961. *Kansas Folklore*. Lincoln: University of Nebraska Press.

Said, Edward. 1978. *Orientalism*. New York: Vintage.

Samper, David. 2002. "Cannibalizing Kids: Rumor and Resistance in Latin America." *Journal of Folklore Research* 39: 1–32.

Samuelson, Sue. 1980. "The Cooties Complex." *Western Folklore* 39: 198–210.

——. 1983. "Notes on a Sociology of Folklore as a Science." *New York Folklore* 9: 13–20.

Sanders, Clinton R. 1999. *Understanding Dogs: Living and Working with Canine Companions*. Philadelphia: University of Pennsylvania Press.

Sandford, Sir D. K., Thomas Thomson, and Allan Cunningham. 1841. *The Popular Encyclopedia*, 7 vols. Edinburgh: Blackie & Son.

Santino, Jack. 1992. "Yellow Ribbons and Seasonal Flags: The Folk Assemblage of War." *Journal of American Folklore* 105: 19–33.

——. 2009. "The Ritualesque: Festival, Politics, and Popular Culture." *Western Folklore* 68: 9–26.

Satterwhite, Emily. 2005. "'That's What They're All Singing About': Appalachian Heritage, Celtic Pride, and American Nationalism at the 2003 Smithsonian Folklife Festival." *Appalachian Journal* 32: 302–38.

Scarborough, Dorothy. 1937. *A Song Catcher in Southern Mountains: American Folk Songs of British Ancestry*. New York: Columbia University Press.

Schatzki, Theodore R. 2001. "Introduction: Practice Theory." In *The Practice Turn in Contemporary Theory*, ed. Theodore R. Schatzki, Karin Knorr Cetina, and Eike Von Savigny, 1–14. London: Routledge.

Scheff, Thomas. 2006. *Goffman Unbound: A New Paradigm for Social Science*. Boulder, CO: Paradigm.

Scheiberg, Susan L. 1990. "A Folklorist in the Family: On the Process of Fieldwork among Intimates." *Western Folklore* 49: 208–14.

Schipper, Mineke. 2003. *Never Marry a Woman with Big Feet: Women in Proverbs from Around the World*. New Haven, CT: Yale University Press.

Schoemaker, George H., ed. 1990. *The Emergence of Folklore in Everyday Life: A Fieldguide and Sourcebook*. Bloomington, IN: Trickster Press.

Searle, John R. 1969. *Speech Acts: An Essay in the Philosophy of Language*. Cambridge: Cambridge University Press.

Sébillot, Paul. 1886. "Le Folklore: les traditions populaires et l'ethnographie populaire." *Revue d'anthropololgie* 2: 290–302.

Seitel, Peter. 1991. "Magic, Knowledge, and Irony in Scholarly Exchange: A Comment on Robert Cantwell's Observations on the Festival of American Folklife." *Journal of American Folklore* 104: 495–96.

Sennett, Richard. 1977. *The Fall of Public Man*. New York: Vintage.

Sharp, Cecil J. 1932. *English Folk Songs from the Southern Appalachians*. London: Oxford University Press.

Sherman, Sharon R., and Mikel J. Koven. 2007. *Folklore/Cinema: Popular Film as Vernacular Culture*. Logan: Utah State University Press.

Shuldiner, David. 1994. "Promoting Self-Worth among the Aging." In *Putting Folklore to Use*, ed. Michael Owen Jones, 214–25. Lexington: University Press of Kentucky.

———. 1998. "The Politics of Discourse: An Applied Folklore Perspective." *Journal of Folklore Research* 35: 189–201.

Silverman, Carol. 1983. "The Politics of Folklore in Bulgaria." *Anthropological Quarterly* 56: 55–61.

Silverman-Weinreich, Beatrice. 1994. "Towards a Structural Analysis of Yiddish Proverbs." In *The Wisdom of Many: Essays on the Proverb*, ed. Wolfgang Mieder and Alan Dundes, 65–85. Madison: University of Wisconsin Press.

Sims, Martha C., and Martine Stephens. 2011. *Living Folklore: An Introduction to the Study of People and Their Traditions*. 2nd ed. Logan: Utah State University Press.

Siporin, Steve. 1992. *American Folk Masters: The National Heritage Fellows*. New York: Harry N. Abrams.

———. 2000. "On Scapegoating Public Folklore." *Journal of American Folklore* 113: 86–89.

Šmidchens, Guntis. 1999. "Folklorism Revisited." *Journal of Folklore Research* 36: 51–70.

Smith, John B. 2004. "Perchta the Belly-Slitter and Her Kin: A View of Some Traditional Threatening Figures, Threats, and Punishments." *Folklore* 115: 167–86.

Smith, Moira. 1995. "Whipping Up a Storm: The Ethics and Consequences of Joking Around." *Journal of Folklore Research* 32: 121–36.

Smith, Peter K. 1997. "Play Fighting and Real Fighting: Perspectives on Their Relationship." In *New Aspects of Human Ethology*, ed. Alain Schmitt, Klaus Atzwanger, Karl Grammer, and Katrin Schäfer, 47–64. New York: Plenum Press.

——, Rebecca Smees, and Anthony D. Pellegrini. 2004. "Play Fighting and Real Fighting: Using Video Playback Methodology with Young Children." *Aggressive Behavior* 30: 164–73.

Smith, Richard D. 2001. *Can't You Hear Me Callin': The Life of Bill Monroe, Father of Bluegrass.* Boston: Da Capo Press.

Snow, Stephen Eddy. 1993. *Performing the Pilgrims: A Study of Ethnohistorical Role-Playing at Plimoth Plantation.* Jackson: University Press of Mississippi.

Sokolov, Y. M. 1971. *Russian Folklore*, ed. Catherine Ruth Smith. Detroit: Folklore Associates.

Sommers, Laurie Kay. 1994. "Festival Imagined, Festival Invented: Producers' Constructs of Michigan on the Mall." *Folklore in Use: Applications in the Real World* 2: 181–200.

——. 1996. "Definitions of 'Folk' and 'Lore' in the Smithsonian Festival of American Folklife." *Journal of Folklore Research* 33: 227–31.

Spradley, James P., and Brenda E. Mann. 2008. *The Cocktail Waitress: Woman's Work in a Man's World.* 1975 rpt, Long Grove, IL: Waveland Press.

Stads, Jan, Paul Spapens, and Henk van Doremalen. 2004. *Werken, werken, werken: De geschiedenis van de gastarbeiders in Tilburg en omstreken 1963–1975.* Utrecht: Nederlands Centrum voor Volkscultuur.

Starnes, Bobby Ann. 1999. *The Foxfire Approach to Teaching and Learning: John Dewey, Experiential Learning, and the Core Practices.* Charleston, WV: Clearinghouse on Rural Education and Small Schools, Appalachia Educational Laboratory.

Stekert, Ellen. 1989. "The Folklorist as Teacher." In *Time and Temperature*, ed. Charles Camp, 41–43. Washington, DC: American Folklore Society.

Stewart, Edward C., and Milton J. Bennett. 1991. *American Cultural Patterns.* Rev. ed. Yarmouth, ME: Intercultural Press.

Stocking, George W., Jr., ed. 1996. *Volksgeist as Method and Ethic: Essays on Boasian Ethnography and the German Anthropological Tradition.* Madison: University of Wisconsin Press.

Stross, Brian. 1999. "The Hybrid Metaphor: From Biology to Culture." *Journal of American Folklore* 112: 254–67.

Strum, Philippa. 2002. *Women in the Barracks: The VMI Case and Equal Rights.* Lawrence: University Press of Kansas.

Súilleabháin, Seán Ó. 1969. *Irish Wake Amusements.* Cork: Mercier Press.

Sullivan, Winnifred Fallers. 2009. "We Are All Religious Now. Again." *Social Research: An International Quarterly* 76: 1181–198.

Sutton-Smith, Brian., and John Roberts. 1972. "The Cross-Cultural and Psychological Study of Games." In *The Folkgames of Children*, by Brian Sutton-Smith, 331–40. Austin: University of Texas Press.

——, John Gerstmyer, and Alice Meckley. 1988. "Playfighting amongst Preschool Children." *Western Folklore* 47: 161–76.

Swart, P.D. 1957. "The Diffusion of the Folktale: With Special Notes on Africa." *Midwest Folklore* 7: 69–84.

Sweterlitsch, Dick, ed. 1971. *Papers on Applied Folklore.* Bloomington, IN: Folklore Forum Bibliographic and Special Series, No. 8.

Sykes, Heather. 2001. "Of Gods, Money and Muscle: Resurgent Homophobias and the Narcissism of Minor Differences in Sport." *Psychoanalysis and Contemporary Thought* 24: 205–26.

Szkaradnik, Mindy. 2015. "The Rise and Fall of State Patty's Day." *Onward State* (February 26). Available at: http://onwardstate.com/2015/02/26/the-rise-and-fall-of-state-pattys-day/

Tabbi, Joseph. 1997. "Reading, Writing, Hypertext: Democratic Politics in the Virtual Classroom." In *Internet Culture*, ed. David Porter, 233–52. New York: Routledge.

Tangherlini, Timothy R. 2013. "The Folklore Macroscope: Challenges for a Computational Folkloristics." *Western Folklore* 72: 7–27.

Tatar, Maria. 1987. *The Hard Facts of the Grimms' Fairy Tales.* Princeton, NJ: Princeton University Press.

Taylor, Archer. 1949. "Folklore." In *Funk & Wagnalls Standard Dictionary of Folklore, Mythology, and Legend*, ed. Maria Leach, 402–3. New York: Funk & Wagnalls.

——. 1951. *English Riddles from Oral Tradition.* Berkeley: University of California Press.

——. 1962. *The Proverb, and an Index to The Proverb.* Hatboro, PA: Folklore Associates.

Temple, Richard Carnac. 1977. *The Legends of the Panjâb. 1894–1900.* rpt. New York: Arno.

Temple, Robert. 1998. "Introduction." In *The Complete Fables* by Aesop, trans. Robert Temple and Olivia Temple, ix–xxiii. London: Penguin.

Theophano, Janet. "'I Gave Him a Cake': An Interpretation of Two Italian-American Weddings." In *Creative Ethnicity: Symbols and Strategies of Contemporary Ethnic Life*, ed. Stephen Stern and John Allen Cicala, 44–54. Logan: Utah State University Press.

Thobaben, Marshelle. 2007. "Horizontal Workplace Violence." *Home Health Care Management & Practice.* 20: 82–83.

Thomas, Jeannie B. 1997. "Dumb Blondes, Dan Quayle, and Hillary Clinton: Gender, Sexuality, and Stupidity in Jokes." *Journal of American Folklore* 110: 277–313.

Thompson, Stith. 1949. "Folklore." In *Funk & Wagnalls Standard Dictionary of Folklore, Mythology, and Legend*, ed. Maria Leach, 403. New York: Funk & Wagnalls.

———. 1951. "Folklore at Midcentury." *Midwest Folklore* 1: 5–12.

———. 1955. *Motif-Index of Folk-Literature*, 6 vols. Revised and enlarged edition. Bloomington: Indiana University Press.

———. 1977. *The Folktale.* 1946 rpt. Berkeley: University of California Press

Thompson, Tok. 2010. "The Ape that Captured Time: Folklore, Narrative, and the Human-Animal Divide." *Western Folklore* 69: 395–420.

Thoms, William. 1965 [1846]. "Folklore." In *The Study of Folklore*, ed. Alan Dundes, 4–6. Englewood Cliffs, NJ: Prentice-Hall.

———. 1876. "The Story of 'Notes and Queries.'" *Notes and Queries*, 5th series, 6 (July 15), 41–42.

Thornbury, Barbara E. 1994. "The Cultural Properties Protection Law and Japan's Folk Performing Arts." *Asian Folklore Studies* 53: 211–25.

———. 1995. "Folklorism and Japan's Folk Performing Arts." *Journal of Folklore Research* 32: 207–20.

Thursby, Jacqueline S. 2006. *Funeral Festivals in America: Rituals for the Living.* Lexington: University Press of Kentucky.

Tinkler, Justine E. 2008. "'People Are Too Quick to Take Offense': The Effects of Legal Information and Beliefs on Definitions of Sexual Harassment." *Law & Social Inquiry* 33: 417–45.

Toelken, Barre. 1979. *The Dynamics of Folklore.* Boston: Houghton Mifflin.

———. 1995. *Morning Dew and Roses: Nuance, Metaphor, and Meaning in Folksongs.* Urbana: University of Illinois Press.

———. 1996. *The Dynamics of Folklore.* Rev. and expanded ed. Logan: Utah State University Press.

Tokofsky, Peter. 1996. "Folk-Lore and Volks-Kunde: Compounding Compounds." *Journal of Folklore Research* 33: 207–11.

———. 2000. "A Tale of Two Carnivals: Esoteric and Exoteric Performances in the Fasnet of Elzach." *Journal of American Folklore* 113: 357–77.

Trend, David, ed. 2001. *Reading Digital Culture.* Malden, MA: Blackwell.

Tschofen, Bernhard. 1999. "The Habit of Folklore: Remarks on Lived *Volkskunde* and the Everyday Practice of European Ethnology after the End of Faith." *Journal of Folklore Research* 36: 235–42.

Tuleja, Tad. 1997. "Closing the Circle: Yellow Ribbons and the Redemption of the Past." In *Usable Pasts: Traditions and Group Expressions in North America*, ed. Tad Tuleja, 311–31. Logan: Utah State University Press.

Turner, Victor. 1969. *The Ritual Process: Structure and Anti-Structure*. Chicago: Aldine.

UNESCO. 2006. "Traditional Knowledge." *Memobpi*. Bureau of Public Information, Paris: UNESCO. Available at: www.unesco.org/bpi/pdf/memobpi48_tradknowledge_en.pdf

Upadhyaya, K. D. 1954. "A General Survey of Folktale Activities in India." *Midwest Folklore* 3: 201–12.

Uther, Hans-Jörg. 2004. *The Types of the International Folktales: A Classification and Bibliography*, 3 vols. Helsinki: Suomalainen Tiedakatemia.

Utley, Francis Lee. 1961. "Folk Literature: An Operational Definition." *Journal of American Folklore* 74: 193–206.

———. 1974. "The Migration of Folktales: Four Channels to the Americas." *Current Anthropology* 15: 5–13.

Van der Zeijden, Albert. 2004. *Volkscultuur van en voor een breed publiek: Enkele theoretische premissen en conceptuele uitgangspunten*. Utrecht: Nederlands Centrum voor Volkscultuur.

Van Gennep, Arnold. 1960. *The Rites of Passage*. Trans. Monika B. Vizedom and Gabrielle L. Caffee. Chicago: University of Chicago Press.

———. 1999. "The Rites of Passage." In *International Folkloristics: Classic Contributions by the Founders of Folklore*, ed. Alan Dundes, 99–108. Lanham, MD: Rowman & Littlefield.

Van Holsteyn, Joop J. M., and Irwin, Galen A. 2003. "Never a Dull Moment: Pim Fortuyn and the Dutch Parliamentary Election of 2002." *West European Politics* 26: 41–66.

Van Schaik, Pim, ed. 2004. *En dat vierenivij! Feesten en vieringen van kinderen in kleurrijk Nederland*. Amsterdam: PlanPlan.

Veidlinger, Jeffrey, ed. 2016. *Going to the People: Jews and the Ethnographic Impulse*. Bloomington: Indiana University Press.

Vellinga, Marcel, Paul Oliver, and Alexander Bridge. 2007. *Atlas of Vernacular Architecture of the World*. New York: Routledge.

Vermeulen, Han F. 2006. "The German Invention of *Völkerkunde:* Ethnological Discourse in Europe and Asia, 1740–1798." In *The German Invention of Race*, ed. Sara Eigen and Mark Larrimore, 123–46. Albany: State University of New York Press.

Virtanen, Leea. 2002. "Estonian Folkloristics Enjoys Its New-Found Freedom." *Folklore Fellows Network Bulletin* 23 (April): 13–15.

Von Sydow, Carl Wilhelm. 1948. *Selected Papers on Folklore*. Copenhagen: Rosenkilde & Bagger.

———. 1999. "Geography and Folk-Tale Oicotypes." In *International Folkloristics: Classic Contributions by the Founders of* Folklore, ed. Alan Dundes, 137–52. Lanham, MD: Rowman & Littlefield.

Walle, Alf H. 1977. "On the Role of Functionalism in Contemporary Folkloristics." *Journal of American Folklore* 90: 68–73.

Ward, Donald. 1988. "New Misconceptions about Old Folktales: The Brothers Grimm." In *The Brothers Grimm and Folktale*, ed. James M. McGlathery, 91–100. Urbana: University of Illinois Press.

Warner, Marina. 1999. *No Go the Bogeyman: Scaring, Lulling, and Making Mock*. New York: Farrar, Straus, and Giroux.

Warnock, G. J. 1989. *J. L. Austin: The Arguments of the Philosophers*. London: Routledge.

Wasik, Bill. 2009. *And There's This: How Stories Live and Die in Viral Culture*. New York: Penguin.

Watts, Linda S. 2006. "Hurston, Zora Neale." In *Encyclopedia of American Folklore*, by Linda S. Watts, 209–10. New York: Facts on File.

Webster, Frank. 2005. "Network." In *New Keywords: A Revised Vocabulary of Culture and Society,* ed. Tony Bennett, Lawrence Grossberg, and Meaghan Morris, 239–41. Malden, MA: Blackwell.

Webster, Richard. 2008. *The Encyclopedia of Superstitions*. Woodbury, MN: Llewellyn.

Weems, Mickey. 2008. *The Fierce Tribe: Masculine Identity and Performance in the Circuit*. Logan: Utah State University Press.

——, Polly Stewart, and Joseph P. Goodwin. 2012. *Qualia Folk*. Available at: www.qualiafolk.com/qegf-introduction-2/

Weiser, Frederick S. 1980. "Baptismal Certificate and Gravemarker: Pennsylvania German Folk Art at the Beginning and End of Life." In *Perspectives on American folk Art*, ed. Ian M. G. Quimby and Scott T. Swank, 134–61. New York: W. W. Norton.

Wells, Patricia Atkinson. 1994. "Helping Craftsmen and Communities Survive: Folklore and Economic Development." In *Putting Folklore to Use*, ed. Michael Owen Jones, 240–50. Lexington: University Press of Kentucky.

——. 2006. "Public Folklore in the Twenty-First Century: New Challenges for the Discipline." *Journal of American Folklore* 119: 5–18.

Wenger, Etienne. 1998. *Communities of Practice: Learning, Meaning, and Identity*. Cambridge: Cambridge University Press.

Wepman, Dennis, Ronald B. Newman, and Murray B. Binderman, comps. 1976. *The Life: The Lore and Folk Poetry of the Black Hustler*. Philadelphia: University of Pennsylvania Press.

Weslager, C. A. 1969. *The Log Cabin in America: From Pioneer Days to the Present*. New Brunswick, NJ: Rutgers University Press.

Westerman, William. 2006. "Wild Grasses and New Arks: Transformative Potential in Applied and Public Folklore." *Journal of American Folklore* 119: 111–28.

Western Folklife Center. 2015. "National Cowboy Poetry Gathering." *Western Folklife Center* website. Available at: www.westernfolklife.org/

General-Information-on-the-Gathering/national-cowboy-poetry-gathering-home-page.html

"What They Say." 1895. *Journal of Education* 41: 227.

Whisnant, David E. 1983. *All That Is Native and Fine: The Politics of Culture in an American Region.* Chapel Hill: University of North Carolina Press.

Whiting, Bartlett Jere. 1989. *Modern Proverbs and Proverbial Sayings.* Cambridge, MA: Harvard University Press.

Widdowson, John. 1977. *If You Don't Be Good: Verbal Social Control in Newfoundland.* St. John's: Institute of Social and Economic Research, Memorial University of Newfoundland.

Wierzbicka, Anna. 1994. "Semantic Universals and Primitive Thought: The Question of the Psychic Unity of Humankind." *Journal of Linguistic Anthropology* 4: 23–49.

Wigginton, Eliot. 1974. "A Reply to the Lesson of Foxfire." *North Carolina Folklore Journal* 22: 35–41.

Wilgus, D. K., and Eleanor R. Long. 1985. "The Blues Ballad and the Genesis of Style in Traditional Narrative Song." In *Narrative Folksong: New Directions,* ed. Carol L. Edwards and Kathleen B. Manley, 437–82. Boulder, CO: Westview Press.

Williams, Clover Nolan. 1994. "The Bachelor's Transgression: Identity and Difference in the Bachelor Party." *Journal of American Folklore* 107: 106–20.

Williams, James C. 2013. "Sailing as Play." *Icon* 19: 132–92.

Williams, Michael Ann. 2006. *Staging Tradition: John Lair and Sarah Gertrude Knott.* Urbana: University of Illinois Press.

Williams, Raymond. 1983. *Keywords: A Vocabulary of Culture and Society.* Rev. ed. New York: Oxford University Press.

Wilson, William A. 1973. "Herder, Folklore, and Romantic Nationalism." *Journal of Popular Culture* 4: 819–35.

Winick, Stephen D. 2003. "Intertextuality and Innovation in a Definition of the Proverb Genre." In *Cognition, Comprehension, and Communication: A Decade of North American Proverb Studies (1990–2000),* ed. Wolfgang Mieder, 571–601. Baltmannsweiler, Germany: Schneider Verlag Hohengehren.

Winter, Claire Ruth. 2010. *Understanding Transgender Diversity: A Sensible Explanation of Sexual and Gender Identities.* N.p.: Claire Ruth Winter.

WIPO: World Intellectual Property Organization. 2015. "Traditional Knowledge." Available at: www.wipo.int/tk/en/#tk

Wojcik, Daniel. 2008. "Outsider Art, Vernacular Traditions, Trauma, and Creativity." *Western Folklore* 67: 179–98.

Woodward, Colin. 2012. *American Nations: A History of the Eleven Rival Regional Cultures of North America.* New York: Penguin.

Wright, Richard A. 1989. "The 'Friendly Student' Exercise." *Teaching Sociology* 17: 484–88.

Yoder, Don. 1974. "25 Years of the Folk Festival." *Pennsylvania Folklife* 23 (Folk Festival Supplement): 2–7.

Zeeland, Steven. 1995. *Sailors and Sexual Identity: Crossing the Line Between 'Straight' and 'Gay' in the U.S. Navy*. New York: Haworth Press.

Zeitlin, Steven J., Amy Kotkin, and Holly Cutting Baker. 1982. *A Celebration of American Family Folklore: Tales and Traditions from the Smithsonian Collection*. New York: Pantheon.

Zelinsky, Wilbur. 1973. *Cultural Geography of the United States*. Englewood Cliffs, NJ: Prentice-Hall.

Zholkovski, Alexandr K. 1978. "At the Intersection of Linguistics, Paremiology and Poetics: On the Literary Structure of Proverbs." *Poetics* 7: 309–22.

Ziolkowski, Jan M. 2010. "Straparola and the Fairy Tale: Between Literary and Oral Traditions." *Journal of American Folklore* 123: 377–97.

Zipes, Jack. 1988. *The Brothers Grimm: From Enchanted Forests to the Modern World*. New York: Routledge.

——. 2012. *The Irresistible Fairy Tale: The Cultural and Social History of a Genre*. Princeton, NJ: Princeton University Press.

Zuidervaart, Lambert, and Henry Luttikhuizen, eds. 2000. *The Arts, Community, and Cultural Democracy*. New York: St. Martin's Press.

Zukin, Sharon. 2004. *Point of Purchase: How Shopping Changed American Culture*. New York: Routledge.

Zumwalt, Rosemary Lévy. 1988. *American Folklore Scholarship: A Dialogue of Dissent*. Bloomington: Indiana University Press.

INDEX